THE UNPUBLISHED POETRY OF
CHARLES WESLEY

Volume III

HYMNS AND POEMS
FOR CHURCH AND WORLD

THE UNPUBLISHED POETRY OF
CHARLES WESLEY

Volume III

HYMNS AND POEMS
FOR CHURCH AND WORLD

Edited by

S T Kimbrough, Jr.
and
Oliver A. Beckerlegge

KINGSWOOD BOOKS
An Imprint of Abingdon Press
Nashville, Tennessee

THE UNPUBLISHED POETRY OF CHARLES WESLEY

VOLUME III

HYMNS AND POEMS FOR CHURCH AND WORLD

Copyright © 1992 by Abingdon Press

Library of Congress Cataloging-in-Publication Data

WESLEY, CHARLES, 1707–1788.
 The unpublished poetry of Charles Wesley / edited by S T Kimbrough, Jr., and Oliver A. Beckerlegge.
   p.   cm.
 V. 2 has also special title: Hymns and poems on Holy Scripture; v. 3 has also special title: Hymns and poems for church and world. Includes bibliographical references and indexes.
 1. Christian poetry, English.   I. Kimbrough, S T, Jr., 1936–.   II. Beckerlegge, Oliver A., 1913–.   III. Title.
 PR3763.W4A6   1988   821'.6   88-19165
 ISBN   0-687-43310-X (pbk.: v. 1: alk. paper)
 ISBN   0-687-43311-8 (v. 2: acid-free paper)

ISBN 0-687-43312-6

Printed in the United States of America
on recycled acid-free paper

TABLE OF CONTENTS*

* Where Wesley supplied no title, the first line of a poem appears in the Table of Contents. Only the first word of each title or first line is capitalized, except for proper nouns and/or adjectives.

SECTION II:
HYMNS AND POEMS FOR ORDINATION

SECTION III:
HYMNS AND POEMS FOR FESTIVALS

SECTION IV:
DEVOTIONAL HYMNS AND POEMS

SECTION VI:
HYMNS FOR MALEFACTORS

SECTION VII:
EPITAPHS AND OTHER POEMS ON DEATH

SECTION X:
FRAGMENTS

SECTION XI:
HYMNS AND POEMS OF DOUBTFUL AUTHORSHIP

INDEXES

FOREWORD

When I was invited to the Center of Theological Inquiry by the late Dr. James I. McCord, founder and then Chancellor of the Center, to research the subject "Charles Wesley as a Biblical Interpreter," I was encouraged by him at mid-point in my work to lay aside that project and to turn my full research attention to the editing and publishing of the unpublished poetry of Charles Wesley. When I described the extent and length of such a project, which has now spanned five years, he replied, "Do not be concerned. We will see you through." Shortly thereafter he sent me this communiqué:

> Sometimes it takes those of us outside a tradition (in this case, the Anglican-Methodist)[1] to see the true values within it. The Anglicans and Methodists have not done well in preserving the works and heritage of Charles Wesley. The publication and dissemination of his unpublished poetry may lead to the kind of spiritual renewal of which we Presbyterians and the church at large are so desperately in need. If you undertake this venture, it will be one of the most important projects for the renewal of the church and its literature which the Center is supporting.

With my colleague, Dr. Oliver A. Beckerlegge, I undertook the venture and now it is completed.

Dr. McCord seemed to possess an innate sense of theological focus, relevance, and urgency. Unfortunately he did not live to see the completion of volumes II and III, though he had perused the material for both. Ever mindful of thoroughness, as the master administrator he was, shortly before his death, though gravely weakened by illness, he asked me for an up-to-date report on this project in which he so strongly believed.

Charles Wesley studies will remain ever in the debt of Dr. McCord and the Center of Theological Inquiry for the vision to support the editing and publishing of *The Unpublished Poetry of Charles Wesley*. A renaissance has begun in the study of his poetical and prose works and their importance for theology, biblical studies, hymnography, spiritual formation, English literature, church history, church music, liturgy, and homiletics. It is perhaps not coincidental that the founding meeting of the Charles Wesley Society, which is committed to the dissemination and interpretation of his works, was held at the Center of Theological Inquiry, October 19–21, 1990. It was preceded in the previous year by a Charles Wesley Colloquium also held at the Center. The papers presented at that time by distinguished scholars

---

1. Editor's parenthetical addition.

from England and the United States have been published under the title *Charles Wesley: Poet and Theologian.* It is fitting that volume III open with this expression of deep gratitude to Dr. James I. McCord, to whom the entire series is dedicated, and to the Center of Theological Inquiry. Charles Wesley's tribute in a epitaph on the death of Charles Perronet is indeed appropriate for Dr. McCord:

> *Here lies, who late a living emblem lay*
> *Of human greatness, in a tent of clay;*[2]
> A pilgrim, wandring through this desart wild,
> Weak as a Reed, and helpless as a Child:
> Whose strengthen'd arm by Faith untaught to yield,
> Oft foil'd the Tempter, and maintain'd the field.
> In wars without, in warring fears within,
> He conquer'd Terror as he conquer'd Sin;
> Look'd for himself to Him, whose potent breath
> Can light up Darkness, or extinguish Death:
> Dart from his eye destruction on the foe,
> And make hell tremble as she hears the blow:
> He look'd, and found what all who look receive,
> Strength to resist, and Virtue to believe;
> Meek, to endure and suffer from his God
> The tender chast'nings of a Father's rod:
> While thus corrected, as by Pain refin'd
> His spirit groan'd to leave its dross behind:
> The dross is left—no more his spirit mourns,
> But spreads her wings, and to her Ark returns;
> Great Ark of Rest—the sufferer's bright abode;
> The Arms of Jesus, and the Ark of God!

Dr. McCord, however, would not have approved of a tribute to him but would have preferred, I am sure, the quotation of two verses from his favorite Wesley hymn:

> Love divine, all loves excelling,
>> Joy of heaven, to earth come down,
> Fix in us thy humble dwelling,
>> All thy faithful mercies crown!

2. Editor's italics.

Jesus, thou art all compassion,
>Pure, unbounded love thou art;
Visit us with thy salvation!
>Enter every trembling heart.

Finish then thy new creation,
>Pure and spotless let us be;
Let us see thy great salvation
>Perfectly restored in thee;
Changed from glory into glory,
>Till in heaven we take our place,
Till we cast our crowns before thee,
>Lost in wonder, love, and praise.

S T Kimbrough, Jr.,
Center of Theological Inquiry
Princeton, New Jersey

PREFACE

This is the final volume of Charles Wesley's unpublished poetry. Much of it dates from the last fifteen years of his life, but unpublished poems from earlier periods are also included.

It was often Wesley's custom to write groups of verse on specific themes such as those represented in this volume: preachers (Section I), ordination (Section II), festivals (Section III), intercession (Section IV), malefactors (Section VI), and death (Section VII). The hymns and poems in those sections include in part large homogeneous groups from manuscripts which are often centered on the themes indicated in the title of each section. However, unpublished texts from other sources, which are frequently thematically related, have been included in the appropriate sections. For example, the poetry in Section III ("Hymns and Poems for Festivals") comes primarily from MS Festivals; however, three poems concerned with festival themes from other sources also appear in this section: (1) "Christmas Day" from MS Preachers; (2) "Jesus from Thy Servants Taken," a poem for Ascension Day from MS Richmond Tracts; (3) hymn I of "Hymns on our Lord's Resurrection" from MS Cheshunt.

In the verse of Section I "Hymns for Preachers" Wesley treated a variety of subjects related to preaching and Methodist preaching in particular. He saw one of his primary tasks as that of improving the state of preaching and he addressed such subjects as lay preaching, *sound* preaching, humility, and penitence.

In Section II "Hymns and Poems for Ordination" one finds Charles Wesley's multi-faceted, negative response to his brother John's ordination of Methodist bishops for America, e.g. Thomas Coke and Francis Asbury. These poems reveal Charles's ideas on apostolic succession, a theology of the priesthood, and the fraternal tension created between John and Charles over the issue of ordination. They are often couched in a biting, sarcastic poetical style quite different from that of his hymn writing. One brief passage suffices to illustrate his compact, eloquent indictment of John for preparing at the time an abbreviated version of the *Book of Common Prayer*.

> Your Liturgy so well-prepared
> To E[ngland]'s Church proves your regard,
> Of churches national the best
> By you, and all the world confest:

21

(Why shou'd we then bad counsel take
And for a worse the best forsake?)
You tell us, with her Book of prayer
No book is worthy to compare;
Why change it then for your Edition,
Deprav'd by many a bold omission?
We never will renounce our creed,
Because of Three but One you need,
No longer the Nicene approve,
The Athanasian Mound remove,
And out of your New book have thrown
God One in Three, & Three in One.[1]

Section III "Hymns and Poems for Festivals" is comprised of poetry for saints' days and other specific days of the church year.

Section IV "Devotional Hymns and Poems" is the largest single section in volume III and is a miscellany of texts from many manuscript sources on a variety of reflective subjects. Some of the dominant themes are: reproach, temptation, trial, uncertainty, penitence, universal redemption, thanksgiving, Holy Scripture, sacrament, grace, and peace.

Most of the "Intercessory Hymns and Poems" of Section V come from MS Misc. Hymns and MS Intercessions and indicate the broad spectrum of Wesley's intercessory concerns, from general themes such as "For the Tempted" and "Those in doubt" to specific names such as "For Miss Durbin" and "Prayer for the Church of England." They embody domestic, social, ecclesiological, theological, and political concerns. Many are imbued with a simple eloquence marked by an economy of words and well chosen metaphors, as the following lines indicate:

O may I never take the praise
Or my own glory spread,
If made thy instrument to raise
A sinner from the dead.
O may I never boast my own
Successful ministry,
But sink forgotten and unknown
And swallow'd up in Thee.[2]

1. See below p. 97.
2. See below p. 311.

Section VI "Hymns for Malefactors" reflects a life-long concern of Charles Wesley for prisoners, particularly those condemned to die. Of a total of eight poems in MS Malefactors four were published in *Prayers for Condemned Malefactors* (London, 1785). The other four are published here for the first time.

Wesley's poetry often reveals a preoccupation with death which is not surprising given the deadly illnesses of his time, the death of nine brothers and sisters, the death of five of his own eight children, and his confidence that death opened to all believers the fullness of union with God. Section VII "Epitaphs and Other Poems on Death" discloses Wesley's concern not only with his own death but also with that of others. His practice of writing poems on the occasion of someone's death is illustrated here in numerous poems written for specific individuals. Hence, these poems are of importance historically for the circle of associates of the Wesleys from the humblest of persons to monarchs.

Section VIII consists of only two epigrams, one of which was written as a mnemonic device for Charles's children to memorize or remember the books of the New Testament. Other epigrams are found concluding longer poems, especially in volume I.[3]

Section IX "Miscellaneous Hymns and Poems" is a mixture of sacred and secular verse covering a wide range of subjects: music, G. F. Handel, the advent of the piano-forte, the King of Poland, the flight of a hydrogen-filled balloon by Vincenzo Lunardi, Calvinism, translations from Latin poets, autobiography, the Countess of Huntingdon, etc.

Section X "Fragments" contains all known fragments of poetry by Charles Wesley. One instance is of special interest as it may illustrate his method of composing verse, i.e. by writing out initial ideas sometimes with blanks to be filled in later.

The final Section XI "Hymns and Poems of Doubtful Authorship" includes poems attributed to Charles Wesley or which sometimes come from his manuscript material but cannot be definitely identified as having been authored by him. For example, the poem which begins "Voracious Learning, often overfed"[4] is found in a letter of Charles to his daughter Sally. Was it a quotation or was it composed by him? If he is the author, it is the only example of blank verse in his entire poetical corpus. Significant questions about many of the poems in this section are raised in the footnotes.

3. See the epigrams in *Unpub. Poetry,* vol. I, pp. 108–9, 151, 167. These epigrams have been published with the MS material to which they are directly related, rather than included separately in Section VIII (Epigrams) of vol. III.

4. See below p. 442.

The poems in volume III are taken from a diverse number of manuscripts which are listed in the Table of Manuscript Sources.[5] Thirty-five of the MS poems published here appeared in Frank Baker's *Representative Verse of Charles Wesley* (1962) and are so designated in the footnotes. Also included are Wesley poems which were published in the *Arminian Magazine* and did not appear in Osborn's collection,[6] as well as a few other poems from Wesley's published sources, which Osborn inexplicably did not publish.

As in volumes I and II manuscript poems of which Osborn published only portions and/or in conglomerate forms are published here for the first time in the fullest form recorded by Wesley in the manuscripts. The footnotes document all such occurrences and the location of the portions of poems published in Osborn's collection.

The contents of the present volume are found on pages 5–16. While there is an affinity in the broad spectrum of poetical styles (both sacred and secular) in volumes I and III of this series, volume II is more unilinearly characteristic of Charles Wesley's hymnwriting. Yet, long narrative poems on biblical passages in volume II are less characteristic of it. The contents of volumes I and II indicate the multi-faceted concerns of his poetical composition and preoccupation:

VOLUME I

The American War and other poems on patriotism
Epistles
Courtship and marriage
Family hymns and poems
John Wesley's marriage

VOLUME II

Hymns and poems based on passages of scripture:
    The Gospel of Matthew
    The Gospel of Mark
    The Gospel of Luke
    The Gospel of John

5. See below pp. 29–30.

6. See volume I of *The Unpublished Poetry of Charles Wesley* (Nashville: Abingdon, 1988, "Foreword," p. 12, and "Preface," pp. 17–18, 21) for a full explanation of the selection process for the poetry in all three volumes of this series.

TECHNICAL MATTERS

Generally the technical matters outlined in volume I on pages 13–15 and in volume II on pages 9–11 are applicable to volume III, except for certain aspects of the use of Holy Scripture by Charles Wesley in volume II, which have little relevance for volume III.

(1) Wesley's spelling and capitalization generally have been maintained as found in the manuscripts. English language orthography was going through major changes in the eighteenth century and some of them are reflected in Wesley's writing which spans some fifty years, ca. 1738–88. For example, his spelling and capitalization are not always consistent. His later writings reflect acceptance of new spellings of many words and a decreased use of capitals. The plethora of capital letters in his early poetical writings tends to diminish in that of his later years.

He often omitted the "l" from the words, *could, should,* and *would,* although he sometimes included an apostrophe in its place, and occasionally employed the "l" in the spelling of the words. These auxiliary verbs are printed as Wesley wrote them. Abbreviations have been expanded for reading purposes: e.g. cd = coud, shd = shoud, wd = woud, wch = which, wo = who, &c = etc., yt = that, yr = your, Xt = Christ. The ampersand (&) has been retained when Wesley used it.

Wesley's spelling of contracted words is not always consistent. For example, one finds *lovst/lov'st* indiscriminately for *lovest* and *knowst/know'st* for *knowest.* Once again his spelling has been retained.

(2) On the whole Wesley's punctuation has been preserved. Commas and other punctuation have been added only for clarity of meaning in reading. Wesley's use of single and double quotation marks is correct, but inconsistent, as he employed both for regular quotations; however, his usage has not been regularized.

(3) In accordance with eighteenth century usage the occurrence of rhyming triplets (three lines which rhyme) within a poem written in rhyming couplets is indicated by a large bracket to the right of the rhyming lines. See pp. 391ff.

(4) Comments by the present editors, such as the manuscript sources of the poems, indentification of names or the occasion of a poem's composition, are designated by the use of footnotes within brackets. English translations of Latin quotations employed by Wesley also appear in bracketed

footnotes. Brackets are used as well in the body of the poems where the editors have filled in a name or word for which Wesley provided only the first and/or last letter. Footnotes without brackets are Wesley's own notes. Where he supplied no title for a poem, the first line appears in brackets as the title. He was not consistent in designating the internal divisions of longer poems, e.g. Part I, Part II, Part III, etc., or the numbering of poems in a sequence. He often omitted the designation of Part I and a Roman numeral for the first poem/hymn in a series, but generally included the designation of subsequent parts and poems/hymns. His use of the words "Part" and "Hymn" as headings is inconsistent.

(5) Biblical quotations are from the Authorized Version (or King James Version) which was used by Wesley, unless otherwise indicated.

(6) Whenever Wesley wrote alternative readings in the margins of the MSS, or above or below lines in the body of a poem, and did not cross out one reading in preference to another, these readings have been indicated in the footnotes.

(7) In a few instances words peculiar to eighteenth century English language usage, or earlier, or to Wesley himself, have been explained and/or noted in the footnotes, e.g. bemir'd.[7]

Finally, the editors express deepest gratitude to the Center of Theological Inquiry, its late founder and Chancellor, Dr. James I. McCord, Trustees, and Advisory Board for supporting the editorial process of the three volumes of *The Unpublished Poetry of Charles Wesley* during Dr. Kimbrough's tenure there and to the Center staff: Kate Le Van and Patricia Grier for technical assistance. The editors are also particularly grateful to Dr. Frank Baker of the Duke Divinity School for elucidation of a variety of technical matters and to Dr. William W. Fortenbaugh of Rutgers University for assistance in Latin linguistics. One must express appreciation for the help given by the staff of The John Rylands University Library of Manchester, and in particular to Miss Alison Peacock, the Methodist Archivist. Acknowledgement of help afforded on specific points is indicated in the footnotes.

This completes then the known corpus of Charles Wesley's unpublished verse and all unpublished portions of poems of which Osborn printed incomplete and/or conglomerate versions. Though the comprehensive evaluation process of Charles Wesley as a poet, spiritual leader, and formative thinker can now begin, there is still a need for a complete edition of his works (poetry and prose) due to the inaccessibility of Osborn and to the multiple inadequacies of his collection. Nevertheless, the three volumes in this series underscore the importance of a new look at Wesley as a poet

---

7. See line three of verse 2 of "Hymns for Redemption" Nr. I on p. 163.

of stature, whose work has yet to be explored fully for its literary value, and who himself has yet to be studied comprehensively as a biblical interpreter come of age, as a poet-theologian who shaped a timeless doxological view of the Christian faith and life, as a keen interpreter of his time, and as one of the most significant authors of Christian hymnic and devotional verse in the English language.

S T Kimbrough, Jr.
Center of Theological Inquiry
Princeton, New Jersey

Oliver A. Beckerlegge
York, England

MANUSCRIPT SOURCES AND ABBREVIATIONS

TABLE OF MANUSCRIPT SOURCES[1]

MS Baker (World Methodist Council Library and Museum, Lake Junaluska, NC)

MS Brothers

MS Cheshunt

MS Clarke: Charles Wesley, Box I.C.45

MS E. T. Clarke Collection (World Methodist Council Library and Museum, Lake Junaluska, NC)

Colman Collection

MS CW I(a): Charles Wesley, Box V

MS CW I(c): Charles Wesley, Box V

MS CW I(e): Charles Wesley, Box V

MS CW I(o): Charles Wesley, Box V

MS CW I(p): Charles Wesley, Box V

MS CW I(t): Charles Wesley, Box V

MS CW III(a): Charles Wesley, Box V

MS CW III(e): Charles Wesley, Box V

MS CW IV, 66–7, 72– 6, 81: Charles Wesley, Box V

MS CW IV, 92: Charles Wesley, Box IV

MS CW Letters

MS CW Letters I, II

MS Death

MS Deliberative

MS Drew

MS Festivals (MS CW IV, 71): Charles Wesley, Box V

MS Gwynne

MS Henderson (MS CW III[f])

MS Hendrix (Duke University, Durham, NC)

MS Intercession (MS CW IV, fo. 68–70): Charles Wesley, Box V, Lamplough Collection

---

1. See Frank Baker, *Representative Verse of Charles Wesley* (Nashville: Abingdon, 1962), pp. 387–94, for a description of the manuscript sources of Charles Wesley's poetry. The box numbers following the sources of the manuscripts indicate the designations of the Finding List of The Methodist Archives of The John Rylands University Library of Manchester, England. MSS Baker and Drew are not described in Baker's volume. See below pp. 361 (fnn. 41, 42) and 421 (fn. 63) for notes on these manuscripts.

MS Letters 25 of Wesley/Langshaw Correspondence (Emory University)
MS Malefactors (MS CW I[h])
MS Misc. Hymns: Charles Wesley, Box I.C.26
MS Misc. 1786 (MS CW III [c], [g])
MS Occasional: Charles Wesley, Box I.C.46
MS Ordinations: Charles Wesley, Box I.C.48
MS Pat. Misc.: Charles Wesley, Box I.C.27
MS Preachers (MS CW I[q]): Charles Wesley, Box V
MS Preachers Extraordinary (MS CW I[i])
MS Preachers 1786 (MS CW I[k])
MS Revd X (MS CW I[j])
MS Richmond
MS Richmond Tracts
MS Samuel Wesley
MS Shorthand: Charles Wesley, Box I.C.40
MS Thirty: Charles Wesley, Box I.C.30
MS Wesley Family Letters

ABBREVIATIONS

Poet. Works = George Osborn, *The Poetical Works of John and Charles Wesley*, 13 vols. (London: 1868–72). Citations from these volumes will be made by the volume and page number, e.g. *Poet. Works*, XI, pp. 302–3.

Rep. Verse = Frank Baker, *Representative Verse of Charles Wesley* (Nashville: Abingdon, 1962). Poems from this volume will be cited by their number followed by the page number, e.g. *Rep. Verse*, No. 245, pp. 272–4.

Short Hymns = Charles Wesley, *Short Hymns on Select Passages of the Holy Scriptures*, 2 vols. (Bristol: Farley, 1762). Citations from these volumes will be made by the volume and page number, e.g. *Short Hymns*, II, p. 219.

1780 Collection = John and Charles Wesley, *A Collection of Hymns for the Use of the People called Methodists* (London: J. Paramore, 1780). See the edition in *The Works of John Wesley*, vol. 7, edited by Franz Hildebrandt and Oliver A. Beckerlegge with assistance of James Dale (Oxford: Clarendon Press, 1983).

Proceedings = *Proceedings of the Wesley Historical Society* (Ilford: Robert Odcombe Associates, date as appropriate. Previous publishers: Ashworth Nuttall, Alfred A. Taberer.)

The Methodist Archives (Manchester) = The Methodist Archives at The John Rylands University Library, Manchester, England.

The Methodist Archives (Madison) = The Methodist Archives and History Center at Drew University, Madison, NJ.

HYMNS FOR PREACHERS

PART 1: HYMNS FOR PREACHERS EXTRAORDINARY

II[1]

1. Lord of the gospel-harvest, hear
   The souls around thy seat,
   And suffer mine, ev'n mine t'appear,
   Self-loathing, at thy feet.

2. I mix with theirs my feeble cry,
   On Thee for mercy call,
   Meanest of all thy servants I,
   Less than the least of all.

3. Less than the least in my own sight
   O may I ever be,
   My own employment and delight
   To serve thy Church and Thee:

4. With all the servants of my Lord,
   Whom on my heart I bear,
   I fain woud live, to preach thy word,
   A life of faith and prayer.

5. The power of praying faith and love
   Into our souls infuse,
   With gifts and talents from above
   Prepare us for thy use:

1. [MS Preachers Extraordinary (MS CW I[i]), pp. 3–4; MS CW I(q) v; MS Misc. Hymns, p. 111. The version printed here is consistent with MS Misc. Hymns, no doubt Wesley's final version.]

6. But O, to every messenger
    The guardian grace impart,
The lowly self-abasing fear,
    The meekly humble heart.

7. Only preserve us, Lord, from pride,
    And we shall never stray;
And I shall never start aside,
    Or fall a castaway.

8. The high, and lofty God shall stoop
    To every contrite One,
And lift his abject servant up
    To his eternal throne.

III²

1. Master of the gospel-feast,
    Thy meanest servants own,
Joining in the same request
    Who now besiege thy throne:
To the hedges and high-ways
    Us if thou indeed didst send,
Bless the heralds of thy grace,
    And keep us to the end.

2. Keep us, O thou lowly Lamb,
    Like Thee distrest and poor,
Simple men without a name,
    And joyfully obscure,
Small, and vile in our own eyes,
    While the wise, and rich, and great
As the trodden dirt despise,
    And spurn us at their feet.

2. [MS Preachers Extraordinary (MS CW I[i]), pp. 4–5; MS Misc. Hymns, p. 112; MS CW I (q) v.]

3. Let us thy great glory seek,
   And not our own applause,
   Still believe, and therefore speak
   The wonders of thy cross,
   Still proclaim thy saving grace,
   Fully our commission prove,
   Spend our latest breath in praise
   Of all-redeeming Love.

FOR SOME OF THE PREACHERS
WRITTEN OCT. 10, 1779[3]

1. Lord over all, thy people hear
   For every favour'd messenger
   Whom Thou hast own'd for thine,
   For every chosen instrument
   Without our rules or orders sent
   To serve the cause divine.

2. Sent forth they *were* to prophesy,
   Their lack of service to supply
   Who sit in Moses' chair,
   But love the world, and seek their own,
   Neglect their ministry, and shun
   The gospel to declare.

3. Because the prophets hold their peace,
   The stones, thy quicken'd witnesses,
   Cried out on every side,
   In streets, and houses, and high-ways
   They spread the news of pardning grace,
   They preach'd the Crucified.

3. [MS Preachers Extraordinary, (MS CW I[i]), pp. 20–23; MS CW IV, 72–3; MS Misc. Hymns, pp. 128–31. *Rep. Verse*, No. 300, pp. 336–8.]

4.   Their doctrine sinsick spirits heal'd,
    The Lord himself their mission seal'd
      By daily signs from heaven,
    Blind souls their inward sight receiv'd,
    The dead were rais'd, the poor believ'd,
      And felt their sins forgiv'n.

5.   By ceaseless toils of humble love
    Thy serv[an]ts sought their faith t'approve,
      They spake, and liv'd the word,
    Simple & poor, despis'd of men,
    They liv'd immortal souls to gain,
      And glorify their Lord.

6.   With tears we own, They *did* run well!
    But where is now their fervent zeal,
      Their meek humility,
    Their upright heart, their single eye,
    Their vows the Lord to magnify
      And live, and die for Thee?

7.   The love of ease, and earthly things,
    The pride from which contention springs,
      The fond desire of praise,
    Have imperceptibly stole in,
    Brought back the old besetting sin,
      And poison'd all their grace.

8.   They now preeminence affect
    Eager to form the rising Sect,
      Some better thing to gain:
    Like hireling priests, they serve[4] for hire,
    And thro' ambition blind, aspire
      Without the cross to reign.

9.   The flock they woud in pieces tear,
    That each may seize the largest share,
      May feed himself alone:
    'Come, see my zeal' at first they cried,
    But now they ask, 'Who's on my side
      Will make my cause his own?'

4. [In the margin "pant" is written as an alternative to "serve."]

10. The men who have their savour lost
    Themselves against the branches boast,
        And dignities despise:
    Their greedy hopes the flock devour,
    As all were left within their power
        To glut their avarice.

11. But O thou Shepherd great & good,
    The sheep redeem'd by thy own blood
        Into thine arms receive;
    If still with England's Church Thou art
    True pastors after thy own heart
        To thy own people give.

12. Thy flock out of their hands redeem
    Who of their own importance dream
        As God had need of man:
    Send whom Thou wilt, in mercy send,
    Thy cause and gospel to defend,
        Thy glory to maintain.

13. And O their faithful hearts inflame
    With love of our Jerusalem,
        Thy Church Establish'd here:
    Still may they cry, & never rest:
    Till Glory, in thy face exprest,
        Throughout our land appear:

14. Till Thee, the Glory of the Lord,
    In truth and righteousness restor'd
        All flesh together see,
    Salute Thee on thy great white throne
    And sink in speechless raptures down
        For ever lost in Thee.

XIII[5]

1.   Yet hear us, O thou patient God,
    For those who once with grace endow'd,
      Confess their faith's decay,
    Renew'd unto repentance, Lord,
    Send them again to preach thy word
      And lengthen out their day.

2.   Able thou art the proud t'abase
    The men that love the highest place,
      In mercy cast them down
    And let them, groveling in the dust,
    Own thy severest sentence just,
      And tremble at thy frown.

3.   If Thou the word of truth revoke,
    And blot their names out of thy book,
      And leave them in their fall,
    Out of the deep regard their cry,
    'Left in our sins, we justly die,
      'Our sins deserve it all.'

4.   Them by thy Spirit now convince
    Of sin, the root of all their sins,
      (Which nature fain woud hide,
    Which turn'd the Seraph to a fiend)
    From every heart the covering rend,
      And show the worms their pride.

5.   Now let them to the dunghill look
    From whence thy will mysterious took
      The basest of the croud—
    Envious to rail at Levi's sons?
    To vie with Bishops on their thrones,
      And hate the Church of God?

5. [MS Preachers Extraordinary (MS CW I[i]), pp. 23–5; MS CW IV, 72–3 (draft).]

6. No: but Thou calldst them forth to be
A pattern of humility,
    Poorest and least of all:
In mercy then, not wrath, chastise
And let them sink in their own eyes,
    And into nothing fall.

7. Repentance true on each bestow,
Tormenting fear, distracting woe,
    Unutterable shame,
The anguish of a broken heart,
Which only Jesus can impart,
    We ask in Jesus' Name.

8. When prostrate in the dust they grieve,
And sad their punishment receive,
    Thy people's prayer attend,
The humbled penitents restore,
Give back with faith their peace and power,
    And love them to the end.

PART 2: HYMNS FOR THE METHODIST PREACHERS

A. HYMNS IN 1786
FOR THE METHODIST PREACHERS

[GREAT GOD, WHO NEVER DOST PASS BY][6]

1. Great God, who never dost pass by,
      Or sin in thy own people spare,
    Regard our penitential cry,
      And let thy Spirit swell the prayer:
    If tempted by the subtle sin,
      We all to pride have given place,
    If every soul hath tainted been,
      Bow every soul by humbling grace.

2. The godly jealousy inspire,
      The deep, divine humility,
    That every preacher may inquire
      Stopt is thy work? & stopt by me?
    Have I & my companions dear
      With unperceiv'd presumption vain
    Usurp'd the sacred character,
      Or sought the praise that comes from men?

3. Surely at first our hearts were right,
      When strangely call'd to preach thy word,
    Little & mean in our own sight
      We only lived to please our Lord:
    Forth without scrip or purse we went,
      And Israel's wandring sheep pursued,
    With food and raiment well content
      With raim[en]t coarse, & scanty food.

6. [MS Preachers 1786 (MS CW I[k]), pp.1–4; in MS CW I(p) xvi, entitled "Preachers VI".]

4. Simple we then remain'd, and poor,
     But safe in our simplicity,
   Vulgar, illiterate, and obscure,
     And ignorant of all but Thee:
   We never join'd the slaves of fame
     In search of pleasure, wealth, or power,
   Jesus was all our hope, and aim,
     Possest of Thee, we ask'd no more.

5. But now the love of earthly things
     Hath imperceptibly stole in,
   And pride, whereof contention springs,
     Revives, our old besetting sin:
   Fulness of bread with worldly praise,
     Hath us for sensual joys prepar'd;
   And unforeseen temptations seize,
     While jealous fear is off its guard.

6. Genteelity we now affect,
     Fond to adorn the outward man,
   Nice in our dress, we court respect
     And female admiration gain;
   As men of elegance and taste
     We slight, & overlook the poor,
   But in the Rich, with servile haste
     Contend to make our Interest sure.

7. With indiscriminating zeal
     To brand our Rivals we presume,
   We who so much in gifts excel
     Those Priests of Babylonish Rome:
   We vent our insolent disdain,
     Those blind Idolators condemn,
   'They stand in need of us, 'tis plain,
     'We scorn to stand in need of Them.'

8. Proud of our numbers, and success,
     We are the men (we boldly cry),
   We are the men of gifts and grace,
     Wisdom and faith with us shall die!

To greater things we now aspire,
    And, studious of our own renown,
Deny, but secretly desire,
    The honors of the Envied *Gown!*

9.   Ambition in our bosom strives
    Inflam'd by the historic page
Delivering our industrious lives
    And portraits, down from age to age;
But now impatient to be known
    We boldly for ourselves declare,
Our plan mature and purpose own
    And claim the hallow'd Character.

10.   Those Reverend Drones who fill *our* place
    And rob the Labourers of their bread,
We soon out of the fold shall chase
    And take possession in their stead:
But while our hopes the land devour,
    And each anticipates his lot,
Thou wilt or'eturn our lofty Tower
    And make us know—*Thou needst us not!*

11.   Those hireling Priests whom we despise
    Thou canst by miracle convert
Render[7] them Stewards good & wise
    And pastors after thy own heart—
A multitude shall feel thy word,
    And to the faith obedient prove,
And witnessing their dying Lord
    Experience and proclaim thy love.

12.   We then our righteous doom shall meet
    As useless vessels cast aside,
Trod under foot, for nothing fit,
    Broken by sin, and marr'd by pride:
Becoming last, we then shall see
    Thy kingdom, Lord, to others given,
Worthy to be shut out by Thee
    Tho' once our Names were wrote in heaven.

7. [The word "Create" is written in the margin as an alternative to "Render."]

[O GOD, WHO DIDST OUT OF THE DUST][8]

1. O God, who didst out of the dust
     An abject beggar raise,
And to so poor a creature trust
     The gospel of thy grace;
I own with grief, & guilty shame,
     I have betray'd thy cause,
'And stole the honors of thy name
     'To build my own applause.'

2. Thy work, alas, too often I
     Deceitfully have done,
My own desires to gratify
     And not thy will alone:
I hid my heart, and woud not know
     Its secret vanity,
And while I spake my gifts to show,
     I preach'd myself, not Thee.

3. But the effects I cannot hide
     Of my unfaithfulness,
My peace is forfeited by pride,
     And eager thirst of praise:
Or'eturn'd my hill, which stood so fast
     Nor ever coud remove:
The salt has lost its savoury taste,
     And I my former love.

4. What can I do, but humbly call
     Upon the Sinner's Friend?
Whose mercies rich are over all,
     Whose miseries never end?
Enter not into judgment, Lord,
     In deep distress I pray,
Nor take out of my mouth thy word,
     Nor cast me quite away.

8. [MS Preachers 1786 (MS CW I[k]), pp. 5–6; MS CW I(p) xvi, entitled "For the Preachers."]

5.   O be not rigorously extreme,
        (While at thy feet I lie,
     A sinner, who myself condemn)
        But freely justify:
     Yet if thou wilt not save, before
        Thou dost my soul release,
     My faith at the last hour restore,
        And let me die in peace.

[O THOU, WHO DOST VOUCHSAFE TO CHUSE][9]

1.   O Thou, who dost vouchsafe to chuse
        The feeble to confound the strong,
     And fit as vessels for thy use
        The least, & meanest of the throng
     That none may rob Thee of thy right,
     Or glory in Jehovah's sight;

2.   Me Thou hast sent, a thing of nought,
        Thy truth & mercy to proclaim,
     To tell the world, so dearly bought,
        Of sure Salvation thro' thy name;
     To wonder at thy sovereign will
     Which blesses, and employs me still.

3.   Or'ewhelm'd with gratitude & fear,
        I thy mysterious counsels own,
     Meanest in my own eyes appear,
        And give the praise to God alone,
     And prostrate in the dust confess
     My own extreme unworthiness.

4.   Master, thy Greatness needs not me
        Thy cause, and kingdom to maintain,
     Who dost in glorious majesty
        At God's right-hand for ever reign,
     Who out of stones canst children raise,
     And preachers of thy pardning grace.

9. [MS Preachers 1786 (MS CW I[k]), pp. 7–9; MS CW I(q) ix, No. VII.]

5. Thou art not to one Sect confin'd,
   Tho' every Sect woud have it so,
   Blows as he lists, the Spirit's Wind,
   And ceases, as he lists, to blow:
   The Pledge, the Witness, & the Seal,
   He calls, & sends by whom He will.

6. If swell'd with self-important pride,
   I seek to build my own renown,
   Canst Thou not set me quite aside,
   A sacrilegious worm cast down,
   Revoke my ministerial grace,
   And justly drive me from thy face?

7. Thou canst , Thou wilt abase the proud,
   Reduc'd to their own nothingness,
   Confound before the listning croud,
   Their testimony *vain* suppress,
   Withdraw their gifts & *boasted* power,
   And trust them with thy word no more.

8. But if I always humbly fear,
   Nor in myself, but Thee, confide,
   Indued with strength to persevere,
   Thou wilt thy trembling Servant hide,
   And keep me, who on thee depend,
   Faithful, and useful to the end.

[HELP, LORD, THE WEAKEST INSTRUMENT][10]

1. Help, Lord, the weakest Instrument,
   Thy sovereign grace hath ever sent
   To publish and proclaim
   The Reigning power & peace of God,
   General redemption in thy blood,
   And pardon thro' thy Name.

10. [MS Preachers 1786 (MS CW I[k]), pp. 9–10; MS CW I(q), viii.]

2. While preaching gospel to the poor,
    My soul impoverish, and secure
        By deep humility,
    Safe in thy wounds a Novice hide,
    Then shall I preach the Crucified,
        And nothing know but thee.

3. T'exalt myself I woud not speak,
    Or proud of my own talents, seek
        The praise of flattering man,
    But serve Thee with a single eye,
    And while thy Name I magnify,
        Thy approbation gain.

4. With pride that I may never swell,
    Or my suppos'd importance feel,
        Vouchsafe me, Lord, the grace
    To loath myself in my own eyes
    Myself deny, renounce, despise,
        And take the lowest place.

5. Here may I covet no reward,
    Nor triffles temporal regard,
        Or reckon earth my home,
    But things invisible desire,
    And wait for my appointed hire
        Till the great Shepherd come.

6. A life of poverty and toil,
    A thousand lives, one gracious Smile
        Of thine will overpay,
    If Thou receive me with *Well done,*
    And for thy faithful Servant own,
        In that triumphant day.

AN *OLD* METHODIST PREACHER'S PRAYER[11]

1.   Jesus, my hope, my life, my Lord,
     A mean dispenser of thy word,
         Wilt Thou not still defend?
     Who hast thro' life my refuge been,
     Preserve from the Satanic sin,
         And save me to the end.

2.   The foe hath thrust at me full sore,
     That I might fall and rise no more,
         But succour'd by thy aid,
     He coud not drag me to the pit,
     He coud not sift a soul like wheat
         For which my Saviour pray'd.

3.   Thou woudst not let the Fiend prevail,
     Or suffer my weak faith to fail
         In trials too severe,
     Trials which long as life must last;
     For O, the danger is not past,
         The tempter still is near.

4.   My faith is to the utmost tried,
     In lofty thoughts ingendring pride
         His fiery darts I feel:
     He temp[t]s me to th'ambitious crime
     Which hurl'd him from a throne sublime
         To the profoundest hell.

5.   He practises his subtlest wiles,
     My heart with soothing hopes beguiles
         Of greater usefulness,
     Woud I my Mother-Church disown,
     Call her the whore of Babylon,
         And look for vast success.

11. [MS Preachers 1786 (MS CW I[k]), pp. 10–13; MS CW I(q) viii under the above title.]

6. He urges me (so rich in grace,
   So great) to take the highest place,
       Superior gifts to *show,*
   To *separate* from the carnal croud,
   And proudly trample on the proud
       Ungodly Priests *below.*

7. Beneath the honors of thy Name
   He teaches me to hide my Aim
       And well-disguis'd intent,
   To make my own provision sure
   My name ennoble,[12] and secure
       An earthly Settlement!

8. O Son of God, whose flaming eyes
   Look thro' th'Angelical disguise,
       The Serpent's closest art,
   Far from my soul *his sin* remove,
   Humble by thy expiring love,
       And fill my humbled heart.

9. O may I every moment feel,
   My prone[ne]ss to the devilish ill,
       If unrestrain'd by grace,
   And never in *my* grace confide,
   Or think myself secure from pride
       Till I behold thy Face.

10. Thy Face I shortly hope to see,
    And partner of thy victory
        To tread the tempter down,
    And more than conqueror thro' thy blood
    By the meer Mercy of my God
        To gain the glorious crown.

12. [The word "perpetuate" is written above "ennoble" as an alternative.]

THE PRAYER OF AN OLD METHODIST PREACHER[13]

1.   God of unbounded patience, hear
   An humble penitent sincere
      Who at thy footstool fall,
   My sins of ignorance confess,
   Since first I tasted of thy grace,
      And offer'd it to All.

2.   A novice full of youthful fire,
   I call'd them to the World's Desire,
      Who woud not One reject;
   I preach'd his love to all mankind
   Nor knew that mine was still confin'd
      To my own narrow Sect.

3.   Elate with controversial pride
   To janglings vain I turn'd aside,
      And mercy show'd to none,
   I did my fellow-servants smite,
   In publishing their faults delight
      But overlook'd my own.

4.   Then, Lord, I had not learnt of Thee
   To melt at man's infirmity,
      To share the Sufferer's sigh,
   To pity Those that went astray,
   And did not find the perfect way
      Or know so much as I.

5.   'Gainst every Sect I fiercely fought,
   Unless with me they spake and thought;
      Myself infallible,
   I scrupled not the sons of Rome
   As Satan's Synagogue to doom
      And send them all to hell.

13. [MS Preachers 1786 (MS CW I[k]), pp. 13–16; MS CW I(p) xvi, under the above title.]

6. The day of smaller things, the wise
    To fear their Lord, I dared despise,
       The Servants of my God
    With Satan's desperate slaves I join'd,
    As those who coud no blessing find
       Before they felt thy blood.

7. Their virtues, alms, accepted prayers,
    Their well-meant deeds, & pious cares
       As splendid sins I deem'd,
    As filth their partial righteousness,
    The work of thy Initial grace,
       I impiously blasphem'd.

8. My strong partition-walls within
    I mock'd as 'Advocates for sin'
       Who saw not with my eyes,
    As all but who my Plan allow'd
    Were, with the unbelieving croud,
       Shut out of paradise.

9. But O! the depth of pardning love!
    Thou dost the middle walls remove,
       Detect the Serpent's art,
    Dost end the dark, Satanic hour,
    And by th'uniting Spirit's power
       Inlarge my wondring heart.

10. Inlighten'd by thy grace, I see,
    The different Sects in One agree
       Essentially the same,
    Who love, or long to love their Lord,
    And hope, believing in thy word,
       Salvation thro' thy Name.

11. The Men whoever hold the Head
    And woud be by thy Spirit led,
       And freely saved by grace,
    To their own forms & modes I leave,
    But Them with open arms receive
       And cordially embrace.

12. With Those that do thy Father's will
    A closer fellowship I feel
        Than nature's dearest tie,
    Whom neither life nor death can part
    I have, I have them in my heart,
        With Them to live, and die.

THE PEOPLE'S PRAYER FOR THE METHODIST PREACHERS[14]

1. Head of thy Church, our prayers attend
   For men Thou didst to sinners send
       With news of sin forgiven,
   Raised from the people's lowest lees,
   Thy messengers to publish peace,
       Peace betwixt Earth and Heaven.

2. Their prayers for Us Thou oft hast heard
   O answer Ours for Them, prefer'd
       In thy prevailing Name,
   Display thy tutelary power,
   Their Guardian in the fiery hour,
       And bring them thro' the flame.

3. Root out that curst self-seeking pride,
   Which woud the little Flock divide
       And into Parties tear,
   That each may make his will the law,
   After himself disciples draw,
       And seize the largest share.

4. Highminded they refuse to hear
   The ruin, and confusion near,
       The Consequences scorn,
   When brethren shall with brethren fight,
   When banish'd peace shall take its flight
       And never more return.

14. [MS Preachers 1786 (MS CW I[k]), pp. 17–19.]

5. They will not see th'impending ills,
   All Israel scatter'd on the hills
       By no kind Shepherd led,
   No longer by their Mother nurst;
   Their children vagabonds, disperst,
       And supplicants for bread.

6. Warn'd by their loving Pastor's care
   To shun the specious Tempter's snare,
       They slight his kind request.
   'Parties distinct ye must not be
   '(Howe'er provok'd, whate'er your plea)
       'Or separate from the rest.

7. 'Have any separated, and sped
   'And prosper'd in the daring deed?
       'Their love and meekness lost,
   'Their influence more and more confin'd,
   'No longer useful to mankind,
       'They sunk into the dust.'

8. Yet resolute These to win the prize
   They stop their ears, and shut their eyes
       And rush into the toils,
   Soon as their long-liv'd Father drops,
   To gratify their greedy hopes
       They fly upon the spoils.

9. The Sword is drawn, the Breach is made!
   But where shall the proud waves be stay'd
       Of controversial strife?
   The Sects against each other spend
   Their bitter zeal, and fighting end
       A vile, litigious life.

10. The kingdom took from Them, by God
    Shall then on others be bestow'd,
        A poor, but fruitful race,
    Contented to be nothing here,
    Who rise by lowly loving fear
        To perfect holiness.

$$II^{15}$$

1. But O my God, shall all be lost
   And the proud foe his victory boast
       Or'e every messenger?
   Surely Thou hast a Remnant still
   Of servants who their weakness feel,
       And always humbly fear.

2. The depths of hell they have not known,
   They do not vaunt, or seek their own
       Or lose their poverty:
   The Salt its savour doth retain
   Nor honour they desire, nor gain
       Nor any good but Thee.

3. They woud not take the tempter's part;
   Thou hearst the language of their heart
       When boded ill is nigh,
   The best suspects himself the worst:
   "Shall I forsake my calling first?
       Shall I my Lord deny?"

4. A difference in their favor make,
   And now into thy bosom take
       The humble and sincere:
   Tell them, they shall not die, but live,
   And to each trembling Servant give
       The grace to persevere.

5. The chaff shall fly, Thou sayst it shall;
   But not one grain of wheat shall fall
       In the wide-scattering day:
   Thou shalt their work & partners show
   To men who woud thy counsel know,
       And all thy will obey.

15. [MS Preachers 1786 (MS CW I[k]), pp. 19–22; MS CW I(q) x.]

6. The weak, the simple, and the poor
   Within thy mercy's arms secure
      With confidence we leave:
   But O the strong, the rich, the wise,
   Ee'r their last spark of goodness dies
      Revisit and forgive.

7. Help us for them in faith to pray,
   Blind Guides, who have mistook their way
      And wander'd far from thine:
   To them again their calling show,
   Raised up to carry on below
      Thy Mercy's chief Design.

8. To the lost sheep of England's fold
   First, be the joyful tidings told
      (Thus their Commission ran)
   Then every Sect & party press
   To know the power of godliness
      And every Child of man.

9. Resolv'd their calling to pursue,
   Do Thou the Preachers' strength renew,
      With double grace inspire,
   Their work with tenfold blessings crown
   To turn the kingdoms upside down
      And set the world on fire.

10. Then let the spreading fire of love
    By Thee rekindled from above
       In every bosom burn,
    Till those that hear, or preach thy word
    See in the clouds their flaming Lord
       And all to heaven return.

III [16]

1.   Lord of the harvest, hear
Our supplicating cry,
And every gospel-messenger
With labouring strength supply,
With well-instructed zeal
To make thy mercy known
Their ministerial work fulfil
And live for Thee alone.

2.   To show forth all thy praise
Let them thy servants live,
Of every virtue, every grace
A bright example give:
Let each by sinking rise,
By self-abasing fear,
And poor, and mean in his own eyes,
And least of all appear.

3.   Still let thy little ones
Thy little ones remain,
Nor e'er despise the prophets' sons* [17]
Or wish like Them to reign:
Out of their hearts expel
The plague of selfish pride,
And in thy secret place conceal
And by thy Presence hide.

4.   Be this their single aim
Thy glorious truth to spread,
As simple men without a name
Who hang on Thee for bread;
Who never seek their own:
In blest obscurity
Content to live and die unknown,
Or known to none but Thee.

16. [MS Preachers 1786 (MS CW I[k]), pp. 22–3; and in MS CW I(q) viii.]
17. *The Clergy. [See MS CW I(q).]

5.   In answer to our prayer
      Thy mind in Them reveal,
That every humbled messenger
      May his own vileness feel;
      That to the faithful race
      They all thro' life may prove
Patterns of purity, and grace,
      Of meek and lowly love.

THE CALL OF THE FIRST
SOUND METHODIST PREACHERS[18]

1.   Godly in Christ resolv'd to live,
      Branded by an opprobrious name,
   The scandal calmly we receive
      Th'impos'd Appellative disclaim:
   The world may either curse, or bless,
   Names cannot make us more or less.

2.   Not the wild Authors of a Sect,
      Not Ringleaders, ourselves we call,
   But messengers of God elect,
      Raised up for preaching Christ to all,
   To Christians not in heart but name,
   Whose lives with heathens save the same.[19]

3.   Not as distinguish'd from the rest
      In a new Party's bounds confin'd
   But sent we run, in spirit prest
      To do the work by God design'd,
   Primeval piety revive,
   And *show* how real Christians live.

18. [MS Preachers 1786 (MS CW I[k]), pp. 24–6; Wesley Family Letters, I, p. 51, with variants.]

19. [Wesley's compressed language is obscure here but he probably suggests the following meaning: part of the preaching task is to proclaim the gospel to Christians who are Christians only in name but not in heart. They can do no more than the heathen, namely, save no one and nothing. MS CW Family Letters, p. 51 has the following concluding line to verse 2: With heathens in the lives the same.]

4.   Born and bred up within the Pale
      Of England's Church, to her we owe
Our first regard; and cannot fail
      Our filial gratitude to show,
And gladly in her service join
Affection natural and divine.

5.   We for our dearest Country feel
      A warmth which words cannot express,
An inextinguishable zeal
      Which patriots false in vain profess;
Nor can we from a Church remove
Which more than life we prize & love.

6.   By civil and religious ties
      United to our brethren here,
Them we respect who us despise,
      Who neither God nor man revere,
But in the deadly darkness dwell
And riot on the Verge of hell.

7.   While plung'd in wickedness and vice
      Our wretched Countrymen we see,
We see them with the Saviour's eyes,
      We feel his y[e]arning sympathy,
Sad Prophet of their woes to come
Who wept the bloody City's doom.

8.   We put his tender bowels on
      Who did his murtherers redeem,
Our lives made willing to lay down,
      To spend, and to be spent for Them
Our brethren, countrymen;—& friends
When hatred in conversion ends.

II[20]

1. But chiefly Those in Moses' seat,
   The Sons of Levi, we revere,
   To all their just commands submit
   Honor their sacred Character,
   Their heavenly Office magnify,
   Servants and Priests of the Most-High.

2. Their Apostolic claim we own,
   Their Right by Providence divine
   From age to age deliver'd down
   God's covenants in his name to sign,
   Watchmen of Israel's house confest,
   To guard and govern all the rest.

3. Of these if some their charge betray,
   And careless, or ungodly live,
   Must they not answer in that day
   When call'd a strict account to give?
   And *shoud* they not our pity move,
   Demand our prayers, and tenderest love?

4. Whoe'er the fiery spirit feel
   Or good and bad alike decry,[21]
   We dare not rail with bitter zeal,
   Or the whole Order vilify,
   Or e'er expose a father's shame,
   And share the curse of impious Ham.

5. The men who as Gamaliel wise,
   Stand still our *whole* design to see,
   Let them our actions scrutinize,
   Till, conquering their neutrality,
   Our lives over their doubts prevail
   And truth weighs down the hovering scale.

20. [MS Preachers 1786 (MS CW I[k]), pp. 26–8; Wesley Family Letters, I, p. 51.]

21. [At the foot of p. 27 of the MS Sally Wesley Junr. has written: "Or call for vengeance from the sky!"]

6. If fiercely some the truth deny,
      Shall we, incens'd, our patience lose,
   Or with invectives keen reply,
      Angry contempt, & foul abuse?
   The wrath of man let God repress;
   It worketh not his righteousness.

7. Humble, dispassionate, and meek,
      As sheep before the shearers dumb,
   Leave we to turn the other cheek
      Till evil we with Good ore'come,
   Their furious enmity remove,
   And melt their hatred into love.

8. But those that labour in the word
      Worthy we count of double praise,
   As abler servants of their Lord,
      Distinguish'd Ministers of grace,
   Their faithful, tho' obscure, Allies
   We trace their footsteps to the skies.

9. O might we gain that heavenly Rest,
      Meanest of all the Prophet's Sons,
   Behold our Guides supremely blest,
      Exalted to superior thrones,
   With joy our elder brethren meet,
   And shout triumphant at their feet!

III[22]

1. Head of thy Church, attend our cry
      For those thou hast redeem'd of old,
   Regard with a propitious eye
      The lambs and sheep of England's fold,
   For whom in earnest faith we pray,
   And glad thy *dear* command obey.

22. [MS Preachers 1786 (MS CW I[k]), pp. 28–30; MS CW I(q) xi.]

2. Thy promise to the Church at large
   For our Particular we plead,
   O make her thy peculiar charge,
   Her children satisfy with bread,
   Bless with a thousandfold increase
   And fill them with eternal peace.

3. Thou hast in our degenerate years
   Reviv'd thine antient work of grace,
   A cloud of witnesses appears,
   Who know thy name, & spread thy praise,
   Redeem'd, and of thy Spirit born,
   With songs to Sion they return.

4. Thou hast ten thousand tokens given,
   That Engl[an]d's Church is still thy care,
   The Holy Ghost sent down from heaven
   Thy truth and mercy doth declare,
   Thine everlasting gospel seals,
   And pardon in our hearts reveals.

5. While Thee remembering in thy ways
   Thou dost thy favour'd people meet,
   In all the channels of thy grace
   We hold with Thee communion sweet,
   The Cloud on our Assemblies rests,
   And glory swells our ravish'd breasts.

6. Thee present in thy Courts we find,
   Thee present at thy table now,
   And while we call thy death to mind
   Thyself Thou to our hearts dost show,
   And nourish'd with immortal food,
   We eat thy flesh, & drink thy blood.

7. Then let us still delight to wait
   Where our dear Lord is pleas'd t'appear:
   Bethel is the celestial gate,
   And faithful souls perceive Thee here,
   And all who here with Thee remain
   The crown of endless life shall gain.

IV [23]

1.   Why shoud we now a Church forsake
     Which Thou our Lord hast not forsook,
  Which Thou thy residence dost make
     And hast into thy bosom took?
  And kept by the good Shepherd's care,
  The lambs & sheep are happy there.

2.   To silent streams his flock he leads,
     And while on Him our souls recline,
  Our souls in pastures green he feeds,
     With Angels' bread of life divine,
  With hidden manna from above,
  The joy of hope, the heaven of love.

3.   Our souls in holiness restor'd
     He marks with his new name unknown,
  Found in the image of our Lord
     From faith to faith he leads us on,
  In pleasant paths of perfect peace,
  And everlasting righteousness.

4.   While walking in the mortal vale
     We cannot fear with Christ our Guide,
  No evil shall our souls assail
     While Jordan's stricken waves divide,
  And stay'd by thine almighty hand,
  With shouts we gain the heavenly land.

5.   Till then Thou dost a table spread
     For us, in presence of our foes,
  With sacred oyl anoint our head,
     And fill'd by Thee our cup o'erflows,
  Our days are all with mercy crown'd,
  Our lives with God for ever found.

23. [MS Preachers 1786 (MS CW I[k]), pp. 30–31; in MS CW I(q) xi, it is numbered II. Note the echoes from verse to verse of Psalm 23.]

6. Here then, while sojourning below,
   We in thy house resolve to dwell,
And to that heavenly Sion go,
   Eternal extacies to feel,
And all who here their Mother love
Shall join with us the Church above.

V^{24}

O PRAY FOR THE PEACE OF JERUSALEM: THEY SHALL
PROSPER THAT LOVE HER, &C. [PS. 122:6]

1. Jesus, our true and faithful Lord,
   Sole Author of assur'd success,
Thou knowst if we can trust thy word
   The Lovers of thy Church to bless;
Thy promise of prosperity
Thou knowst if it belongs to me.

2. To us commission'd in thy name
   To preach glad tidings to the poor,
May we not confidently claim
   The word to pious children sure,
Who dutiful affection show
The Church to which their birth they owe?

3. All wise, omniscient as Thou art,
   Thou dost our secret passions see,
The drop which now o'reflows my heart,
   The tenderness of piety
From the pure, heavenly Fountain flow'd:
The grace Thou hast thyself bestow'd.

4. Thy word Thou hast to us fulfill'd,
   Least of our Church's duteous Sons,
Our ministerial labours seal'd
   On multitudes of quicken'd stones,
Hast prosper'd us weak things of nought
And wonders by meer sinners wrought.

24. [MS Preachers 1786 (MS CW I[k]), pp. 32–3; MS CW I(q) xi. The AV reads:
"Pray for the peace of Jerusalem: they shall prosper that love thee."]

5.   But bless us, Lord, and prosper still
        Who in the good old ship abide,
    (And fight our passage up the hill,
        God, and the martyrs on our side)
    For Sion still our love declare
    In all the fervency of prayer.

6.   Peace be within her walls, and grace,
        Plenty be in her temples found,
    Let all the fruits of righteousness
        In our Jerusalem abound,
    That faith may from the least proceed,
    And knowledge to the Greatest spread.

7.   For other Sects' & Churches' sake
        We seek to do our Sion good,
    That They her blessings may partake,
        Plenteous redemption in thy blood,
    That the pure life her children find
    May reach, and quicken all mankind.

[O THOU TO WHOM ALL HEARTS ARE KNOWN][25]

1.   O Thou to whom all hearts are known,
    Who dost for thy disciples own
        The simple and the poor,
    Omniscient Son of God & man,
    Come with thy winnowing Spirit's fan,
        And throughly purge thy floor.

2.   Who rashly ran uncall'd, unsent,
    And forging thy commission, went
        With us to the high-ways,
    Arrest, & lay them, Lord, aside,
    And every false Pretender hide
        In his own proper place.

25. [MS Preachers 1786 (MS CW I[k]), pp. 34–5.]

3.   The men who did not count the cost,
    The Salt that hath its savor lost
      Out of thy Church[26] remove;
    But let them in the ship remain,
    The men Thou didst thyself ordain
      Who Thee & Sion love.

4.   Still let the little leaven spread,
    The remnant small, the faithful seed,
      Throughout our happy land;
    Exert thy power, till every knee,
    Till every heart bows down to Thee
      And blesses thy command.

5.   But first, Thou all-refining Fire,
    With purifying faith inspire
      The Sacerdotal race,
    That multitudes of priests may know
    Their heavenly Lord reveal'd below,
      And preach thy pard'ning grace.

6.   Why shoud They be the last that bring
    Home to their hearts their gracious King
      Who comes with man to dwell,
    Their sins & troubles to remove,
    And with the signal of his Love
      True Israelites to seal?

7.   Who bear the vessels of the Lord,
    Cleans'd by the Spirit & the word,
      Thy converts let them rise,
    Strengthen their brethren's hearts, & gain,
    And urge them with their guides t'obtain
      A kingdom in the skies.

26. [The phrase "Far from thy work" is written in the margin as an alternative to "Out of thy Church".]

8. Thy Priests be cloth'd with righteousness,
    Thy flock a thousand-fold increase,
        A witness of thy power
    Till each with God himself acquaints
    And Britain shines, an Isle of saints,
        Till time shall be no more.

PRAYER FOR THE UNCONVERTED CLERGY[27]

1. Thy Priests commanded to revere,
        We pay them the respect we owe;
    But can we, Lord, with heart sincere,
        More than external honor show?
    Howe'er unwilling to displease,
        And Governors & Fathers blame,
    Thy Church's Guides we must confess
        In every nation still the same.

2. Their outward call to minister
        In things divine is plainly prov'd:
    But few, ordain'd by man, we fear,
        Are inly by thy Spirit mov'd:
    Yet These, devoid of sacred power
        Who nothing know, or understand,
    Suffer'd by Thee, thy flock devour,
        And all thy houses in the land.

3. But hast Thou, Lord, thy church forsook,
        And let thy faithful promise fail?
    Sion is founded on the Rock;
        The gates of hell cannot prevail:
    Thou dost thy people's wants supply,
        And some of every Order raise
    In every age, to testify
        Thy truth, & power, & pardning grace.

27. [MS Preachers 1786 (MS CW I[k]), pp. 36–8.]

4. Jesus, thy witnesses increase,
   And let thy gospel-trumpet sound
To rouse the men, who take their ease
   In luxury, and pleasure drown'd:
Break, & bind up the broken heart
   Of every stranger to his Lord—
Convince the Pastors, & convert,
   And send them forth to preach thy word.

5. Open their eyes the signs to see,
   The tokens of this gospel-day,
Of Sion visited by Thee
   Who comst to take our sins away:
To the lost sheep of England's fold,
   Is not the great Salvation sent?
Thine Arm reveal'd let them behold
   And gladly answer thy Intent.

6. Saviour, at thy benign command
   A troop of preaching Priests shall rise,
And Israel's Masters understand
   The mysteries hidden from the wise,
Themselves begotten from above,
   Made conscious of their sins forgiven,
Renew'd in holiness & love
   And meet for all the joys of heaven.

B. OTHER HYMNS FOR METHODIST PREACHERS

[FATHER & FRIEND OF ALL MANKIND][28]

1. Father & Friend of all mankind,
    Who hast to every soul assign'd
        His destin'd work below,
    On us who serve thy blessed will,
    While we our daily task fulfil,
        Thy promis'd grace bestow.

2. We hear thy Providential call,
    Things honest in the sight of all
        Industrious to provide,
    "Go forth with the ascending ray
    Our travel[29] for our bread to pay,
        As still in thee confide."

3. Thy blessing makes our work succeed,
    Thy bounty gives our daily bread;
        And nourish'd from above
    We here our proper place maintain
    And pay our *only* debt to man
        In pure, fraternal love.

4. Assur'd Thou wilt direct our ways,
    Who Thee in all events confess,
        And in thy mercy trust,
    With chearful hearts we labour on
    Till nature lays her burthen down,
        And dust returns to dust.

28. [MS Preachers 1786 (MS CW I[q]) xviii; also in MS Misc. Hymns, p. 273 with the title "Hymns for some called to earn their bread!"]
29. [The *Oxford English Dictionary* quotes two examples of "travel" with the meaning of "bodily or mental labour" in the eighteenth century and none later.]

[O GOD WHO DIDST THE SEERS INSPIRE][30]

1. O God who didst the Seers inspire,
    If Thee sincerely I desire
        To know, revere, obey,
    Thy all-inlightning grace afford,
    And by the Spirit, & the word
        Point out my heavenly way.

2. While from fallacious man I cease,
    To none, for real happiness,
        But to Thyself I go:
    They only find, who learn of Thee,
    The science of felicity
        And life eternal know.

3. In vain the Partisans of Rome
    Divine authority assume
        And all mankind condemn,
    "God cannot help us to believe,
    Unless implicit we receive
        The written word from Them."

4. But he that reads, thy Spirit perceives
    Breathing throughout the sacred leaves
        Interpreting thy will;
    The soul o'rewhelm'd with doubts and fears
    The Voice of whispering Wisdom hears,
        "To know thy God, be still!"

5. Faith comes by hearing of thy word,
    And witnessing of Christ the Lord
        Thy Spirit seals it thine;
    Thou dost confirm thy word of grace,
    Which true believers all confess
        The Saving power divine.

30. [MS Preachers (MS CW I[q]), xxvi.]

6.   Spirit and life, thy words, convey
       A power the Speaker to obey
          In all that Thou hast said;
       The evangelic faith impart
       To every unopposing heart,
          And bring to life the dead.

7.   Wher[e]fore, if thou the grace permit,
       Attentive at my Teacher's feet
          I wait, till Christ appears!
       Now, Lord, eternally the same,
       Speak, and declare thy Father's name,
          For now thy Servant hears.

8.   Determin'd here I still abide,
       Scripture my rule, and God my Guide;
          And when my Lord I love,
       And when the Truth I fully know,
       In glorious liberty I go,
          To sing thy praise above.

PREPARATORY[31]

1.   Father, Thou knowst I need
          Pardon & Purity
      To make me free indeed
          And meet thy Face to see,
    Free from the guilt & stain of sin,
    And saved, & glorious all within.

2.   My double want supply
          For Jesus' sake alone,
      And make before I die
          Thy truth & mercy known;
    Before I yield my fleeting breath,
    Redeem my soul from endless death.

---

31. [MS Preachers (MS CW I[q]), p. 4.]

1784[32]

1. O God, who dost the motives know
From which our various actions flow,
    And what we now intend,
If Thee our Lawful Purpose please
Prevent, accompany, and bless
    With a successful end.

2. Unmov'd by avarice or pride
Things honest, L[or]d, we woud provide
    According to thy will,
And, (while thy hand points out our way,)
The providential call obey
    And thy designs fulfil.

3. By thy paternal love decreed
To labour for our daily bread,
    Our business we pursue,
In every step look up to Thee,
And ask, with meek docility,
    What woudst Thou have us do?

4. Who dost from man his purpose hide,
If from thy path we turn aside,
    Our wandring feet repress,
Stop us impatient to proceed,
Nor let us snatch with eager speed
    At dangerous success.

5. Deceiv'd by each appearance fair,
The specious bait, the secret snare,
    Thou know'st we cannot shun,
Unless we thy direction find,
Who promisest to bring the blind
    A way we have not known.

32. [MS Preachers (MS CW I[q]), pp. 1–2. The poem exists with variants in a manuscript at Drew University, where it is entitled "Prayers for the Divine Blessing on a Temporal Undertaking. Sept. 1784."]

6. But thro' the world's insidious arts,
    The labyrinth of human hearts,
        Thou wilt thy children lead,
    Who biddest us of men beware,
    Thou wilt with kind continued care
        Supply our every need.

7. Thee then we joyfully confess,
    In all our purposes and ways,
        Disposer of thine own,
    And satisfied with God our Friend,
    Soul, body, and estate commend
        Into thy hands alone.

8. We trust our never failing Guide,
    Thou wilt for all our wants provide,
        And all our paths attend,
    Giver of every gift and grace,
    Till happily our earthly race
        In life immortal end.

[TREMENDOUS GOD, SEVERELY JUST][33]

1. Tremendous God, severely just,
        Beneath thy mighty hand we fall,
    For mercy, prostrate in the dust,
        In Jesus' name for mercy call,
    While humbly we our sins confess
    And mourn our nation's wickedness.

2. The perilous, vindictive times,
        The long-impending plagues are come,
    And Britain's complicated crimes
        Loudly demand her instant doom;
    The vial bursts, the curse takes place
    And swallows up our faithless race.

33. [MS Preachers (MS CW I[q]) vii, p. 4.]

[JUDGMENT IS AT THY HOUSE BEGUN][34]

Judgm[en]t is at thy house begun:
  Our brethren once belov'd of Thee,
Thy followers in a world unknown
  They scorn thy lifted Hand to see,
And rush on their own flesh & blood
To death pursuing—& pursued.

[WHILE BLACKEST CLOUDS INVOLVE THE SKIES][35]

1. While blackest clouds involve the skies,
    And discord's maddest waves arise,
      Ah! whither shall we flee!
    To whom for sure protection run,
    Or how the dire contagion shun
      Of factious anarchy?

2. Thee, Jesus, Thee whoe'er confess,
    Thine Israel's strength, thy people's Peace,
      From age to age the same,
    A covert from the storm & wind,
    A Tower impregnable we find
      In thy Almighty Name.

3. Who bow to thy supreme command,
    The meek & quiet in the land,
      O may we still appear,
    Our faith by our obedience show,
    And in thy Delegate below
      The King of kings revere.

34. [MS Preachers (MS CW I[q]) vii, p. 4. It is possible that this verse is a continuation of the last. It appears after a space, perhaps for other verses, on the same page of the MS.]
  35. [MS Preachers (MS CW I[q]) vii, p. 8.]

[TO WHOM IN PERIL & DISTRESS][36]

1. To whom in peril & distress
   While growing ills our Land oppress,
   Shoud we for refuge fly?
   Jesus, from age to age the same,
   We find, confiding in thy Name,
   The strength of Israel nigh.

2. Of wars & rumour'd wars we hear,
   But thy command forbids our fear,
   And unbelieving haste;
   In Thee our quiet souls we hide
   And safe beneath thy wings abide,
   Till every storm is past.

3. Our only care thy grace to gain
   And stedfast in the faith remain
   Which sweetly works by love,
   To prove thine accept[abl]e Will
   And all thy dear com[mands] fulfil
   As angels do above.

4. Us, whom thy mind & Spirit arm,
   Nor sword nor pestilence can harm,
   Nor earth nor hell annoy;
   The plagues that on the wicked seize
   Can never interrupt our peace,
   Or rob us of our joy.

5. We thus to meet our God prepare[37]
   By constant watchfulness & prayer,
   By toils of love renew'd,
   Assured that all events shall join
   Accomplishing thy blest design
   In our eternal good.

36. [MS CW IV, '75–6.]
37. [In the margin in shorthand appears the following alternative to lines one and two:
    We thus to meet our God prepare,
    Labouring and watching into prayer.]

6. O Son of Man, O God most high
    We on thy faithful word rely
        For persevering[38] grace,
    Till fully saved & counted meet
    We stand, in Holiness compleat,
        Before thy glorious Face.

[O THOU WHO DOST THE PROUD WITHSTAND][39]

1. O Thou who dost the proud withstand,
    While those that stoop beneath thy hand,
        Thy hand sets up on high,
    Behold the men whose load we bear
    Who, sprung out of the dunghill, dare
        Themselves to magnify.

2. The self-exalting worms abase,[40]
    Ambitious of the highest place,
        Into the lowest thrust,
    Compel'd to feel thine angry frown;
    Their Luciferian pride cast down
        And humble to the dust.

3. Down to the dust, but not to hell,
    Abase the men who long have fell
        From their humility,
    Who now at wealth & honour aim
    Audacious for their own to claim
        The sheep redeem'd by Thee.

38. [The words "All-sufficient" and "all-preserving" are written in the margin as alternatives to "persevering."]
39. [MS CW IV, 72.]
40. [In MS CW IV, 75, there is a draft of this verse in shorthand included as an additional verse to "To whom in peril and distress," but transferred to this hymn. The draft reads:
    7. The self-exalting worms abase,
        The men who love the highest place,
            In their own merits trust,
        On all their fond devices frown,
        Their Luciferian pride cast down
            And down into the dust.
Wesley began a further verse, "Into the dust, but not to hell," but left it incomplete.]

4. Wild havoc of the flock they make
   For power & filthy lucre's sake
      And into parties rend,
   Unless thy mercy interpose
   And save thy people from their foes
      And save them to the end.

5. Our gracious & almighty Lord,
   According to thy faithful word
      In which thy Church confide,
   Stand Thou before the poison spread
   Betwixt the living & the dead
      And stay the plague of pride.

6. Now, now the dire contagion stop,
   The source of bitter strife dry up,
      The stumbling block remove,
   That all may think & speak the same
   And breathe the Spirit of the Lamb
      In meek & lowly love.

HYMNS AND POEMS
FOR ORDINATION

ON JOHN WESLEY'S ORDAINING DR. COKE, &C.[1]

1.　Wesley himself & Friends betrays
　　By his good Sense forsook,
　　When suddenly his Hands he lays
　　On the hot Head of Coke:

2.　Yet we at least should spare the weak,
　　His weak Co-evals we;
　　Nor blame a hoary Schismatick,
　　A Saint of eighty three.

[A ROMAN EMPEROR, 'TIS SAID][2]

A Roman emperor, 'tis said,
His favourite horse a consul made:
But Coke brings greater things to pass—
He makes a bishop of an ass.

1. [MS Samuel Wesley, p. 2; MS Ordinations, No. (1); *Rep. Verse*, No. 325, p. 367. The former is in the hand of Samuel Wesley, the son of Charles. See below the poem entitled "Epigram" on p. 89.]

2. [The poem is printed in William Guirey's *The History of Episcopacy* (Raleigh, NC: Gales, 1799), p. 332. In a footnote Guirey states: "These lines are to be found in the possession of the Reverend Mr. Samuel Bradburn, in Mr. Wesley's own handwriting; and if I mistake not, Mr. Bradburn told me he was present when Mr. Wesley wrote them." For this reference the editors are grateful to Dr. Frank Baker, who says in a personal letter, "I have a file of Bradburn material, but see no reference to this. But in the MS Ordinations there are suggestions of missing material, and the stubs of leaves, and it may well have been that Bradburn did actually have Charles Wesley's copy of the poem." John A. Vickers cites the poem in his volume *Thomas Coke: Apostle of Methodism* (London: Epworth, 1969), p. 102. Baker comments further, "Vickers mentions the poem as 'later', and implies it is 1787, and it may well have been associated with Coke's 'Letter to the author of Strictures on Dr. Coke's Ordination Sermon' (of Asbury), London, 1786 (see Vickers, p. 378). But although there is some speculation here, I think that the poem is almost certainly genuinely by Charles Wesley, and that the almost contemporary vouching for this by Guirey from Bradburn is good evidence, though not absolute proof."]

ALL MY GEESE ARE SWANS[3]

The Methodists must all allow
Their Preachers taken from the Plough;
In Schools they pick'd up little Knowledge,
Nothing beholden to the College;   *4*
To Science they had no Pretence,
To Dress, or Taste, or Elegance;
To Labour, not to Learning bred,
Yet most of them could write & read;   *8*
And some, by Mother's care, knew how
To doff their Hats, & make a Bow.

Small their Acquaintance with their Betters,
With Men of Fashion, or of Letters;   *12*
They aim'd at no Distinctions here,
Of Place, or Rank, or Character.

But lo! thro' a fond Father's Aid
They all at once become well-bred;   *16*
And instantaneously polite;
Spring up like Mushrooms in a night;
Equals to Men of high Degre,
The very Pink of Courtesy;   *20*
Worthy superlative Esteem,
For why?—they all belong to HIM
Whose ev'ry Goose is a black Swan,
Whose ev'ry *Jack's a Gentleman*.   *24*

TO DR. COKE, MR. ASBURY, AND OUR
BRETHREN IN NORTH AMERICA

IX[4]

Happy the days, when Charles and John
By nature and by grace were One
The same in office as in name,
Their judgment and their will the same: *4*

3. [MS Samuel Wesley, p. 3, dated 1786.]
    4. [MS Brothers, pp. 31–5. MS Brothers is a notebook dated Bristol, Sept. 10, 1784. Only the pages cited here remain.]

True Yokefellows, they join'd to draw
The galling burthen of the Law,
And urg'd with unremitting strife
Each other on, to work for life: *8*
Chearful beneath the Legal Load,
Joyful to do imperfect good,
And all the Lord's commands t'obey,
Before they knew in Christ The Way.   *12*

   In infancy their hopes and fears,
In youth, and in their riper years,
Their hearts were to each other known
Attun'd in perfect Unison.   *16*
No private End, no selfish art
Did then the faithful Brothers part,
No flatterer the Friends divide,
Who each from each coud nothing hide,   *20*
Neither injoy'd a good alone,
Or call'd what he possess'd his own,
Their good supream with humble zeal
To know, and do the Master's will.   *24*

   To both at once their Lord reveal'd
His counsel from the Wise conceal'd,
His will to chuse the weak and base
And save a much-lov'd world by grace.   *28*
To the highways and hedges sent
They both with one Commission went,
Zealous immortal souls to win,
And force the Vagrants to come in.   *32*
He bad them first for England care,
And to her Church the truth declare
To love his own Jerusalem,
To spend, and to be spent for Them,   *36*
Outcasts of men, a thoughtless Herd,
Who sinning on with conscience sear'd,
Rush'd down the steep, by Satan driven,
As far from God, as hell from heaven.   *40*

Jesus, who sent them out by pairs,
Prosper'd his gospel-messengers,
HE their united labours bless'd,
Their flock abundantly increas'd,   *44*
Increas'd their word-begotten Sons,
And preachers rais'd from stocks & stones.

But rais'd out of the people's lees,
Raw, inexperienc'd Novices,   *48*
They soon their low Estate forgot,
And of themselves too highly thought,
While the ambitious Fiend stole in,
And poisoning them with his own sin,   *52*
Used as his Agents to inspire
With lofty thoughts their flatter'd Sire.

They urg'd the Elder Presbyter
Himself a Bishop to declare,   *56*
And then to answer their demands
By laying on his hasty hands;
The mighty Babel to erect,
And found a new Dissenting Sect,   *60*
His Mother-Church to rend, disclaim,
And brand the Party with his Name.
But for a length of years he stood,
By a whole Army unsubdued,   *64*
By friendship kept, refus'd to yield,
And all their fiery Darts repel'd,
And check'd the Madness for a space
Of Corah's[5] bold, rebellious race,   *68*
Who heard, like Eli's sons[6] unmov'd,
His words too tenderly reprov'd,
"In vain you tempt me to do ill
"For separate I never will—   *72*
"Will never with my Brother break,
"Will never die a Schismatic!"

5. [*Cf.* Numbers 16.]
6. [*Cf.* I Samuel 2–4.]

O had he died *before* that day,
When W[esley] did himself betray,   76
Did boldly on himself confer
The Apostolic Character!
O that we both had took our flight
Together to the realms of light,   80
Together yielded up our breath,
In life united, and in death!
Leaving an honest Name behind,
We then assur'd that Rest to find   84
Had past the valley undismay'd,
Nor fear'd to meet a Father's shade,
A Cloud of Witnesses inroll'd
In heaven, the sheep of England's fold,   88
A noble host of Martyrs too
Who faithful unto death, and true,
Spent their last breath for Sion's good,
And strove resisting unto blood.   92

God of unbounded power and grace,
Whose pleasure is to save and bless,
At whose omnipotent Decree
Things most impossible shall be,   96
Who only, cancelling our sin,
Canst make it as it ne'er had been;
Thine energy of love exert
And change thy favour'd Servant's heart,   100
Thy own prevailing Plea we plead—
In ignorance he did the Deed,
The Deed with endless mischiefs fraught,
Alas, he did he knew not what.   104
Pity the Blind who went astray
And turn'd the Lame out of the way;
Whom still Thou dost vouchsafe to own—
Undo the evil he hath done,   108
Incline him humbly to revoke
The fatal Step his haste hath took,
And his true heart again shall be
Turn'd back to England's Church and Thee.   112

Stir up thy faithful people, Lord,
To urge their suit with one accord,
And rescue thro' the Strength of prayer
Their Father, Guide, and Minister.   *116*
His prayers for us have reach'd thy throne,
And brought us many a blessing down:
Thy blessings all on Him be shed;
With glory crown his reverend head.   *120*
Found in the way of righteousness
There let him stay, and die in peace:
Let all the children of his prayers,
Seals of his Ministerial cares,   *124*
To him by his Redeemer given,
Compose his Crown of joy in Heaven!

II [7]

C[oke] in his spritely youth for Honor tried
And fair Preferment—on the Church's side.
For Church & King the valiant Champ[io]n fought,
And from the powerful Great a Living sought: *4*
But sick of hope delay'd, he turn'd his coat,
Rail'd at 'the Antichristian Church,' & wrote;
Abjur'd his King, on Congress fawn'd so civil,
And cring'd & held a candle to the Devil.   *8*

Resolving now a nobler Prize to gain,
The Curate views a Living with disdain:
On meaner souls her Gifts let Fortune shower,
His Object is Authority and Power;   *12*
A supple Courtier, an obsequious Tool,
He creeps to climb, & humbly stoops to rule.
Till curst with his imaginary power
He swells, a spurious Bishop for an hour,   *16*
Destroys a Church, to consequences blind,
Goes out in smoak,—& leaves his Stink behind.

---

7. [MS Ordinations, No. 2. The following group of poems numbered through roman numeral X are from MS Ordinations and are not parts of the immediately preceding poem "To Dr. Coke, Mr. Asbury, and our Brethren in North America."]

So when Erostratus[8], with fruitless aim
By virtuous Action had aspir'd to fame,   *20*
He chang'd his plan; and better to succeed
Determin'd by some bold, atrocious Deed:
Th'Ambitious Wretch, the daring Felon fir'd
A Temple thro' the universe admir'd,   *24*
By sacrilege immortaliz'd his Name,
And damn'd himself—to everlasting Fame.

III[9]

OCCIDIT, OCCIDIT![10]

1.   And is it come to this? and has the Man
       On whose Integrity our Church relied,
     Betray'd his trust, render'd our boastings vain,
       And fal'n a Victim to Ambitious Pride?

2.   Whose seal so long her Hierarchy maintain'd,
       Her humble Presbyter, her duteous Son* [11]
     Call'd an High-priest, & by Himself Ordain'd,
       He glorifies himself, & mounts[12] a Throne.

3.   Ah! where are all his Promises and Vows
       To spend, & to be spent for Sion's Good,
     To gather the lost sheep of Israel's house,
       The Outcasts bought by his Redeemer's bl[oo]d?

4.   Who won for God the wandring Souls of men,
       Subjecting multitudes to Christ's command,
     He shuts his eyes, & scatters them again,
       And spreads a thous[an]d Sects throughout the land.

8. [Herostratus (of Ephesus) is intended by Wesley. Under torture he confessed (356 B.C.E.) that he had fired the temple of Artemis to immortalize himself. *Cf.* Strabo, xiv, 640; Cicero, *De Natura Deorum*, 2. 27, etc.]

9. [MS Ordinations, No. 3; *Rep. Verse*, No. 327, pp. 368–9.]

10. ["Fallen, fallen!" Horace, *Odes*, 4, iv, 70. The Ode was written to celebrate victories by Augustus's stepsons Tiberius (future emperor) and Drusus in the Eastern Alps, 15 B.C.E.]

11. *His usual signature was E.A.P.J. [Frank Baker suggests that these initials stand for "Ecclesiae Anglicanae Presbyter," plus "jure" or "juratus," or some such word.]

12. [The word "claims" is written beneath "mounts" as an alternative.]

5. The great Restorer of Religion pure,
        Ah! why shoud he a meaner style affect,
    His friends, his principles in death abjure,
        Head of a Kirk, & Leader of a Sect?

6. His Charge, departing to the Wolf he leaves
        (For Who so fit to keep the Flock as He?)
    And to that fawning Beast unwary gives
        'His power, & seat, & great authority.'

7. W[ha]te'er of weak, or human in his Plan,
        Wood, stubble, hay built on the Solid Base,
    (His own by-laws, his own inventions vain)
        He leaves his furious Successor to raze.

8. Secure he now the sacred Pale o'releaps,
        (Tau[gh]t by audacious C[oke] to slight the guilt)
    And with that Besom of destruction sweeps
        The Babylon which his own hands had built.

9. How is the Mighty fallen from his height,
        His weapons scatter'd, & his buckler lost!
    Ah! tell it not in Gath, nor cause delight
        And triumph in the proud Philistine Host.

10. Publish it not in Askelon, to make
        The world exult in his disastrous End!
    Rather let every soul my Grief partake,
        And ah! my Father,[13] cry, & ah! my Friend!

11. The pious Mantel or'e his Dotage spread,
        W[i]th silent tears his shameful Fall deplore,
    And let him sink, forgot, among the dead
        And mention his unhappy name no more.

13. [The word "Brother" is written beneath "Father" as an alternative.]

IV[14]

Happy America, whose ruinous wars,
  Direful calamities, & loss extreme,
One single man, (above man's height) repairs,
  In rank sublime, in dignity supreme:
To gain a C[oke] is "ample Compensation,
For half a million slain and general Desolation!"* [15]

EPIGRAM[16]

1. So easily are Bishops made
      By man's, or woman's whim?
    W[esley] his hands on C[oke] hath laid,
      But who laid hands on Him?

2. Hands on himself he laid, and *took*
      An Apostolic Chair:
    And then ordain'd his Creature C[oke]
      His Heir and Successor.

3. Episcopalians, now no more
      With Presbyterians fight,
    But give your needless Contest o're,
      'Whose Ordination's right?'

4. It matters not, if Both are One,
      Or different in degree,
    For lo! ye see contain'd in John
      The whole Presbytery!

14. [MS Ordinations, No. 4; *Rep. Verse*, No. 329, p. 370.]

15. *Witness himself in his Ordination Sermon at Baltimore. 1784. [This is Wesley's own note on the quotation from Coke's sermon.]

16. [MS Ordinations, No. 5; *Rep. Verse*, No. 326, p. 368. The first verse of this epigram would appear to be based on a skit (a short satirical piece of writing) at the time of the Reformation:

  "Barlow on Parker his hands he laid,
    But who laid hands on him?"

Parker was consecrated on Dec. 17, 1559 by four bishops, including William Barlow, Bishop of St. David's, of whose consecration, however, there is no record. For other epigrams see above pp. 23, 81 and below p. 375, etc.]

VI[17]

W[esley] beset, assail'd on every side
By his own Sons become the Sons of Pride,
By every argument and every plea
Of Scottish craft, and Irish Flattery,   *4*
T'immortalize his name by noblest deeds
By laying hands on their hot giddy heads,
Firm on the Church's ground, & unsubdued
Against their growing multitude he stood   *8*
And nicely managing their hopes & fears,
Held out a siege of more than forty years.
'To found a Church, his modesty declines,
'His strength unequal to such vast designs.   *12*
'To found a Church a life of care demands,
'And wisdom more than mine, & abler hands:
'The Plan shoud be to full perfection brought
'By deeper skill, & more extensive thought: *16*
'Be patient then, my sons, that you & I
'May in the Church of England live and die.'

    He speaks: when lo! the man app[ea]rs unsou[gh]t
'Of deeper skill, and more extensive thought,'   *20*
Of wisdom to secure the ablest friends
And properest means for compassing his ends;
Resolv'd to reach the top of fortune's wheel
But skilful[18] his ambition to conceal;   *24*
Bold without fear, or shame, or self-mistrust;
Whate'er his point, it shall be done, and must   }
By one who runs, & flies, & creeps, & licks the dust.
Nor reason's aid, nor conscience's he needs   *28*
To plant the cabbage with inverted heads,
Implicit ready at his Patron's call
To pull the Temple down, or burn the Capitol.

    Who cou'd so choice an instrument refuse   *32*
So versatile, and fit for every ruse,
So forward with his tongue, & feet, & hands
And close-shut eyes, to execute commands:

17. [MS Ordinations, No. 6.]
18. [The word "careful" is written beneath "skilful" as an alternative.]

His merit must be by his foes confest,   *36*
His total worth—th'Obedience of a beast!* [19]

    No marvel he shoud soon mislead his Guide
And circumvent him on the weaker side.
Who cou'd resist the servile flatterer's skill,   *40*
Practis'd on Age, which loves to have its will?
But giving Age its will & pressing on
The servile flatterer obtain'd his own.
Glory invites, a Mitre is the Prize!   *44*
He all his arts, all his manouvres tries,
Argues, and urges him his pow[e]r to show,
Sooths, and intreats, and will not let him go.
The Sum of all his importunity: *48*
'Ordain yourself, & then lay hands on me!'

    Feeble, & self-betray'd, the Prophet hears
The voice of Satan and his messengers;
He faints; he strives against the stream no more,   *52*
Lays on his hands (with neither right nor pow[e]r),
And yields himself at last their Captive at Fourscore!

VII[20]

1.   Who can the odd Phenomenon explain?
    A Bishop new, who doth himself ordain,
    And hands extends beyond th'Atlantic main?

2.   Sends his intrepid Suffragan before,
    To found (for Presbyterians to adore)
    His Church *Episcopal* at Baltimore!

3.   'Tis done! the deed adventurous is done!
    The sword is drawn, the civil war begun.
    And John at last has pass'd the Rubicon!

19. *Obedientia jumenti. [The Latin word "jumentum" means "beast of burden." It has proved impossible to trace the classical allusion.]
20. [MS Ordinations, No. 7; *Rep. Verse*, No. 328, p. 369.]

4. A troop of Jeroboam's priests appears[21]
For, after a long life of fourscore years,
Poor John had Rehoboam's Counsellers.

5. But you who censure his ductility,
His hoary hairs with *my* compas[sio]n see,
And own—'Twas Age that made the breach, not He.

VIII[22]

W[esley] permits ambitious C[oke] to rule,
Duped by himself, and Tool of his own Tool;
While C[oke] in all his towering house succeeds,
By nicest flattery of obsequious deeds.   *4*
Impatient to revive the good old Cause,
Zealous for all his patron's rules and laws,
Him he in every fav'rite triffle apes,
Swears to his words, & puts on all his shapes.   *8*
On horseback set, he spurs his fiery steed,
And furiously rides o're the hoary head,
Well satisfied in office to appear
Either as Judge, or Executioner,   *12*
Minds neither right nor wrong, nor good nor evil, ⎫
Is rough, or smooth, is insolent or civil,   ⎬
On villains fawns, & holds a candle to the devil. ⎭

IX[23]

1. Our Champion for a length of years,
Like Samson[24] shorn, has lost his crown:
Th'Uncircumcis'd in heart and ears
With an old house have pull'd him down:

---

21. [*Cf.* I Kings 12.]
22. [MS Ordinations, No. 8.]
23. [MS Ordinations, No. 9.]
24. [*Cf.* Judges 16:17–21.]

2. They count him now their lawful prize
  As taken captive at their will:
  His Preachers have put out his eyes
  And keep him—grinding at their Mill!

X[25]

We hear a Romish Founder say
'Cast—not your sins, but—shoes away;'
Another bids, in whining note,
'Strip off the buttons from thy coat:'
A Third adorns the Sisters' shapes
With jackets, and their head with Caps:
But the supreme Reformer cries
'Your wrists, and elbows circumcise!'

VERSES WRITTEN BY CHARLES WESLEY, ON HEARING THAT HIS BROTHER JOHN WAS ORDAINING MINISTERS FOR AMERICA [1784][26]

1. Christ our merciful High-Priest,
  With thy people's grief distrest,
  Help us for our guide to pray
  Lost in his mistaken way:

2. By a show of good misled
  Lest he farther shoud proceed,
  Stop, restrain him, and defend,
  Till the hour of darkness end.

3. Hide him from the thing design'd
  Not according to thy mind;
  Save him from the purpos'd Ill
  After his, but not thy will.

25. [MS Ordinations, No. 10.]
26. [The original MS is at the New Room in Bristol.]

4. We, alas, can nothing do,
   But present him to thy view,
   Weeping at thy feet complain
   All the help of man is vain.

5. 'Gainst the truth he stops his ears,
   Will not see his children's tears,
   Shuts his eyes against the light,
   Sure, that He alone is right.

6. Whom we cannot undeceive,
   Lord, we to thy mercy leave;
   Seize him for thy mercy's sake,
   Bring our wand'ring Shepherd back.

7. We concerning this agree
   In thy Name to ask of Thee,
   Pity on thy Servant show,
   Show him what he dreads to know.

8. Of his ignorance convince,
   Of his least-suspected sins,
   Zeal, a name and sect to raise,
   Love of power, and thirst of praise.

9. Mov'd by our united prayer
   Pluck his feet out of the snare,
   Guide of our bewilder'd guide,
   Save him from the gulph of pride;

10. Rescu'd by Thy Spirit's groans
    Pleading in his pious Sons,
    Led to his Reward above,
    Thro' the path of humble Love.

TO THE REVD.—[JOHN WESLEY][27]

Your little Sketch, and sage Advice
To the free States has bless'd my eyes,
On which permit me, Sir, to send
The strictures of a faithful Friend,   *4*
Who wishes you his doubts to clear
Touching your own great Character.

You say, 'Th'Americans distrest
'Unite your Counsel to request:'   *8*
I doubt, if they indeed require it,
Or you desire them to desire it:
I fear, your pure benevolence
And care of souls, is meer pretence   *12*
Your own desires to gratify,
That dying, you may never die,
But vindicate your sacred Claim,
And purchase an immortal Name.   *16*

For King,[28] (at last you let us know)
Convinc'd you many years ago,
'Bishops and presbyters, in name
'Distinct, in Order are the same;'   *20*
And [you] th'undoubted Right possess
Now to ordain whom e'er you please.
Yet have for peace and order sake,
Refus'd your lawful Right to take,   *24*
As loth to violate, or wrong
The Church whom you had own'd so long.
Your Preachers importun'd in vain,
They cou'd not get you to Ordain: *28*
Hard-pressing you on every side
To gratify their secret pride,
(Eager the Envied Priests to ape,
And gain a feather in their cap.)   *32*

27. [MS Revd X (MS CW I[j]), pp. 1–11.]

28. [Sir Peter (afterwards Lord) King (1669–1734) was a Presbyterian by upbringing who became Lord Chancellor, and wrote his "Enquiry into the Constitution, Discipline, Unity and Worship of the Primitive Church" in 1691.]

Superior to the swelling floud,
A Rock impregnable you stood,
Nor cou'd S[i]r Peter self subdue,
Till you was turn'd of Eighty-two.   36

Wou'd King's weak reasons have prevail'd,
Had not your Solid judgment fail'd,
Had not your wavering heart misled,
And got the better of your head?   40
To prove a Point, you never was,
You never *will* be, at a loss,
(To prove, and to disprove it too)
Just as you wish it false, or true.   44

In British realms you wa[i]ve your Right,
Which justly exercise you might,
Where in America appear
Nor Bishop, Priest, nor Presbyter.   48
Wherefore abroad your scruples end;
Elders to Them you boldly send;
Tho' here you fear'd to do the same
'Where Bishops jurisdiction claim: 52
'You *fear'd t'invade their Character.*'
Alas! how weak and insincere!
You was not by that *fear* restrain'd
From sending Preachers thro' the land;   56
You chose the place of their abode,
You bad them leave it to your Nod,
And for a course of forty years
Appointed all *your* Ministers.   60

Now to your utmost height you rise,
And your whole Office exercise,
Nor Presbyters, nor Bishops need
To lay their hands upon *your* head,   64
But nobly, self-appointed, dare
To seize an Apostolic Chair,
And on the creatures of your will
Your glorious ministry fulfil.   68

And first your sacred hands are laid
On giddy Coke's aspiring head,
Your throne Prelatical t'inherit
Worthy thro' dint of pure demerit:　　　　　　72
Then, to secure a doubtful Friend,
The consecrated pall you send,
A douceur, cross th' Atlantic Sea,
To independent Astbury.[29]　　　　　　76
Two Elders, from the people's lees,
Ordain'd for holy services,
Shall your high Dignity make known,
And prove, the Church is all your own!　　　　　　80

Your Liturgy so well-prepar'd
To E[ngland]'s Church proves your regard,
Of churches national the best
By you, and all the world confest:　　　　　　84
(Why shou'd we then bad counsel take
And for a worse the best forsake?)
You tell us, with her Book of prayer
No book is worthy to compare?　　　　　　88
Why change it then for your Edition,
Deprav'd by many a bold omission?
We never will renounce our creed,
Because of Three but One you need,　　　　　　92
No longer the Nicene approve,
The Athanasian Mound remove,
And out of your New book[30] have thrown
God One in Three, & Three in One.　　　　　　96

The Articles curtail'd must be,
To compliment Presbytery:
The Saints alas & Martyrs are
All purg'd out of your Calendar,　　　　　　100
Since you for Saints acknowle[d]ge none
Except the Saints of Forty-One,
With their fanatical Descendants,
The noble House of Independants!　　　　　　104

---

29. [Charles Wesley has transcribed "Asbury" incorrectly or simply misspelled the name.]
30. [John Wesley's version of the *Book of Common Prayer*.]

Such is your Church, above the rest
Extol'd[31] and better than the best;
The Basis sure you laid *alone,*
You rais'd at once the crowning-stone: 108
And now if any man, you say,
Will point you out a wiser way
To govern these poor Sheep, and feed,
And safely thro' the desart lead;   112
You gladly will his counsel take:—
But careful *first* all sure to make,
You steal the steed, and (not before)
You bid us—shut the stable door.   116

How is it possible to hide
From your own heart its closest pride?
Pride only gave the dire occasion
Of your clandestine Ordination: 120
Pride furnish'd the usurping power,
The garret and the secret hour:
Studious to hide from human sight
A deed that cou'd not bear the light,   124
Did you your dearest Brother join
In council on your dark design?
Him you pass'd by for reasons good,
Who ready at your elbow stood,   128
And wisely your Exploit conceal'd
To none but *fav'rite Tools*[32] reveal'd,
Not to your Partners in degree,
Not to your own Presbytery.   132
Surely you meant to verify
By after-facts the Popish Lie,
And in your hugger-mugger[33] fashion
To act the Nag's head Ordination,   136
And power Pontifical assume
Greater than all the Popes of Rome.

31. [The word "Exalted" is written in the margin as an alternative to "Extol'd".]
32. [The word "favorites" is written in the margin as an alternative to "fav'rite Tools."]
33. ["Hugger-mugger" means "secret." Shakespeare used the word in Hamlet, IV, v, 83.]

Why woud you aim at things so high
Why on your Self alone rely?   140
How frivolous your strongest Plea
Of self-impos'd Necessity!
'You ask a Bishop to ordain
Whom you believe a proper man,'   144
A proper Man *your* friends esteem,
But *his* a Man improper deem:
You trust your friends, to you best known,
Best known to Him He trusts his own!   148
And who can his refusal blame,
When all men wou'd have done the same?

This urges you to let him see
You are a Bishop, good as He,   152
And need not ask his Lordship's leave
For power you to yourself can give,
Or make, after one flat denial,
Upon the rest a farther[34] trial: 156
For if they shou'd ordain your sons,
They wou'd not do it *all at once*:
No instantaneious starts they know,
So cool, deliberate, and slow,   160
You can't for their proceedings stay,
The thing admitting no delay:
(Yourself was doubtless in such haste
Lest help from hence shou'd come too fast)   164
And if our Bishops shou'd ordain,
They wou'd expect the Rule to gain
To govern the whole Church and guide,
Whereas you wou'd yourself preside,   168
And modestly yourself esteem
A fitter Governor than Them,
Somebody owed you, Sir, a shame
Or this you had forborn to name,[35]   172

34. [The word "fruitless" is written in the margin as an alternative to "farther."]
35. [The words "never woud proclaim" are written in the margin as an alternative to "had forborn to name."]

For by your self-preferring brag
You let the Cat out of the bag,
And vanity too strong for art
Betrays the weakness of your heart.   *176*

But grant the Bishops *shou'd* bow down,
And you their great Superior own,
Must they to abject Coke submit
Who licks the dust under your feet?   *180*
Does Coke deserve to reign supreme?
Or can you give your spirit to Him?
Your reign will be concluded soon,
And where is Coke, when you are gone?   *184*
Will Asbury to Coke give place,
Or fly in his Archbishop's face,
Against his Consecrator swell
'And all his own importance feel?'* [36]   *188*
And while the little flock they tear,
Be sure to gain the largest share.

But grievous ills you apprehend
Unless Yourself superintend,   *192*
And rescue from despotic sway
The Brethren in America.
For as the State's and Church's yoke
Is from their neck so strangely broke,   *196*
So disintangled from the chain
Why shou'd we hamper them again?
Freed from the English Hierarchy,
Your people you exult to see,   *200*
Left at discretion to pursue
The Scriptures—as explain'd by you,
And the primeval Church to own
Where Priests and Bishops are but One.   *204*

YOU JUDGE IT BEST (& much you love
To judge and your own Acts approve)
You judge it best, that they shou'd stand
Subject to none but your command,   *208*

36. *See B[ishop] Coke's Ordination Sermon.

(As You and Providence design'd)
From England totally disjoin'd,
As who their Mother never knew,
As loose, and disengaged—as You.   212

But we bewail their wretched state,
(Whom you alas, congratulate)
Griev'd, that triumphant Wickedness,
Rebellion curst with sad[37] success,   216
Traitors, & Gaul, and furious Zeal,
Murther, and Anarchy, and Hell
Have giv'n the States their liberty,
Yet God, you say, has made them free!   220

---

37. [The word "its" is written in the margin as an alternative to "sad."]

HYMNS AND POEMS
FOR FESTIVALS

PROLOGUE[1]

Readers, accept at this thrice solemn Time
The humble Tribute of an Annual Rhyme,
Accept with Smiles, from such a Bard as me,
Plain artless Trust transcending Poesy:
Let Others in Superiour Strains aspire,
Charm the gay Crowd, & strike the tuneful Lyre,
Suffice it if to me kind Heaven impart
A good Intention and an honest Heart.

TO THE WORSHIPFUL THE MAYOR AND ALDERMEN OF THE CITY OF BRISTOL[2]

Ye worthy Ministers of Righteousness,
Who Piety promote, & Vice suppress,
Ye Guardians of our Liberties & Laws,
Patrons of Virtue's & Religion's Cause,
Go on your high Commission to fulfil,
Commend The Good, and terrify The Ill,
Till HE who did the powers on Earth ordain
Receive You with Himself in Heavenly Bliss to reign.

ON ST. MICHAEL[3]

See from his Throne by the Archangel driven,
The Dragon falls, as Lightning, out of Heaven!
To Hell he falls: but bursts th'Infernal Den,
And fiercely wars against the Sons of Men:
Yet Michael shall again or'ecome the Foe,
Jesus shall Him, & all his Host or'ethrow,
And take us up their Places to supply,
First of Created Things, and nearest the Most High!

1. [MS Festivals (MS CW IV, 71), No. 1. The numbering of the poems in MS Festivals which appears in the footnotes of this section is Wesley's original sequence. He renumbered them, however, and the poems are printed here in his revised sequence.
2. [MS Festivals, No. 2.]
3. [MS Festivals, No. 3.]

ON ST. ANDREW [4]

'Saints in old Times there were (the World allow)
'But only Fools pretend to Saintship now.'
What fools like Those who senselessly divide,
And blasphemously mock *the Sanctified?*
All *must* be Saints, or Lost. Who will not be
Holy Themselves, our God shall never see;
Who scoff his Saints below, shall never prove
The Glorious Fellowship of Saints above.

ON CHRISTMAS DAY [5]

Favour & Peace on Earth & Praise in Heaven!
To us a Son is born, a Child is given!
To day Jehovah lays aside his Crown,
To day the Saviour of the World comes down,
God over all supream, who all things made,
Cloath'd with our Flesh & in a Manger laid,
Is on this happy Morn to Mortals given:
Favour & Peace on Earth, & Praise in Heaven!

CHRISTMAS DAY [6]

1.   Stupendous mystery!
        GOD in our flesh is *seen*
   (While angels ask, how can it be?)
        And dwells with sinful men!
        Our nature He assumes,
        That we may his retrieve;
   He comes, to our dead world He comes,
        That all thro' Him may live.

---

4. [MS Festivals, No. 5.]
5. [MS Festivals, No. 8; *Rep. Verse*, No. 147, p. 204.]
6. [MS Preachers (MS CW I[q]), p.3. This poem does not appear in MS Festivals.]

2.　　The true, eternal Word
　　　To us a Child is given,
　The sovereign God, th'Almighty L[or]d,
　　　Who fills both earth & heaven;
　　　Our God on earth appears
　　　To take our sins away,
　And guide us thro' the vale of tears
　　　To realms of endless day.

ON INNOCENTS' DAY [7]

We blame the Savage King whose Cruel Word
Gave up his Subjects' Children to the Sword;
We praise our *doting* selves, who every Hour
Yield our own Babes to the Destroyer's Power:
Which to poor Innocents doth heavier prove,
The Tyrant's Hatred, or the Parents' Love?
His Fury on their slaughter'd Bodies fell,
Our Fondness sends their pamper'd souls to Hell.

ON ST. THOMAS' DAY [8]

Happy the Man by Jesus' grace subdued,
Who saw, & cried at last, My Lord, my God!
They too are blest, whose Lives & Actions own
Their Lord & God, beheld by Faith alone,
Blest with the Consciousness of Sin forgiven,
Blest with the Seal, and Antepast of Heaven,
Blest with their Full Inheritance above,
Blest with a glorious Crown of everlasting Love.

7. [MS Festivals, No. 10; *Rep. Verse*, No. 258, p. 295.]
8. [MS Festivals, No. 6.]

ON THE KING'S BIRTH-DAY [9]

With Joy we see th'auspicious Day return,
When Heaven on Brittain smil'd, and George was born!
Born for the General Good, by Fate design'd
A Parent, King, a Patron of Mankind!
Long may He bless the Nations with his Sway,
See the calm Sunset of his glorious Day
With golden Beams thro' all th' Horison shine,
And late return to Heaven in Majesty Divine!

ON THE PRINCE OF WALES [10]

Hail happy Prince, in whom combin'd we see
Imperial State, and mild Humanity!
In thee let every Virtue still be join'd,
To constitute the Darling of Mankind:
And when your Royal Greatness shall supply
The Throne of GEORGE, translated to the Sky,
With Equal Mercy may You use your Power,
And leave a Race of Kings, till Time shall be no more.

ON ST. STEPHEN'S DAY [11]

O for a Zeal like His, who scorn'd to fear
The hoary Murtherers in Moses' Chair!
O for a Faith like His, whose streaming Blood
First seal'd the Truth of the Atoning GOD!
A Meekness Evil still with Good t'oppose,
A Love that prays for its relentless Foes,
A Fiery Car, to mount like Dying Stephen
And seize the glittering Crown, reach'd out by God in Heaven!

9. [MS Festivals, No. 4; *Rep. Verse*, No. 259, p. 295. The king mentioned is George II who died in 1760.]
10. [MS Festivals, No. 7; *Rep. Verse*, No. 260, p. 295. The Prince of Wales did not succeed his father, George II, as he died before him. *Cf.* the poems on pp. 278, 339, 341.]
11. [MS Festivals, No. 9.]

[WHO WOULD NOT WISH TO HAVE THE SKILL][12]

Who would not wish to have the skill
Of tuning instruments at will?
Ye powers who guide my actions, tell
Why I, in whom the seeds of music dwell,
Who most its power and excellence admire,
   Whose very breast itself a lyre
   Was never taught the happy art
      Of modulating sounds,
And can no more in concert bear a part
Than the wild roe that o're the mountain bounds.

[JESUS, FROM THY SERVANTS TAKEN][13]

1. Jesus, from thy Servants taken!
     Taken up this solemn Day,
  See us seemingly forsaken
     To surrounding Wolves a Prey:
  In a World of Tribulation,
     In a Vale of Misery,
  Prest with manifold Temptation,
     Looking, gasping after Thee.

2. To thine own Eternal Glory
     Thou triumphantly art gone,
  Where the Angels fall before Thee
     Seated on thine Heavenly Throne:
  Yet Thou hear'st thy Servants mourning,
     Feel'st whate'er thy members feel,
  Us, who long for thy Returning,
     Earnestly rememberest still.

3. Touch'd with exquisite Compassion
     For thy feeble followers here,
  Answer, Lord, our Supplication,
     Send us down The Comforter:

12. [MS Festivals; *Rep. Verse*, No. 277, p. 311. It has been transcribed by Frank Baker from Wesley's shorthand at the end of MS Festivals (MS CW IV, 71).]
13. [MS Richmond Tracts, pp. 171–2. The hymn is appropriate to Ascension Day.]

Breathe into our Hearts thy Spirit,
    Witness of thy Dying Love,
Seal of all we hope t'inherit,
    Earnest of our Joys above.

4. Ever in thy Spirit near us
        Let us now thy Spirit feel,
    By thy faithful Mercies chear us,
        By the Gift unspeakable:
    Shew th'Intent of thine Ascending,
        Answer it on All & me,
    Every soul on Thee depending,
        Draw us, Saviour, up to Thee.

5. All the Virtue of thy Passion,
        All the Benefits apply,
    Visit us with thy Salvation,
        Pardon, Lord, and sanctify:
    By thy Resurrection raise us
        To that sinless Life unknown,
    By thine Exaltation place us
        On thine Everlasting Throne.

HYMN ON THE RESURRECTION[14]

1. Join all the Friends of Jesus,
        The Church of his election,
            Called to confess
            In songs of praise
        The Saviour's resurrection:
    Let every member witness
        With rapturous exclamation,
            He lives indeed,
            Our quickning Head,
        Our Life and our Salvation.

14. [MS Misc. Hymns, pp. 193–4. The origin of this metrical form, the vehicle of such hymns as "Head of Thy Church triumphant," has hitherto baffled identification. It is, however, the metre of John Gay's verse "O ruddier than the cherry" in Handel's *Acis and Galatea*, though in that song line one rhymes with lines two and five.]

2.   For Jesus' sake forgiven,
      Partakers of his merit,
        We know our Lord
        To life restor'd
      By his attesting Spirit;
    The virtue of his Rising
      Brought every true believer
        Out of their graves;
        And still he saves,
    And lives in us for ever.

3.   Risen with Christ, in newness
      Of life, we stand before him
        And seek in love
        The things above
      Where all his host adore him:
    Above all height exalted,
      The Partner of our nature,
        He sits inthron'd,
        By Seraphs own'd
    Our glorified Creator.

HYMN ON OUR LORD'S RESURRECTION[15]

1.   All ye that seek the Lord who died,
    Your GOD for Sinners crucified,
    Prevent the Earliest Dawn, & come
    To worship at his Sacred Tomb.

2.   Bring the sweet Spices of your Sighs,
    Your contrite Hearts, & streaming Eyes,
    Your sad Complaints, & humble Fears;
    Come, & embalm Him with your Tears.

15. [MS Cheshunt, pp. 178–80; MS Clarke, pp. 185–6. Verses 1–8 and 10–12 appear in *Poet. Works*, IV, pp. 129–30.]

3. While thus ye long your Souls t'employ,
    Your Sorrow shall be turn'd to Joy!
    Now, now let all your Grief be o're,
    Believe, & ye shall weep no more.

4. An Earthquake hath the Cavern shook,
    And burst the Door, & rent the Rock,
    The Lord hath sent his Angel down,
    Lo! He hath roll'd away the Stone.

5. As Snow behold his Garment white,
    His Countenance as Lightning bright,
    He sits, & waves a flaming Sword,
    And waits upon his Rising Lord.

6. The Third Auspicious Morn is come,
    And calls your Saviour from the Tomb,
    The Bands of Death are torn away,
    The yawning Tomb gives back its Prey.

7. Could neither Seal nor Stone secure,
    Nor Men, nor Devils make it sure!
    The Seal, & Stone are both cast by,
    And all the Powers of Darkness fly.

8. The Body breath[e]s, & lifts his Head,
    The Keepers sink, & fall as dead,
    The Dead restor'd to Life appear,
    The Living quake, & die for Fear.

9. No Power a Band of Soldiers have
    To keep One Body in its Grave;
    Surely it no Dead Body was
    That could the Roman Eagles chase.

10. The Lord of Life is ris'n indeed,
    To Death deliver'd in your Stead,
    His Rise proclaims your Sins forgiv'n,
    His open Grave hath open'd Heaven.

11.   Haste then, ye Souls who first believe,
      Who dare the Gospel-Word receive,
      Your Loving Faith with Joy confess;
      Be bold; be Jesus' Witnesses.

12.   Go tell the Followers of your Lord,
      Their Jesus is to Life restor'd.
      He lives, that They his Life may find,
      He lives to quicken All Mankind.

DEVOTIONAL HYMNS AND POEMS

EPINICION[1]

1. Praise to the Wonder-working GOD!
   Proclaim his glorious Praise abroad,
   Let Earth his Arm unshortened sing,
   Let Earth rejoice, the Lord is King!
   O're all his furious Foes He reigns,
   And holds the Powers of Hell in Chains.

2. Evil before his Presence flies
   Scattered by Jesus' flaming Eyes,
   His flaming Eyes pierce thro' the Snare,
   And lay the Depths of Satan bare,
   And blast his well-concerted Plan,
   And make his surest Triumph vain.

3. Where is the Fury of our Foe
   With all his Wisdom from below?
   Thou, Lord, hast crossed his dire Design
   T'orethrow the Gracious Work Divine,
   To sift thy Messengers like Wheat,
   And whelm them in the Burning Pit.

4. Howl the defrauded Fiends beneath
   And clank their Chains, and gnash their Teeth,
   To see us clean escaped away
   (Their Captives sure, their lawful Prey)
   While Judah's Lion tears the Toils,
   And Jesus glories in his Spoils.

5. Shout to the mighty Jesus' Name
   Thro' which we now our Foes or'ecame,
   His Name hath cast th'Accuser down,
   His Name the Fight hath more than won,
   His Name shall still our Souls defend,
   His Name shall save us to the End.

1. [MS Richmond, p. 9; MS Misc. Hymns, p. 2. Epinicion: i.e. an ode celebrating a victory, a song of triumph. It apparently refers here to Wesley's release in Ireland. *Cf.* the previous poem in MS Richmond which appears in *Poet. Works*, VIII, p. 396.]

6. Safe in his Name's celestial Tower
    We tread on all the Adverse Power,
    We spurn them now beneath our Feet
    And soon at GOD'S Right hand shall sit,
    Arraign them at his righteous Bar,
    And shout their just Damnation there!

[THE COLLIER'S HYMN][2]

1. Salvation to GOD,
    Who freely bestow'd
    Salvation on Man:
    In Thanks let us give Him his Blessings again,
    Throughout our glad Days
    His Benefits praise,
    His Goodness adore,
    And praise Him forever, when Time is no more.

2. Thou, Jesus, hast been
    Our Saviour from Sin,
    By Nature set free,
    We surely have found our Red[emptio]n in Thee.
    The Sense of thy Love
    We joyfully prove,
    Of Pardon possesst
    Even now in the Arms of thy Mercy we rest.

3. Since first we Believ'd,
    And Pardon receiv'd,
    What Grace hast Thou shewn,
    What Wonders of Pity & Goodness unkn[ow]n!
    Not all our Excess
    Of Sin could suppress
    That Affection of Thine,
    That Flame of unquenchable Mercy Divine.

2. [MS Richmond, pp. 61–2. The poem is incomplete.]

4.   Thy Spirīt[3] of Grace
Hath seen all our Ways,
Our Stubbornness born,
And waited, & griev'd for our hearty Return:

[THEE, FATHER, WE PRAISE][4]

1.   Thee, Father, we praise,
So plenteous in Grace,
So able and willing to save a lost Race!

2.   With Angels above
Thy Goodness we prove,
And joyfully join in the Triumph of LOVE.

3.   In Sins we were dead,
LOVE ran to our Aid,
And quicken'd, & rais'd us with Jesus our Head.

4.   Thy merciful Word
Our Spirits restor'd,
And sweetly inspir'd with the Life of our LORD.

5.   The Word of thy Grace
In a Moment took place
And caught us away to the Sight of thy Face:

6.   Come up hither, it cried,
For whom Jesus hath died,
And share in his Glory, & sit by his Side.

7.   By Faith we ascend
With our Saviour & Friend,
And begin the Injoyment that never shall end.

3. [Frank Baker remarks in a personal note: "Note line over second syllable in 'Spirīt,' showing that in this case the full value should be given to that syllable. The assumption surely is, therefore, that in the numerous cases where 'Spirit' is to be scanned as one syllable, it is 'spir't' and not 'sp'rit.' At long last a piece of evidence!"]

4. [MS Richmond Tracts, pp. 169–70.]

8.   With Fellowship sweet
Our Elders we meet,
And in Heavenly Places with Jesus we sit.

9.   Transported in Prayer
Our Spirits are there,
And our Bodies shall shortly to Sion repair.

10.   They already *are* gone,
With Christ to thy Throne;
He is Flesh of our Flesh, He is Bone of our Bone.

11.   The meek Son of Man,
Who suffer'd our Pain,
Hath carried our Nature to Heaven again.

12.   In Immanuel we
Thy Majesty see,
And our Life is all hidden with Jesus in Thee.

13.   Our Advocate prays,
Our Harbinger stays
For The Moment of Time to make ready our Place.

14.   He keeps us above
In the Depth of his Love
Till again He appear, & his Members remove.

15.   This, this is the Prize,
We together shall rise,
And our Glorified Bodies shall fly to the skies.

16.   This, this is our Aim,
Thy Fulness we claim,
Thy Heaven of Heavens in Jesus's Name.

IN REPROACH [5]

1. O Thou, who didst my Burthen bear
   Still let me cast on Thee my Care,
      And tell Thee all my Grief:
   My Soul is vexed with Fiends and Sin,
   With Wars without, and Fears within,
      And cannot find Relief.

2. My Brother comes with Armed Bands
   (My brother with the hairy Hands)
      Against this helpless Soul:
   I fear, his cruel Hate I fear;
   Ah! rescue me from Esau near,
      And all his Rage control.

3. To Thee my feeble Heart I tell,
   My Littleness of Faith reveal,
      I dread the Ruffian's Force,
   Least he the trembling Children slay,
   Or turn the Lame out of the Way
      Or stop the Gospel's Course.

4. I would not, Lord, the Doom decline,
   Were all the threatned Evil mine,
      The death-inflicting Shame:
   I long to rest my weary Head
   And lose among the Quiet Dead
      My wretched worthless Name.

5. But if they triumph in my Fall,
   Will they not cast reproach on All
      The People of my GOD?
   Will they not GOD Himself blaspheme
   Who died his People to redeem,
      Who washed us in his Blood?

5. [MS Richmond, p. 21; MS Misc. Hymns, p. 76.]

6. O GOD, stir up thy Jealousy,
    Nor let thy Truth be blamed for me,
        The Fool's and madman's Scorn;
    Thou GOD of all the Earth, arise,
    Scatter their Evil with thine Eyes,
        Or to thy Glory turn.

7. Look to thy Cause, I ask no more,
    But suddenly my Soul restore,
        And let me hence retire,
    Secure the Honour of thy Name,
    Content I sink beneath my Shame,
        And quietly expire.

WRITTEN UNDER REPROACH[6]

1. Thou, Lord, hast bid th'Afflicted pray
    And promised in his Evil Day
        To hear thy Mourner's Prayer,
    To save him by thy timely Grace,
    That He may his Deliverer's Praise
        To all the World declare.

2. O wouldst Thou grant my Soul the Power
    With Thee to wrestle in this Hour
        Of my extreme Distress,
    While all the Rage of Hell is joined
    With all the Malice of Mankind
        To tear away my Peace.

3. O might thy Spirit intercede
    And help me at my greatest need,
        To tell Thee all my Care,
    By Tears to make my Anguish known,
    In speechless Agonies to groan
        Th'inexplicable Prayer.

6. [MS Richmond, p. 50.]

4. Pity my Grief, and Fear, and Shame,
   The Gift I ask in Jesus' Name
       For Jesus' sake bestow,
   The Spirit of Supplicating Grace,
   To soften my extreme Distress,
       And sanctify my Woe.

5. Worn out with toil, defamed, opprest,
   I dare not ask for Instant Rest,
       But strength my load to bear,
   Afflict me to my latest Hour,
   But let my troubled Spirit pour
       The never-ceasing Prayer.

6. Give me but This, I ask no more,
   Mine Honour, Strength, and Friends restore
       At that tremendous Day,
   But let me, till I see thy Face,
   With broken Heart implore thy Grace,
       But let me always pray.

IN REPROACH [7]

1. My worthless life, O Lord, receive,
       Can I to thy glory live?
           Alas, the fond desire
   Is blasted by the dragon's breath;
   Then let me from the world retire,
       And praise thee by my death.

2. The fiend hath laid mine hon[ou]r low,
       Mangled by a deadly blow:
           My race of glory's ore:
   O that my race of shame were past,
   O might I bear my sin no more,
       But weep & groan my last!

7. [MS Misc. Hymns, p. 75; MS Richmond, pp. 121–2; MS Occasional, p. 29.]

3. Why shoud I live in fruitless pain,
        Suffer on, & all in vain!
            Why as an evil-doer
    Shoud I, to shame thy people, stay?
    Now, Lord, my sinsick Spirit cure
            And call me hence away.

4. Speak, Sav[iou]r, speak the welcome word,
        Pardon, & receive me, Lord,
            Shut up my mournful years,
    From all my sins & sorrows save,
    And let me quit this vale of tears,
            And rush into a grave.

5. O might I now lay down my head,
        Weary sink among the dead
            Beyond the tempter's power,
    Escap'd from life's tempestuous sea
    O might I gain the happy shore
            Of calm Eternity!

6. Regard, regard my vehement cry,
        Hallow, Lord, & let me die,
            In answer to my prayer,
    The death-presiding Angel send,
    And let my pain, & grief, & care
            In life eternal end!

IN TEMPTATION [8]

1. Prest, or'ewhelm'd with sore temptation,
            Lord, must I
            Faint and die,
        Purchase of thy passion?

2. Bought by Thee, shall Satan have me?
            God of love,
            From above
        Haste, to help and save me.

---

8. [MS Misc. Hymns, pp. 83–4.]

3. Let the sprinkled blood that cleanses
    From all sin,
    Speak within,
    Blot out my offences.

4. Sovereign Lord of earth and heaven,
    Cleanse and keep
    Me, who weep
    At thy feet forgiven.

5. From presumptuous sins defend me,
    Every hour
    Wisdom, power,
    Love divine, attend me.

6. In the Spirit of inspiration,
    Jesus, come
    To thy home,
    With thy great salvation.

7. Come, and take intire possession,
    Christ, my life,
    End the strife,
    Finish the transgression.

8. Then my sin no more shall grieve thee,
    When Thou art
    In my heart,
    Then I cannot leave Thee.

IN TEMPTATION [9]

I

1. A present Help in deep distress,
   Arise, and bid the tempest cease,
   Thou whom the winds and seas obey,
   Appear, and end this evil day:

9. [MS Misc. Hymns, pp. 297–8.]

My strength is spent, my struggle's o're,
I sink, I can hold out no more,
I faint, if still thy face Thou hide,
I die, for whom thy Son hath died.

2. No succour in myself I have,
But quite despair myself to save,
All weakness, sin, and misery,
Unworthy to be saved by Thee:
My sins have made thy mercies void,
I perish by my sins destroy'd;
And when thy utmost wrath I feel,
I'l clear the righteous God in hell.

3. But while I to my doom submit,
Wilt Thou not snatch me from the pit?
A wretch Thou dost so oft reprieve
Wilt Thou not finally forgive?'
Surely if Thou hadst quite forsook,
And blotted me out of thy book,
Thou woudst not let me now intreat
And gasp for mercy at thy feet.

IV [10]

1. Ah! woe is me, a Wretched Man!
Still of my misery I complain,
With no deliverance nigh,
Afraid, when all my strife is past,
To perish in my sins at last,
And unconverted die.

2. I must of my salvation doubt,
Till I have fully wrought it out,
And all my sins are gone:
Till perfect love hath fear expell'd,
And by th'indwelling Spirit seal'd,
I serve my God alone.

10. [MS Misc. Hymns, pp. 301–2. The poems numbered II and III appear in *Poet. Works*, XIII, pp. 253–5.]

3. My God, for help I cry to Thee,
   Ah, why hast Thou forsaken me
     In this infernal snare,
   Expos'd, assail'd on every side,
   Tempted above my strength, and tried
     With more than I can bear!

4. Or shorten my extreme distress,
   Or larger influence of grace
     To a weak worm impart,
   My Keeper in this fiery hour,
   Omnipotent in saving power,
     And greater than my heart.

5. O might my heart, to ill inclin'd,
   Continually thy Spirit find
     Restraining me from ill,
   Till ripe in holiness and love,
   I mount to meet my Lord above
     On the celestial hill.

IN TEMPTATION[11]

1. Jesus, in every time and place
     On Thee for help I call,
   Preserve me by thy promis'd grace,
     Or into sin I fall;

2. By day and night my Keeper be,
     My strength and righteousness,
   And every moment water me
     And every moment bless.

3. From all iniquity avert
     My feeble, tempted soul,
   And keep the issues of my heart,
     And all my foes controul;

11. [MS Misc., 1786 (MS CW III[g]), p. 15.]

4.   Erase the deep, original stain
        Thro' love's almighty power,
     And I shall never sin again,
        Shall never grieve Thee more.

[HELP, O MY GRACIOUS SAVIOUR][12]

1.   Help, O my gracious Saviour,
        (If Help on thee is laid)
     And shield me by thy favour
        Who humbly ask thine Aid,
     Throughout my fierce Temptation
        Continue with my Soul,
     And all these storms of passion,
        And all these sins controul.

2.   Balm of the wounded Spirit,
        Thy pretious Blood apply,
     And save me by thy Merit,
        O save me, or I die:
     Wash out my Sin's Infection
        And arm me with thy Blood,
     Thy Blood be my Protection
        And quench the Wrath of GOD.

WRITTEN IN D[UBLI]N[13]

1.   Far from my Native Land remov'd
        Far from all I priz'd & Lov'd,
           In a black Wilderness
     I ask my Soul, What dost Thou here,
     Thou poor afflicted Sojourner,
           This Earth is not thy Place.

---

12. [MS Richmond, p. 156.]

13. [MS Richmond, pp. 67–8; MS Occasional, pp. 77–8; *Rep. Verse*, No. 237, pp. 263–4. MS Occasional adds at the title: "To—With Pity, Lord, etc." The poem would appear to date from 1747–8, when Charles Wesley often faced mobs in Ireland.]

2. Nothing beneath my Heart commands,
        Hope & I have shaken Hands,
            And parted long ago.
    Inur'd to Pain, & Shame, & Grief,
    I ask, I look for no Relief,
        For no Delight below.

3. Happy, forever happy, I
        Suffer'd to escape, & fly
            To that eternal Shore
    Where all the Storms of Life are past,
    And Exiles find their Home at last,
        And Losers weep no more.

4. Come then, ye threatning Sons of Rome,
        Kindly to my Rescue come,
            And set my Spirit free,
    Nor tremble at th'Avenger near
    No Justice is for Christians here,
        For slaughter'd Sheep—or me.

5. An Outcast for my Master's sake
        Haste, ye Ruffian Band, to take
            This mournful Life of mine;
    A Life by Sin & Sorrow stain'd,
    A Life, which I have long disdain'd,
        And languish'd to resign.

THE FIERY TRIAL[14]

1. Where is the GOD of Shadrach? where
        Abednego's & Meshach's Power,
    Thro' whom we may the Furnace bear,
        The Violence of Hell's hottest Hour!

14. [MS Richmond, p. 69. The poem, probably on the same subject as the last, is incomplete as indicated by the number "7" for an additional verse which Wesley did not write.]

2. Be Thou omnipotently near,
   Whose Form is as the Son of Man,
   Amidst the raging Flames appear,
   And all their burning Power restr[ai]n.

3. Thou knowst, O Lord, in thy great Name
   Unshaken Confidence we have,
   Send us the promis'd Help we claim,
   Now, Jesus, & forever save.

4. The World's Infernal King exclaims,
   Whose Image we disdain'd t'adore,
   At his Command the Furnace flames,
   Flames seven times hotter than before.

5. His mighty Chiefs have cast us in,
   Behold, ye Heathen, & admire,
   Loose from our Bands we here are seen
   And walk unhert amidst the Fire.

6. We walk throughout our evil Day,
   Our Leader in the Furnace see,
   The lambent Flames around us play,
   And own the present Deity.

7. [unfinished]

[REJOICE, YE PROUD PHILISTINES][15]

1. Rejoice, ye proud Philistines,
   Your dreaded foe is taken,
       In me survey
       Your helpless prey
   As now by all forsaken!
   Maliciously successful,
       Your rage at last has found me,
       My brethren's hands
       In surest bands
   At your command have bound me.

15. [MS Richmond, p. 110. The poem is incomplete. Page 111 of the MS is blank for intended continuation. It is clearly based on the story of Samson in Judges 16.]

2. Ye Aliens, shout against me,
   Over your captive glory;
   But at the sound
   I rise unbound,
   And drive you all before me.
   That everlasting Spirit
   Let him to me be given,
   And all your host
   Shall fly like dust
   Before the whirlwind driven.

3. Cut off from all dependance
   Of human help & favour,
   Thee, Lord, alone
   My strength I own,
   My all-sufficient Saviour.

FRIDAY, 31 MARCH, 1749[16]

1. O my GOD, my gracious GOD,
    I seek for Help to Thee,
    Crush'd beneath a Mountain-Load
    Of sad Perplexity:
    Thou alone canst grant me Ease,
    And take the Mountain-Load away,
    Help my deepest, last Distress,
    And give me Power to pray.

2. Sore beset on every Side
    With Dangers, Doubts & Snares,
    Can I from my Saviour hide
    The Weight my Spirit bears?
    Still these cruel Fears oppress,
    And fill my Soul with huge Dismay,
    Help my deepest, &c.

16. [MS CW Letters, I, 33. The last two lines of verse 1 are abbreviated by Wesley, when repeated in verses 2–7: Help my deepest, &c.]

3.   Least the Enemy prevail
And tear away my Hope,
While my Fate is in the Scale,
These feeble Hands lift up:
Least the Word its Captive seize,
And Sense my softned Soul betray,
Help my deepest, &c.

4.   Jealous for thy People be,
And for thy glorious Cause,
Leave them not, great GOD, thro' me
To suffer Shame or Loss;
Let not Sin thro' me increase,
But roll the dire Reproach away,
Help my deepest, &c.

5.   If to me in Drawing Love
Thou didst of old appear,
Still attract me from above,
And keep my Heart sincere,
If thy Mercies never cease,
Support me in this evil Day
Help my deepest, &c.

6.   Could I ask the promis'd Grace,
I shoud the Grace obtain,
Never Sinner sought thy Face,
And sought thy Face in vain;
Sure I am of full Success,
If Thou vouchsafe a Pitying Ray,
Help my deepest, &c.

7.   Open, Lord, my willing Ear,
And my Obedient Heart,
Let my loosen'd Tongue declare
How wise & good Thou art;
That I may thy Praise express
Pronounce the sighing Ephphatha,[17]
Help my deepest, &c.

17. [*Cf.* Mark 7:34.]

8.   Saviour, Friend of sinful Man,
           I will not let Thee go,
       Till the Secret Thou explain,
           And all thy Counsel shew;
       Never will I hold my peace
       But still with strugling Anguish say,
       See my deepest, last Distress,
           And give me Power to pray.

WRITTEN BEFORE A TRIAL AT TAUNTON, APRIL—1767[18]

1. Jesus, to Thee thy Church looks up,
        And cannot pray in vain:
    Forgive our fond, unwary hope
        Redress from men to gain:
    From men to whom Thou art not known
        What help can we receive?
    The world will always love its own,
        And only them believe.

2. But sufferers in a righteous cause
        By persecuting power,
    Protection from our Country's laws
        May we not, Lord, implore;
    To kings and magistrates appeal,
        The men Thou didst ordain
    Impartial equity to deal,
        And peace and truth maintain?

3. Thy ministers of righteousness
        To these we calmly flee,
    Nor look for succour, or success,
        Without a Nod from Thee:
    Thou art the Judge supremely just;
        And suitors at thy throne,
    Not in an arm of flesh we trust,
        But hang on Thine alone.

18. [MS Misc. Hymns, pp. 163–5. It has proved impossible to trace to what trial this poem refers.]

4. The hearts of all are in thy hand,
        Defender of the poor;
    And Thou dost by thy servants stand,
        From evil to secure;
    Dost from unrighteous judges save,
        And hide our life above:
    And Truth our Advocate we have,
        And all-commanding Love.

5. If such the counsel of thy will,
        The world shall justice show,
    And earth assist the Woman still,
        Against her furious foe;
    The sons of violence and pride
        Shall bow to those they scorn,
    And justice roll her rapid tide
        Too strong for them to turn.

6. In judgment then, great God, arise,
        Assume thy power, and reign,
    Sole Arbiter of earth and skies,
        Thy people's Cause maintain:
    Now let thine outstretch'd arm be shown,
        In all the heathen's sight,
    And force the alien host to own
        Thou dost for Israel fight.

7. So shall the Church surround thy throne
        With ceaseless songs of praise,
    Extol the wonders Thou hast done,
        And magnify thy grace:
    "Thou givst to us the victory,
        And we ourselves resign
    A living sacrifice to Thee
        Thro' endless ages Thine."

II[19]

1.   Arise, O God, arise,
    Thy righteous Cause maintain,
Attentive to thy people's cries,
    Opprest by lawless men:
    Trampled beneath their feet
    Thou knowst what we indure,
And never can thy love forget
    The persecuted poor.

2.   The foes to us and peace
    Boast their tyrannic power,
And confident of full success
    Thy injur'd flock devour;
    They mock with scornful pride
    Our hope of justice here,
And (for the world is on their side)
    Nor man, nor God they fear.

3.   But Thou shalt take our part,
    Who to thy promise flee,
Almighty Love for us Thou art
    Who put our trust in Thee,
    Ourselves to Thee commit,
    The helpless sinner's Friend,
And prostrate at thy mercy-seat
    Thy just award attend.

4.   Jesus, the matter take
    Into thy sovereign hand,
And those who lies their refuge make
    Their counsel shall not stand:
    Thou wilt cast down the foe,
    Put all his tools to shame,
Their dire confederacy o'rethrow,
    And blast their surest aim.

19. [MS Misc. Hymns, pp. 165–7.]

5.   But if our faith to try
Thou grant our foes success,
Still let us on thy love rely,
Thy power and faithfulness,
Thy good, permissive will
Implicitly obey,
And lodge with Thee our just Appeal
Against thy righteous day.

AFTER THE TRIAL[20]

1.   Righteous, O God, thy judgments are,
If now unsearchable,
We humbly in the dust declare
Thou hast done all things well!
Wisely Thou dost the world permit
Over our heads to ride,
And tread us down beneath their feet
With justice on our side.

2.   But blacken'd, and refus'd our due,
We stand to thy award,
The instruments of wrong look thro',
And cry, It is the Lord!
We neither threaten, nor complain
Of man's iniquity,
But turning to our Rest again,
Commit our souls to Thee.

20. [MS Misc. Hymns, pp. 167–8.]

3.   They coud have no injurious power
      Unsuffer'd[21] from above,
Or crush for one triumphant hour
      The objects of thy love:
They only serve thy secret will,
      Accomplishing their own,
O'rerul'd, and order'd to fulfil
      Thy purposes unknown.

[O HOW ARE THEY INCREAS'D][22]

1.   O how are they increas'd
      That vex & trouble me!
By Men & Fiends distress'd
      I cry, O Lord, to Thee:
They persecute with cruel Hate
      Whom Thou hast wounded sore
Till Nature faints beneath the Weight
      And Life can bear no more.

2.   Why then dost Thou detain
      My fleeting Spirit here,
And hold me still in Pain
      With lasting Ease so near?
O woudst Thou now renew my Heart,
      From all my Sins release,
And bid me quietly depart,
      And bid me die in peace!

21. [The *Oxford English Dictionary* has no example of this rare word in the sense of "not permitted" as here.]
22. [MS Occasional, p. 30.]

IN A STORM[23]

1. Omnipot[en]t Lord, We sing of thy Power,
   Thy Wonderful Word With Joy we adore,
   Thy dreadfullest Creature, The billowing Flood,
   Submits to a Greater, Confesses a God.

2. The tyrannous Winds Are subj[ec]t to Thee,
   Thy Providence binds, Or lets them go free:
   And now they are risen, And blow as they list,
   Releas'd from their Prison Of Jesus's Fist.

3. But Thou by a Look Their Race canst restrain,
   The Billows rebuke, And still them again:
   And while they are roaring, We know thou art near,
   And hearst us imploring Our Lord to appear.

4. Come, Jesus, & show Thyself on the Wave,
   Appear in our View, Almighty to save,
   [Unfinished]

IN UNCERTAINTY
AT SETTING OUT FOR BRISTOL, NOV. 20, 1779[24]

1. I know not what to do,
   But till thy hand I see,
   And gain the Providential clue,
   Mine eyes are unto Thee:
   What is my Father's choice?
   Explain thy own design,
   And lo, I come, make haste, rejoice
   To do the will divine.

2. Ah, send me not up hence,
   Unless thy truth and grace,
   Thy wisdom, and omnipotence
   Attend on all my ways;

23. [MS Richmond, p. 85. The poem is incomplete.]
24. [MS Misc. Hymns, pp. 241–2.]

Unless thy Spirit lead
By pure, unerring light,
And shine on every destin'd deed,
And order all things right.

3. This token, Lord, for good
Be on thy servant shown,
Appear my tutelary cloud,
And lead me safely on:
My soul on Thee reclin'd
Patient may I possess,
Blest with a meek and lowly mind,
And kept in perfect peace.

4. I in thy strength proceed,
If Thou art with me still,
And closely in his footsteps tread
Who did thy utmost will;
With glorious liberty
Thy utmost will I prove,
When all my works are wrought in Thee,
When all are wrought in Love.

IN UNCERTAINTY [25]

1. I know not what to do—but wait
With lifted eyes intent on Thee!
Lord over all, thy will is fate;
Whate'er thy will ordains, shall be:
And here with humble faith I rest,
Whate'er thy will ordains, is best.

2. So foolish, ignorant, and blind
I see not what thy love intends;
Thy Providence a way shall find,
A way which human thou[gh]t transcends,
Which turns my counsel upside down,
That thine, O God, may stand alone.

25. [MS Misc. Hymns, pp. 282–3.]

3. Thou canst from man his purpose hide,
   When poison he mistakes for food,
   Canst turn the deadly draught aside,
   Or change the evil into good,
   Make darkness light before his face,
   And charm his nature into grace.

4. Expecting[26] then before thy throne,
   I long to prove thy welcom will:
   Saviour, to make thy counsel known,
   By plainest signs infallible
   The doubt resolve, the cloud remove,
   And show thyself Almighty Love.

II^{27}

1. In absolute, extreme despair
   To help a soul, whose doom I see,
   Father, I breathe my plaintive prayer,
   And bring my last distress to Thee.

2. A thousand ways to man unknown
   Thou hast t'avert the threatned ill,
   T'arrest his haste to be undone
   And save the wretch—against his will.

3. [unfinished]

26. [Expecting: this intransitive use of the verb in the sense of "to wait, to defer action," was already essentially obsolete in Wesley's day. The last such use quoted in the *Oxford English Dictionary* is in 1765.]

27. [MS Misc. Hymns, p. 283. At least one more verse was intended, since the rest of the page and page 284 of the MS are left blank.]

WRITTEN AT BRISTOL, NOV. 28, 1779[28]

1.   Hasty in spirit I,
Hasty in word and deed,
To Thee, mine only refuge, fly,
My help in time of need;
Jesus, thy servant guard,
While after Thee I go
To walk in all the works prepar'd,
To serve thy Church below.

2.   What woudst Thou have me do?
When certain of thy mind,
My way I chearfully pursue,
And do the thing design'd:
What woudst Thou have me say?
Instruct me in that hour,
And all my words shall then display
Thy wisdom, and thy power.

3.   All-wise, almighty Lord,
My lips in silence seal,
That no one rash unguarded word
May contradict thy will,
That with a single eye
I at thy praise may aim,
And think, and speak, and live, and die
A follower of the Lamb.

WRITTEN AT BRISTOL, DEC. 7, 1779[29]

1.   My God, be Thou my Guide,
My strength and wisdom be,
And far from danger, and from pride
Shut up my soul in Thee:

28. [MS Misc. Hymns, pp. 242–3; MS CW I(t). The poem was possibly written by Wesley when he was in Bristol to deal with a violent attack on his brother. *Cf.* the following two poems and "Jesus, thy hated servant own" (p. 304), and also Jackson's *Life of Charles Wesley*, II, p. 317.]
29. [MS Misc. Hymns, pp. 243–4.]

Not in myself, Thou know'st,
But in thy guardian power,
Thy truth and grace I put my trust,
Till all the storm is o're.

2.   Constrain'd with men to deal
Of deep, serpentine guile,
Who mischief in their hearts conceal
By words as smooth as oil;
For succour I look up,
For meekness from above,
For stedfast faith, and patient hope,
And all-victorious love.

3.   My nature's haste restrain
By thy o'reruling hand,
While strenuous I thy cause maintain,
And by thy people stand;
Rais'd up for England's fold,
I stand in her defence
Against the wolves divinely bold,
And sworn to drive them hence.

4.   To a good warfare, Lord,
I at thy charges go,
The shield of faith, and Spirit's sword
Shall conquer every foe;
But arm me with thy mind,
And lo, my work I see,
And life, and all things cast behind,
To serve thy Church and Thee.

ANOTHER[30]

1. Thee, Lord, my prostrate soul adores,
   And humbled in the dust implores
     Thy help in time of need:
   I cannot in this trial stand,
   Unless Thou hold me by thy hand,
     And by thy wisdom lead.

2. Thy hand upon thy Servant lay,
   The whirlwind of my will to stay,
     Superior power exert,
   So shall my weaken'd spirit own
   That Thou art God supreme, alone,
     And greater than my heart.

3. Longsuffering, pitiful, and kind,
   Endued with thy all-patient mind,
     Thy meek humility,
   O might I thro' thy wondrous Name
   Appear a follower of the Lamb,
     A Copy, Lord, of Thee!

4. Give me thy only will to seek,
   Thy words, & not my own, to speak,
     Thy tempers to express,
   That all to Thee may glory give,
   And for thy only sake receive
     The messenger of peace.

5. If anger once begin to rise,
   Behold me with thy watchful eyes,
     Thine eyes of darted flame,
   And check'd by thy controuling frown
   Command the leopard to lie down,
     And sink into a lamb.

30. [MS Misc. Hymns, pp. 245–6.]

6. Happy, for ever happy I
    Indulg'd at thy dear feet to lie,
        A penitent forgiven,
    Less than the least myself t'abase,
    Till Thou the chief of sinners raise
        To find my place in heaven.

[HELP OF THEM THAT SUCCOUR NEED][31]

1. Help of them that succour need,
    Wilt Thou break a bruised reed?
    Wilt Thou quench the smoaking tow?
    Rather thy salvation show.

2. List'ning to my feeble cry,
    With balsamic virtue nigh,
    Perfect in infirmity,
    Manifest thy strength in me.

3. Healer of my languid soul
    Thou canst make my body whole,
    Nature's wasted powers repair,
    All my sins & sorrows bear.

4. Jesus, on thy saving Name,
    Now as yesterday the same,
    I for double health rely,
    Sick in soul and body I.

5. Now my spirit's cure begin,
    Binding up the wounds of sin;
    Pouring in the balm Divine
    Tell my heart that God is mine.

31. [Lamplough Collection.]

[THOU RIGHTEOUS GOD, WHOSE PLAGUE I BEAR][32]

1.   Thou righteous God, whose Plague I bear,
     Whose Plague I from my Youth have borne,
   Shut up in Temporal Despair,
     Ordain'd to suffer, & to mourn;

2.   If now I had forgot to grieve,
     As every Penal Storm were or'e,
   Forgive, the Senseless Wretch forgive,
     And all my Chastisement restore.

3.   Asham'd of having hop'd for Rest,
     Or Ask'd for Comfort here below,
   Lo! I revoke the rash Request,
     And sink again in desp'rate Woe.

4.   Submissive to the Stroke again
     I bow my faint devoted Head,
   Till Thou discharge the latest Pain,
     And write me free among the Dead.

5.   Ah! what have I to do with Peace,
     Or Converse sweet, or Social Love?
   From Man, & all his Help, I cease,
     From Earth, & all her Goods remove:

6.   Waking out of my Dream of Hope
     I see the fond Delusion end,
   And give the whole Creation up,
     And live and die—without a Friend.

---

32. [MS Occasional, p. 19; MS Deliberative, p. 23. In the latter it is entitled: XI. To—Sinners, Obey the Gospel-Word. *Rep. Verse,* No. 239, pp. 265–6.]

[O HOW SORE A THING & GRIEVOUS][33]

1. O how sore a Thing & grievous
      'Tis to make
      God forsake
   And to Satan leave us!

2. None can tell but those that bear it
      All the Pain
      We sustain
   In a Wounded Spirit!

3. How for Grace in vain we languish,
      Pine away,
      And decay
   Thro' the knawing Anguish;

4. Fear, & Grief, & sore Temptation,
      Guilty Care,
      Sad Despair,
   Finish the Vexation.

5. Doom'd to late but vain Repentance,
      Can we feel
      Out of Hell
   A severer Sentence?

6. Yes, an heavier Curse besets us;
      Who fulfil
      Our own Will
   GOD in Anger *lets* us.

7. Suffers us our Sin to cover,
      Dark, & void,
      Dead to GOD,
   While He gives us over.

8. Senseless of its lost Condition
      Sleeps the Soul,
      Seems as whole,
   Needs not a Physician.

33. [MS Occasional, pp. 70–2.]

9. Neither asks, nor looks for Healing,
   Nought afraid,
   Doubly dead,
   Past remorse & feeling.

10. Conscience sear'd by Sin's hot Iron,
    Nothing knows
    Of the Woes
    That our Soul inviron.

11. Now our Heart again is harden'd,
    GOD is lost,
    Vain our Boast
    That we once were pardon'd.

12. Such a desperate Self-deceiver
    I have been,
    In my Sin
    Seem'd a True Believer.

13. But the Lord once more hath shook me,
    Ee'r I fell
    Into Hell
    And with Thunder woke me.

14. Me He hath not quite rejected,
    But with Pain
    Once again
    Dreadfully corrected.

15. Conscious of my Condemnation,
    Now I wou'd
    Turn to GOD,
    Hope for His Salvation.

16. Fain I woud retrieve his Fav[ou]r,
    Taste the Grace,
    See the Face,
    Of my injur'd Saviour.

17.   Would, but O! I want the Pow[e]r,
        Sigh in vain
        To regain
    That Accepted Hour.

18.   Whether I shall ee'r regain it
        Only He
        Knows, for me
    Who expir'd t'obtain it.

PENITENTIAL[34]

1.   If thy Justice, Lord, demands
        That I shoud suffer Pain,
    Let me fall into the Hands
        Of GOD, & not of Man:
    Cruel all his Mercies are,
    But Pity in thy Strokes we feel;
        Pity moveth Thee to spare
        And love thy Children still.

2.   Thou a self-condemning Soul
        In Measure dost chastize,
    Mercy will not let thy whole
        Displeasure to arise:
    Though Thou visit with the Rod
    My Sins, & angrily reprove,
        Wilt Thou cast me off, my GOD,
        And quite withdraw thy Love?

3.   Father, to thy just Decree
        I quietly submit;
    Lay thy Chastning Hand on me,
        While weeping at thy Feet;
    Strike—but O! remember still
    Him, who thy Justice satisfied,
        Then the helpless Sinner kill
        For whom thy Son hath died.

34. [MS Richmond, p. 20.]

PENITENTIAL[35]

1. Wretched Sinner that I am,
   What doth all my Strife avail?
Sin, my dire Reproach, & Shame,
   Character indelible
Can my utmost Powers erase,
Can my Tears, or Blood deface?

2. Lo! the Beastly Mark is seen,
   Lo! the Inbred Sin is found,
Written with an Iron Pen,
   With a pointed Diamond,
Deep engrav'd by hellish Art
On the Marble of my Heart.

3. Forty long & mournful years[36]
   Have I strove to purge the Stain,
Still it mocks my ceaseless Tears,
   Baffles all my Efforts vain:
Lord, at last to Thee I fly,
Help, or I forever die.

4. Faith I surely have in Thee,
   Sins Thou canst forgive *below*,
Red as Scarlet though they be
   Thou canst wash them white as snow,
Canst blot out the thickest Cloud,
Justify me by thy blood.

5. Flows a Fountain from thy Side
   For Impurity & Sin,
Plunge me in the Purple Tide
   Purge me, & I shall be clean,
Wash'd from all my guilty Stains
Sav'd from Sin, & Sin's Remains.

35. [MS Richmond, p. 24.]
36. [The MS probably dates from about 1749. Charles was born on December 18, 1707.]

ANOTHER[37]

1. Dreadful—sin-chastising GOD,
   Must I always bear thy Rod?
   Wilt Thou still persist to chide,
   Never lay thy Wrath aside?
   O for Mercy sake release;
   When Thou hast restor'd my Peace,
   Bear my wretched Soul away,
   Take me from the Evil Day.

2. End these dire Effects of Sin,
   Wars without & Fears within,
   Publick, & intestine Strife,
   All the Bitterness of Life:
   Wherefore shoud I longer live,
   Live, to suffer, & to grieve?
   Bear my wretched Soul away,
   Take me from the Evil Day.

3. All my Happiness is fled,
   All my Hopes of Joy are dead,
   Only Sin remains in me,
   Desperate Sin & Misery:
   Lord, Thou knowst the Pains I feel,
   Guilt, that knawing Worm of Hell;
   [Bear my wretched Soul away,
   Take me from the Evil Day.][38]

37. [MS Richmond, p. 25.]
38. [The last two lines are not in the original MS, hence the use of brackets. The two lines which conclude verses 1 and 2 were no doubt intended to complete the final verse.]

PENITENTIAL HYMNS

I[39]

1.   What shall I say, Preserver, Lord
      Of all the helpless Sons of Men?
  Shall I presume to plead thy Word,
      Or sue for pardning Grace again?

2.   Is it in all thy Depths of Love
      To cover such a World of Sin,
  So huge Destruction to remove,
      And wash so foul a Leper clean?

3.   The Infinite of Grace Divine
      In vain I labour to conceive,
  Thy ways & Thoughts are not like mine,
      If me Thou ever canst forgive.

4.   It seems impossible that Grace
      Shoud save a Wretch so lost as me,
  Or all thy cleansing Blood efface
      The Stain of mine Iniquity.

5.   If yesterday Thou canst recall,
      Or save a Soul shut up in Hell,
  Thou mayst at last repair my Fall,
      And make me as I ne'er had fell.

6.   But O! my tortur'd Conscience cries,
      Thy Justice must reject my Prayer—
  Thou must abhor my Sacrifice
      And leave me to extream Despair.

7.   Alas! I dare no longer hope,
      The Door is shut, the Day is past,
  Mercy itself has giv'n me up,
      To perish in my Blood at last.

39. [MS Misc. Hymns, p. 56; MS Richmond, pp. 78–9; MS Occasional, p. 81. The variants of MS Occasional suggest that it preceded MS Richmond. Similarly Charles Wesley's note "transcribed" in MS Richmond and the fact that the poem is scored through vertically, suggests that MS Misc. Hymns was copied from MS Richmond. The above version corresponds to MS Misc. Hymns which apparently was Wesley's final version.]

8. Yet for thy Cause & People's sake
        Indulge me in this One Desire:
    Take me away, in Judgment take,
        But let me *silently* expire.

9. Prevent the proud Philistine's Boast,
        The Ruin, Lord, be all my own,
    Bring me with Sorrow to the Dust,
        A Wretch unpitied & unknown.

10. Soon as on Earth I disappear,
        O might I all-forgotten be,
    Perish my sad Memorial here,
        And let my Name be lost with me.

II[40]

1. O my GOD, my GOD forbear
        Thine utmost Wrath to show,
    Spare the chief of Sinners, spare,
        Nor give the Final Blow,
    Weeping in the Dust I lie,
    If haply yet there may be Hope,
        If thy yearning Bowels cry,
        "How shall I give thee up?"

2. By reiterated Crimes
        I have thy Spirit griev'd,
    Twice ten thous[an]d thous[an]d times
        Forgiven, or repriev'd,
    None of our Apostate Race
    Matches my vile Apostasy,
        None hath so abus'd thy Grace,
        And dar'd thy Wrath, as me!

3. Yet for thy Compassion sake
        And never failing Love,
    Call the Storms of vengeance back,
        The bitter Cup remove;

40. [MS Misc. Hymns, p. 58; MS Richmond, pp. 79–80; MS Occasional, p. 82.]

Once again in Jesus' Name
For Pardon & Release I cry,
   Sav'd from all my Sin, & Shame,
   O let me love, & die.

III [41]

1. My God, my God, I hear thy call
     But dare not lift my guilty eyes;
  Confounded by another fall,
     Why shoud I still attempt to rise?
  I cannot draw this bearded dart,
  Or tear this nature from my heart.

2. My heart (how contrary to Thee!)
     Is still a cage of birds unclean,
  A sink of all impurity;
     My spirit, soul, and flesh is sin,
  And tired to death in vain I groan,
  To lay my life, my burthen down.

3. What woud I give to feel and know
     That I shall never sin again?
  A thousand worlds? they all shoud go,
     Might I the precious grace obtain,
  Assur'd by love's abiding power
  That I shall never grieve thee more.

4. Love only can renew my heart,
     And fix, that it no more shall rove:
  O woudst Thou, Lord, ev'n now impart
     The power of thy forgiving love,
  Ev'n now to bid my wandrings cease,
  And seal mine everlasting peace.

41. [MS Misc. Hymns, p. 59.]

ACCEPTING PUNISHMENT[42]

1. Ah! Lord, I do, I do repent,
        My vileness & thy justice own,
    Humbly accept my punishment,
        And scarse presume my griefs to groan,
    Give my rebellious murm'rings ore,
    And kick against the pricks no more.

2. Holy, & just are all thy ways,
        Most fitly contrary to me,
    I see thy awful righteousness,
        The wisdom of thy wrath I see,
    My sin in every judgment read,
    And meekly bow my guilty head.

3. Convinc'd I hear th'instructive rod,
        Which brings my secret faults to mind,
    My long forgetfulness of GOD,
        I now, of GOD forgotten, find.
    Nor can I ask, who fled from thee,
    Ah, why hast thou forsaken me!

4. I woud not use the proffer'd Power,
        Or warn'd, thy Spirit's calls obey,
    And now I cannot watch one hour,
        I cannot for one moment pray,
    The stony o're my heart is spread,
    And my dead soul is doubly dead.

5. Dead, dead to GOD, but still alive
        To sin, I make my feeble moan,
    Who in thy strength refus'd to strive,
        Thy strength I find withdrawn & gone,
    To every tempting lust give place,
    And faint—without thy *slighted* grace.

42. [MS Richmond, pp. 116–17.]

6.   To good averse, to ill inclin'd
      Left to my own rebellious will,
   The hatred of the carnal mind
      An hundred fold increas'd I feel,
   Yet cannot I my GOD accuse,
   Who gives me but the thing I chuse.

7.   Me if thou never more incline
      In humble fear to sue for grace,
   I cannot at my doom repine,
      Or charge thee with unrighteousness,
   But merit all the plagues I feel,
   And vindicate my GOD in hell.

[O MERCIFUL CREATOR][43]

1.   O merciful Creator,
      An helpless Soul receive,
   Thy Property & Nature
      Is always to forgive;
   With eyes of kind compassion
      A guilty Sinner see,
   And grant me the Salvation
      Thy Son procur'd for me.

2.   For Jesus' sake release me
      From all these Chains within,
   O send thy Son to bless me
      By turning me from sin,
   In honour of my Saviour
      And Advocate above
   Reveal thy gracious favour,
      Display thy pardning Love.

43. [MS Richmond, p. 155.]

[BURST, STRUGLING SOUL, THE BANDS OF SIN][44]

1.   Burst, strugling Soul, the Bands of sin,
         The corruptible Body leave,
       If that can quench the Fire within,
         My Heart's last Drop of Blood I gave,
       To 'scape the Inbred Tyrant's Power,
       And die that I might sin no more.

2.   Tir'd with the greatness of my Way,
         Weary alas! to Death I am,
       Ten thousand times I curse my Day;
         I cannot bear my Load of Shame.
       In Rage my sinful Flesh I tear,
       In all the Madness of Despair.

3.   What Help or Hope remains for me,
         A fallen, damn'd, apostate soul!
       No distant Ray of Light I see:
         The Measure of my Sin is full:
       Since first from Pard'ning Grace I fell
       I have debas'd Myself to Hell.

4.   Conscience, the Worm that never dies,
         Distracts & knaws my bleeding Heart,
       Sin always meets my blasted eyes:
         I cannot from myself depart;
       O wretched Man of Sin, I cry,
       And groan, till I forever die.

5.   But let me first the Justice clear
         Of God who turns me into Hell:
       No dire Decree of His is here
         Compelling me the Death to feel,
       He doth not drive me from His Face
       For Want, but for Abuse of Grace.

44. [MS Thirty, pp. 126–7.]

6. Because I did receive the Seed,
    Th'Immortal Seed of God in vain;
   The Talent of my Lord I hid,
    And did not Other Talent gain,
   I would not live, I would rebel,
   And thus from Saving Grace I fell.

7. I fell, but not by His Decree,
    He never preordain'd my Fall;
   His Saving Grace appear'd to me;
    And freely offers Life to all;
   I Him denied who me had bought,
   He came, but I receiv'd him not.

8. Tophet is now my just Reward,
    By Sin I made it my own Place,
   For Devils, not for me prepar'd—
    Yet there I clear th'All-pard'ning Grace,
   In Hell disprove their Hellish Lie,
   And self-destroy'd forever die!

WAITING FOR FULL REDEMPTION [45]

1. Let all who know the Sinner's Friend
    With us their Faith confess,
   Stir themselves up to apprehend
    The Lord their Righteousness.

2. Thro' Jesus' Righteousness alone
    We feel our sins forgiven,
   And find Eternity begun,
    And antedate our Heaven.

3. But shall we rest in Pardning Grace,
    On this side Jordan stop?
   No, Lord, we look to see thy Face,
    And after Thee wake up.

45. [MS Richmond, p. 55.]

4. A glorious Prize is still behind
    For those that dare believe,
    And we the Second Rest shall find,
    The perfect Gift receive.

ANOTHER[46]

1. Saviour of a rebellious Race,
    My ever-loving Saviour,
    How have I forfeited thy Grace,
    Slighted thy Frown & Favour!
    How have I rose against the Rod,
    Strong in my Provocation,
    Weary of waiting on my GOD,
    Murmuring for Salvation!

2. O what an hardned Wretch was I
    So to provoke, & grieve Thee,
    Threaten, if Thou delaydst, to fly
    Back to my Sins, & leave Thee!
    Lord, if thy Love had dwelt in me,
    Could I have so offended?
    Nay, but I then had look'd to Thee,
    Till all the Storm was ended.

3. O that I could my Soul possess
    In Humbleness & Patience,
    Hoping in Wars for perfect Peace,
    Joyful in Tribulations!
    O might I for a Moment prove
    Some Token of thy Favour!
    Say to my Soul, Thou art my Love,
    Look unto me, thy Saviour.

46. [MS Richmond, pp. 56–7; MS Cheshunt, p. 211. The unusual metre of the poem, with its reversed and stressed accent at the beginning of each line, is the metre of "The True Use of Musick," set to the tune of "Nancy Dawson." See *Rep. Verse*, p. 117.]

4. Jacob of old to gain a Wife
        Twice seven Years could tarry,
    Chearful in Toil he spent his Life,
        Labour'd, & was not weary:
    And shall I count it long to stay
        With GOD Himself before me,
    Sure of the Lamb in that glad Day,
        Sure of the Crown of Glory!

5. Jesus, tho' late I now submit,
        Execute all thy Pleasure,
    Weeping I fall before thy Feet,
        Willing to wait thy Leizure.
    What are a Sinner's Toils or Tears,
        If he but hope to gain Thee?
    Who would not wait a thousand Years,
        Could he at last obtain Thee?

UNIVERSAL REDEMPTION[47]

1. Saviour of All, whose Bowels move
        To all the Souls Thy Hands have made,
    Whose Sovereign Everlasting Love
        For All a Bleeding Ransom paid;

2. All-good, All-gracious to redeem,
        To Thee my loftiest Songs I raise,
    Gladly resume my darling Theme,
        And glory in thy General Grace.

3. I sing Thy Grace Divinely free,
        Let all Mank[in]d Thy Grace adore,
    That vast unfathomable Sea
        Without a Bottom or a Shore,

4. Not all the first-born Sons of Light
        Thy Glorious Grace can fully tell,
    The Length, & Breadth, & Depth, & Hei[gh]t
        Of Love Incomprehensible.

47. [MS Thirty, pp. 111–12. In v. 5 Wesley is either inconsistent in his use of verb forms or regards "army" as both a singular and plural subject.]

5. Thy Love th'Angelic Army sings
  And tremble at Thy Gracious Power,
  And wrap their Faces in their Wings,
  And fall, & silently adore.

6. Like them I long on Thee to gaze,
  Like them before Thy Throne to fall,
  With Joy unutterable praise
  The Love Divine that died for All.

ANOTHER[48]

1. Captain of my Salvation hear,
  And stand in all thy Power confest,
  And arm thy Soldier for the War,
  And breathe Thy Spirit into my Breast.

2. With stedfast, calm, deliberate Might,
  With temper'd Zeal my Heart inspire,
  And teach my feeble Hands to fight
  And touch my Lips with hallow'd Fire.

3. Vilest of all the ransom'd Race,
  I hear, & answer to thy Call,
  Assert thy free unbounded Grace,
  And witness Thou hast died for All.

4. To Thee my worthless name I give,
  Here at the Altar of Thy Cross
  I plight my Faith to die & Live
  To vindicate Thy Mercy's Cause.

5. Thro' Thee to Heaven I lift my Hand,
  The Purpose of my Soul declare;
  With All that dare Thy Love withstand
  I vow to wage an Endless War.

48. [MS Thirty, pp. 112–14.]

6. An endless War, yet free from Rage
    Or cruel Hate, or proud Despight,
With Satan, & his World I wage,
    And suffer in Thy Mercy's Right.

7. To Battle in Thy Strength I go
    Against the Trampler on Thy Grace,
The Hellish Reprobating Foe,
    The Molock of our Helpless Race.

8. The Fiend who counterfeits Thy Seal,
    Consigns as by Thy Dire Decree
Whole Nations with their Babes to Hell,
    And damns from All Eternity.[49]

9. Sworn Enemy to All his Art,
    And Pains to wash the Ethiop white,
Jesu, till Soul & Body part,
    With Satan in Thy Strength I fight.

10. Whether he damns or passes by
    The wretched Reprobated Brood,
His utmost Efforts I defy
    To stain the Mercy of my God.

11. Long as in me Thy Breath remains,
    Long as the Circling Blood shall flow,
I spend my Soul, & Strength, & Pains
    To reprobate Thy Hellish Foe.

12. To pluck the Prey out of his Teeth,
    On every Soul of Man to call,
And testify in Life & Death
    Who died for me hath died for All.

49. A quotation from Calvin. [This is Wesley's note regarding lines three and four of verse 8.]

UNIVERSAL R[EDEMPTIO]N[50]

1. O All-embracing Love Divine,
   O All-illuminating Light,
   Throughout the World victorious shine,
   Victorious or'e the Shades of Night.

2. The Smoak that issues from the Pit,
   And darkens Heaven's All-chearing Face,
   Scatter, & bruise beneath our Feet
   The bold Blasphemer of Thy Grace.

3. Let him blaspheme Thy Grace no more,
   Or mock us while he calls it free,
   Silence his reprobating Roar,
   Cancel his Horrible Decree.

4. Drive the Old *Fatal*ist to Hell
   Nor longer let him Refuge take
   In Kirk,[a] or School,[b] or Mosque,[c] or Cell,[d]
   Not ev'n in his own Leman-Lake.[e][51]

5. Spare the poor Advocates for Sin,
   But let their Master's Kingdom fall,
   Destroy the Frogs, the Spirits unclean
   That croak, 'Thou didst not die for all.'

HYMNS FOR REDEMPTION[52]

I

1. And must I still in groans complain,
   A weak, intangled, wretched man,
   From good averse, to sin inclin'd
   O how shall I redemption find?

50. [MS Thirty, p. 124; *Rep. Verse*, No. 120, p. 167.]
51. [The footnotes a - e are Wesley's.] a. of Scotland. b. Of Zeno, the heathen Philosopher. c. Of Mahomet the Impostor. d. Of Dominick the Popish Friar—All Predestinarians. e. Of Geneva.
52. [MS Misc. Hymns, p. 80.]

2. I see the gospel-summer past,
   And still in deepest clay stick fast,
   Bemir'd,[53] opprest by my own sin,
   I am not saved, I am not clean.

3. Jesus, thy only grace can heal
   This strong propensity to ill,
   A soul idolatrous convert,
   And turn the bias of my heart.

4. Weary I come for rest to Thee,
   Inslav'd, for power and liberty,
   Redemption from my sinful load
   O might I find it in thy blood!

5. If Thou the power of faith bestow,
   The stream shall to the Fountain flow,
   My heart shall pant with pure desire
   And all my soul to heaven aspire.

6. My heart which cannot cease from sin
   Shall never lodge a thought unclean,
   But, fill'd with love and holiness,
   Abide in everlasting peace.

II[54]

1. God of uncreated love,
      God of spotless purity,
   Send thine image from above
      Breathe thy Spirit into me,
   Purge mine evil heart from sin,
   Make my inmost nature clean.

53. ["Bemi'rd" is a rare word. The only eighteenth century example quoted in the *Oxford English Dictionary* is from John Wesley: "Doubt. . . bemires the soul." (*Works*, 1872, VI, p. 36.]
    54. [MS Misc. Hymns, pp. 81–2.]

2. Smiting this polluted breast,
        For thy purity I groan,
    Never shall my spirit rest,
        Till with thine intirely one,
    Till in holy love renew'd
    Sin I loath, and cleave to God.

3. O how distant from my hope,
        How unlike my God am I!
    Yet thy grace to me can stoop,
        Yet thy blood can sanctify;
    Let it now my soul inflow,[55]
    Make me as my Lord below.

4. Jesus, full of balmy grace,
        Now thy virtuous power exert,
    Foulest of the filthy race,
        Lo, I offer Thee my heart,
    Form it, Lord, averse from sin,
    Cleanse the house by entering in.

5. By th'indwelling God restor'd
        To my pure, original state,
    I shall never grieve my Lord,
        Never do the thing I hate,
    I shall all thy ways approve,
    Love thee with a perfect love.

6. Come then, O my heart's desire,
        Strength'ning me t'abide thy day,
    Sit as a Refiner's fire,
        Throughly purge my dross away,
    All my creature-love consume,
    Come, my utmost Saviour, come!

55. [The word "inflow" was obsolete in Wesley's time. The only transitive use of the verb in the *Oxford English Dictionary* is from the seventeenth century.]

III[56]

1. Say, thou Almighty Jesus,
        If Jesus is thy name,
   How long shall sin oppress us,
        Our burthen, grief, and shame?
   How long shall we go mourning,
        With short repentance vain,
   And to our vomit turning
        Implunge[57] in guilt again?

2. Thou art a present Saviour
        Of them that can believe,
   Thy property is ever
        To pity, and forgive;
   Thy bowels of compassion
        To helpless sinners move,
   Thine office is salvation,
        And all thy heart is love.

3. My Friend and Mediator
        O had I faith to see!
   Jesus, display thy nature,
        Answer thy Name to me.
   My long-imprison'd spirit
        Release, and bring to God,
   As ransom'd by thy merit,
        And pardon'd thro' thy blood.

FOR REDEMPTION [58]

1.   How long shall I complain
       Of the fierce war within,
   The importunity and pain
       Of this rebellious sin;

56. [MS Misc. Hymns, pp. 82–3.]

57. [The *Oxford English Dictionary* gives no example of the intransitive use of the verb "implunge." It is rare even as a transitive verb. Charles Wesley used it in Hymn No. 76 in the *1780 Collection:* "Implunged in the crystal abyss."]

58. [MS Misc. Hymns, pp. 306–8. The poem numbered II, which follows this poem in the MS, was published in *Poet. Works*, XIII, p. 252.]

Which tempts me night and day
To violate thy commands,
And strives to tear my soul away
Out of my Saviour's hands?

2.   In life's extremest hour
I find the fight renew'd,
And tremble at th'oppressive power
Of passions unsubdued:
Departing hence, I dread
With evil to comply,
And, (while I bow my hoary head,)
To sin, despair, and die.

3.   But, Lord, I must confess
Thy justice and thy truth
In age condemns me to possess
Th'offences of my youth:
The gracious God I clear,
If now my day is past,
If I have sought salvation here,
And die unsav'd at last.

4.   Yet will I feebly cry
With my expiring breath
To Him who died himself, that I
Might gasp his name in death,
Jesus, appear within,
And bid my soul be free,
For ever separated from sin,
For ever *One with Thee.*[59]

---

59. [In the margin "join'd to Thee" is written as an alternative to "One with Thee."]

III [60]

1.   Is there no balm in Gilead found,
     Is there no kind Physician there,
  To cure a bleeding spirit's wound,
     To mitigate my sad despair,
  Before th'intolerable smart
  My God and me for ever part?

2.   No helps medicinal have I,
     But soon the second death must feel,
  Unless my God the grace supply
     My plague original to heal,
  Unless his Son, on me bestow'd,
  Pour in the balm of his own blood.

3.   Hope of the sinsick, dying soul,
     Me at my latest gasp receive:
  O that thy wounds might make me whole,
     O that thy death might bid me live;
  Live, my Physician to proclaim,
  And spread the powers of Jesus' name.

4.   If virtue, Lord, from Thee proceed,
     This loathsom Issue shall be dried,
  While fully saved, and truly freed,
     Restor'd, and wholly sanctified,
  My happy soul exults to prove
  A perfect cure in perfect love.

60. [MS Misc. Hymns, pp. 309–10.]

THANKSGIVING[61]

1. Sons of GOD, your Father praise,
    Praise him in alternate lays,
    Lift your hearts & voices higher,
    Emulate the angel-quire.

2. Day & night they chant above,
    Praise his everlasting love,
    Joyful all again they sing
    Glory to our heavenly king.

3. King of heaven's exalted powers,
    Him we call thro' Jesus ours,
    Humbly bow before his throne,
    Boldly claim it for our own.

4. Christ hath paid the mighty price,
    Bought our mansions in the skies,
    Equal praise to Christ be given,
    Fellow to the GOD of heaven.

THANKSGIVING FOR FAIR WEATHER[62]

1.   Jehovah's praise declare,
            Who makes his mercies known,
        Our God that hears the prayer
            Presented thro' his Son:
        Ev'n now He answers to our cry,
        And stays the bottles of the sky.[63]

61. [MS Richmond, p. 113. Though the poem seems complete, there is space left in the MS for two more verses at the foot of the page, and for three more at the top of the next page.]

62. [MS Misc. Hymns, pp. 89–90.]

63. [*Cf.* Job 38:37.]

2.   Father, accept our praise,
            Who dost thy power reveal,
        In wrath remembring grace
            Thou art our Father still;
        Thy mighty love we magnify
        Which shuts the windows of the sky.

3.   Thy sovereign word obey'd,
            Thy gracious will is done,
        The plague of water stay'd,
            The rain is o're and gone,
        Thankful we lift our heart and eye,
        And see with joy the smiling sky.

4.   Smile on us still from heaven,
            Thou Giver of all grace,
        Eternally forgiven
            Till we behold thy face,
        And hail thee with thy saints above
        Inthron'd in everlasting love.

THANKSGIVING FOR ONE NARROWLY ESCAPED ASSASSINATION— MR. THOMAS STOKES[64]

1.   Let every tongue my Saviour Praise
        Who for his Servant cares,
     And watches over all my ways,
        And numbers all my hairs;
     In danger's unsuspected hour
        Who hides my life above,
     And saves from the destroyer's power
        The object of his love.

2.   Thou only dost the rage restrain
        Of my infernal foe,
     And arm'd with death, beyond his chain
        Th'assassin cannot go;

64. [MS Misc. Hymns, pp. 189–90.]

The fatal weapon cannot speed—
    A wall of brass withstands,
And angels hover round my head,
    And bear me in their hands.

3.   A bird escap'd the fowler's snare,
    A brand out of the fire,
My kind Deliverer I declare,
    My Guardian God admire;
A pledge of greater mercies still
    My ransom'd life receive,
And live to serve thy blessed will,
    And to thy glory live.

4.   For this Thou didst my soul allure
    With early tastes of grace,
In health preserve, in sickness cure,
    And rescue in distress:
For this Thou hast my manners borne,
    And spar'd from year to year,
Nor let me quite to sin return,
    Or quite throw off thy fear.

5.   I now as from the grave restor'd,
    By miracle divine,
Enter into thy counsel, Lord,
    And answer thy design;
For heavenly joys at last compel'd
    With earthly things to part,
Lover of souls, I yield, I yield,
    I give Thee all my heart!

THANKSGIVING AFTER A FALL
JULY 30, 1781[65]

1.   My spirit magnifies the Lord,
    Who doth salvation send,
And those that hang upon his word
    In danger's hour defend:

65. [MS Misc. Hymns, p. 91.]

Distinguish'd by his guardian grace
  We all his goodness prove,
With songs our kind Preserver praise
  And triumph in his love.

2. While One remov'd by sudden death
    We see before our eyes,
  Jehovah spreads his arms beneath
    And bids the fallen rise:
  We rise unhurt, nor feel the shock,
    Nor suffer from the fall,
  And not one single bone is broke,
    Because He keeps them all.

3. We live, by miracle, we live
    Still greater things to see,
  Reserv'd for good, and kept to give
    Our loving hearts to Thee:
  Saviour, accept our sacrifice,
    Inspire us with thy love,
  And bid our new-born souls arise
    To sing thy praise above.

WRITTEN AFTER A FALL[66]

1. Let fools and infidels revere
    And bow to Fortune's shrine,
  No chance, or accident is here,
    But Providence divine.

2. Thou, Lord, hast suffer'd me to fall,
    That I again may prove
  My worthless hairs are numbred all,
    My life secur'd above.

66. [MS Misc. Hymns, p. 92; *Rep. Verse*, No. 297, p. 333.]

3. Thankful the token I receive
    Of greater things to come,
    And trust, thy love will never leave,
    But bring me safely home.

4. For when I fall into the grave,
    I only fall to rise,
    Whom Thou dost to the utmost save
    And bear above the skies.

BEFORE READING THE SCRIPTURES[67]

1. Son of God, to Thee I look
    Teach me the mysterious Book;
    Take my weakness by the hand,
    Make my dulness understand.

2. With thy grace anoint my eyes,
    Make me to salvation wise,
    Wisdom from above impart,
    Give me the believing heart.

BEFORE READING THE SCRIPTURE[68]

III

1. O God, to whom for light I look
    How shall I know this ancient book,
        If it indeed be thine,
    Unless thy Spirit breaks the seals,
    And to my heart the Sense reveals
        As oracles divine.

2. The Church that did from Christ proceed,
    Whose many parts and members spread

67. [MS Richmond, p. 106.]
68. [MS CW I(p) 3–4.]

Throughout the Earth I see,
Not one, but all in every age
Have handed down the sacred page
    And left it pure to me.

3. Not one particular alone,
    The Universal Church I own,
        But all with one accord,
    Churches diffus'd from East to West,
    Conspire unanimous t'attest
        The heaven-descended word.

4. The Fact historical is plain,
    But standing on the words of man
        I am not satisfied,
    I want a more substantial ground,
    A Rock on which my faith to found
        Which always may abide.

5. What is that Rock, but Christ alone:
    O were He to my soul made known,
        The Truth infallible,
    Son of the living God supream!
    The faith, the Church, that's built on Him
        Defies the gates of hell.

6. His Spirit in these mysterious leaves
    Unerring testimony gives
        To Christ the Lord most high:
    O woud He take of Jesus' blood,
    Blood of the true,[69] eternal God,
        And to my heart apply!

7. The Witness of thy truth I need
    (Which whosoe'er believes indeed
        Doth in himself possess)
    To testify that I am thine,
    To fill with righteousness divine
        And love, and joy and peace.

69. [The word "one" is written above "true" as an alternative.]

8. Possest of Him I doubt no more,
   But God in spirit and truth adore,
     My Father and my Friend,
   Till the bright Image of his Sire
   I see with all his angel-quire,
     My glorious Lord descend!

IV[70]

1. In search of the Religion true
   O God, I know not what to do,
     But humbly look to Thee,
   Who only canst direct me right,
   Illumine with celestial light
     And give me eyes to see.

2. That truth I in the means may find,
   A candid, free, impartial mind
     To me vouchsafe to give,
   With judgment sound, and reason clear,
   So shall I weigh, and read, and hear
     And all thy mind receive.

3. Obstinate prejudice remove,
   That I may all religions prove,
     And hold the balance even:
   Make me indifferent to the Way
   (Whate'er it be) which safely may
     Conduct my soul to heaven.

4. From sloth, and pride, and passion free
   And wilful ignorance, to me
     The worship pure make known,
   Most acceptable in thy sight,
   In which Thou chiefly dost delight,
     And wilt with glory crown.

70. [MS CW I(p) 5–6.]

5. Thine Oracles the answer give,
   They teach me to repent, believe,
     And Christ my Lord confess,
   My faith by my obedience prove,
   Worship Thee in the Spirit of love
     And truth of holiness.

6. While thus I worthily adore
   My God, I can inquire no more,
     Assur'd that mine Thou art,
   Who dost in Christ thyself reveal;
   I own thy manifested will
     And give Thee all my heart.

V[71]

1. The word of God, by all confest
   Of truth th'indubitable test
     My perfect Rule I own,
   The Word which doth his mind reveal
   To those that woud perform his will,
     And worship Him alone.

2. 'Tis here I seek, and hope to find
   My Lord, who hath my heart inclin'd
     Himself to serve and please:
   I ask his Spirit's promis'd light
   To guide my wandring feet aright
     Into the way of peace.

3. Scripture doth Christ The WORD declare,
   The Spirit, his own Interpreter,
     Doth testify of Thee;
   Son of the living God most high,
   Born for a sinful world to die,
     Thy death hath ransom'd me.

71. [MS CW I(p) 6–8.]

4.   The Spirit doth the power infuse,
     Thro' which I now my Chuser chuse:
         He breaks my heart of stone:
     From Him my holiness proceeds,
     My faith, and hope—and love that leads
         Directly to thy throne.

5.   Thro' Him the Crucified I know
     And let all other knowledge go,
         As trivial, void, and vain;
     And blest with evidence divine,
     And certified, that Thou art mine,
         Eternal life I gain.

6.   The Spirit doth the truth reveal,
     The pledge, the witness, and the seal,
         To all believers given,
     Thy word of all-sufficient grace
     Prepares me for that happy place,
         And builds me up to heaven.

VI[72]

1.   See, Lord, thy meanest servant set,
     Humbly attentive at thy feet,
         Thy welcome will to prove;
     Help me to chuse the better part,
     And teach my inexperienc'd heart
         The lessons of thy love.

2.   Thou only knowst what is in man;
     Me, Saviour, to myself explain,
         And true repentance give;
     Bid me from sin this moment cease
     And then I follow after peace
         And in thy presence live.

72. [MS CW I(p) 8.]

3. Author of faith, the grace bestow
    Thro' which I may my Saviour know,
    And feel thy blood applied,
    In Thee my Lord and God believe
    And by thy hands and feet perceive
    Jehovah crucified!

4. Me let thy dying love constrain
    To love my loving Lord again
    And walk in all thy ways,
    And never from thy footsteps move
    Till call'd to meet Thee from above,
    I see thy heavenly face.

BEFORE READING THE SCRIPTURE[73]

1. Come, divine Interpreter
    Of thy own most sacred word,
    The deep things of God declare,
    Testify of Christ the Lord,
    Life, eternal life impart,
    Speak the truth into my heart.

2. Christ, the Truth, the Life, the Way
    Thine alone it is to show:
    Help me for thy help to pray,
    Teach me God in Christ to know,
    Christ the Lord *my* Lord to prove,
    Mine to call, adore, and love.

3. Him the self-existent God,
    Sole, supreme, in me reveal,
    Witness with Jehovah's blood,
    Taste of joys unspeakable,
    Seal, and bid my soul arise,
    Give me wings to reach the skies.

73. [MS Misc. Hymns, p. 228.]

BEFORE PREACHING AT ST. EUDY [74]

1.   Come, O thou mighty Lord,
         Come, O thou Prince of Peace,
      Give out the Gospel-Word,
         And crown it with success,
Now to thy ransomed ones appear,
And plant thy heavenly Kingdom here.

2.   Claim as thy lawful Right
         The souls before thee bowed,
      From Darkness turn to Light,
         From Satan's Power to GOD,
That they may all thy Love receive,
And saved from Sin forever live.

3.   In this Accepted Hour
         A gracious Token shew,
      And make us own thy power
         And groan ourselves to know,
Weep for our sins, and deeply mourn,
And to a pardning GOD return.

4.   Gather the Outcasts in
         Who feel their guilty Load;
      Redeem the Slaves of Sin,
         And point them to thy Blood,
Thy Blood be to their hearts applied,
And speak them freely Justified.

74. [MS Richmond, p. 158. "St. Eudy" is Wesley's spelling of "St. Udy," a frequent contemporary error for "St. Tudy" (Cornwall). Charles Wesley preached there on Monday, August 11, 1753. This poem appeared in *Hymns for Divine Worship* (the hymnbook of the Methodist New Connexion) in 1863.]

THE PRAYER OF AN AGED MINISTER BEFORE PREACHING

III[75]

1. Jesus, supreme, almighty Lord,
      The kingdom and the praise is thine,
   Thine is the everlasting word;
      Demonstrated by power divine
   Now let it on the hearers be,
   And now extend thy grace to me.

2. Open my mouth, and utterance give,
      Open their hearts, and faith bestow.
   And who by faith already live,
      Let them in grace and knowledge grow,
   Bring forth the hundred-fold increase,
   The fruit of ripest holiness.

3. Empty the word cannot return,
      But must thy kind design fulfil,
   While sinners of the Spirit born
      Rejoice to prove thine utmost will,
   Obedient as the host above,
   And perfect in their Father's love.

4. Then, Saviour, then thyself descend,
      And let us meet thee in the air,
   Receive our faith's triumphant End,
      Th'unutterable rapture share,
   Where Seraphs on their faces fall,
   And Thou, O God, art all in all.

75. [MS Misc. Hymns, pp. 231–2.]

SACRAM[EN]T—HYMN [76]

1. Author of everlasting Bliss,
       To All who thy Commands obey,
    By Faith impower us to *do this,*
       Here let us for thy Coming stay,
    Kept by thy sure unerring Word,
    Girt with thy Spirit's two-edg'd Sw[or]d.

2. Thou knowst our feeble wav'ring H[ear]t,
       So often weary of thy Ways,
    So fain, & ready to depart
       And leave the Channels of thy Grace,
    So prone to fleshly Liberty,
    So sick of waiting long for Thee.

3. Thou knowst the Number of our Foes,
       Their cunning Craftiness & Power,
    Who Thee, & Thy Commands oppose;
       Watchful thy People to devour,
    They still our every Path beset,
    And hunt our Souls with Satan's Net.

4. Servants of Sin, by Nature led,
       Freedom they promise us, & Peace,
    Friends to the World, & free indeed
       From real, inward Righteousness.
    [Unfinished]

SACRAMENTAL [77]

1.   O Jesus our Head,
       Who hast died in our stead,
    Thy Promise of Faith & Repentance we plead,

76. [MS Richmond, p. 27. The poem is incomplete. Space for four lines has been left at the foot of the page and p. 28 is blank.]
    77. [MS Richmond, pp. 63–4.]

Now let it take place,
Pour out on our Race
The Spirit of Prayer, & Contrition, and Praise.

2.   While thus we record
Our Crucified Lord,
Be mindful of Us, & accomplish thy Word.
Thy Promise is past,
We shall see Thee at last,
And our Souls on thy Bloody Atonem[en]t be cast.

3.   Stretch'd out on the Tree,
Thou saidst, They shall see,
My Murtherers surely shall look upon me.
The Stones shall relent,
The Rocks shall be rent
And the Hearts more obdurate than Marble lament.

4.   Now then let us turn
To Jehovah's First-born
And look upon Thee we have wounded, & mourn;
In Bitterness cry
That the Prince of the Sky,
GOD's Only-begotten, we doom'd Him to die.

5.   Our Sins were the Cause
Of his Sorrow & Loss;
By our Sins we pursued Him & nail'd to the Cross;
We inflicted the Pain;
We have pierc'd Him again;
And O! shall He suffer so often in v[ai]n?

6.   The Sense of thy Smart,
O Jesus, impart,
And break by thy Death the Inflexible Heart:
By thy Passion alone
The Deed can be done;
Appear in thy Wounds, & our Heart is Thine own.

[SACRAMENTAL]—HYMN 3[78]

1. Father, Friend of Human Race,
   Trusting in thine only Grace,
   I a feeble sinful Worm,
   I have vow'd, & will perform.

2. I in Jesus' Name have sworn,
   I will not to Sin return,
   Stedfastly resolv'd I am
   Sin to'eschew in Jesus' Name.

3. Strength alas! in me is none,
   I my utter Weakness own,
   Sin t'eschew, I know, & feel,
   Is with Man Impossible.

4. By ten thous[an]d Snares beset
   Sin at every Turn I meet,
   Sin I always bear within;
   How should I abstain from Sin?

5. Answer, O Thou mighty One,
   Partner of thy Father's Throne,
   Canst Thou by thy Promis'd Power
   Keep me, that I sin no more?

6. Closely urg'd on every Side,
   Tried, & to the utmost tried,
   May I on thy Love depend?
   Wilt Thou save me to the End?

7. Yes, I know, Thou canst, Thou wilt,
   On The Rock my Faith is built,
   Israel's Rock, which cannot move,
   Jesus' Truth, & Power, & Love.

8. By the Spirit of thy Grace
   Thou shalt keep me all my Days;
   On thy Truth, & Love, & Power
   Standing, I shall fall no more.

78. [MS Richmond, pp. 65–7.]

SACRAMENT—HYMN [79]

1.   O the Blood, the pretious Blood,
      That streams from yonder Tree!
  Glory to th'Incarnate GOD
      Who suffers Death for me!
  Me to save from Endless Pain,
      Me to mount above the Skies,
  GOD becomes a Mortal Man,
      And bows his head, & dies.

2.   Him as on the Altar laid
      Ev'n now by Faith I view,
  Suffering in the Sinner's stead
      The Death to Sinners due:
  Say not ye, The Deed is *past,*
      Now his mortal Pang I feel,
  Still he pants, & groans his last,
      He dies for Sinners still.

3.   Close beneath the cursed Wood
      My prostrate Soul remains,
  Gasping for the Balmy Blood
      That starts from Jesus' Veins:
  Wilt Thou not One Drop afford?
      Yes, Thou *dost* the Comfort give;
  O my bleeding, loving Lord,
      Thou diedst that I may live.

4.   Rivers of Salvation flow
      And springs of Life from Thee,
  Sav'd from Sin, I live, I know
      Thy Blood hath ransom'd me:
  Now I catch the healing Tide
      Now I taste how good Thou art,
  Now I feel the Blood applied,
      The Pardon to my heart.

79. [MS Richmond, pp. 82–3; MS Occasional, p. 87.]

SACRAMENT—HYMN [80]

1. How dreadful is the Place
   Where GOD appoints to meet
   Sinners that humbly seek his Face,
   And tremble at his Feet.
   Where to th'Assembled Crowd
   His Promis'd Grace is given:
   This is the solemn House of GOD,
   This is the Gate of Heaven!

2. His Ordinance Divine
   He now vouchsafes to own,
   Blessings herein & Duties join,
   And GOD & Man is One:
   The Sacramental Rite
   Which Jesus' Love commands
   Heaven & Earth by Faith t'unite
   Like Jacob's Ladder stands.

3. On this mysterious Tree
   Where our Redeemer hung,
   Descending & ascending see
   The bright Angelick Throng!
   They fill the hallow'd Place
   While we his Death record,
   And lost in silent wonder gaze
   On our *redeeming*[81] Lord.

4. By Jesus' Cross sustain'd
   Our Souls to Heaven aspire,
   Blessings by Jesus' Cross descend
   And raise our raptures higher.
   The Ministers of Grace
   Swift to our succour move,
   Our Guardians fill the middle space
   And GOD appears above!

80. [MS Richmond, pp. 105–6.]
81. [In the margin "expir-"(ing) is written as an alternative to "redeeming."]

184

5.   He calls us to the skies,
     And lo! we spurn the ground,
Light on the sacred Ladder rise,
     And gain the topmost Round;
     Of Everlasting Life
     The glorious Pledge is given,
Another Step shall end the Strife,
     And lodge us all in Heaven!

SACRAMENTAL HYMNS

I[82]

Commemorating the Death,
     We woud thy life receive,
Breathe on us, Lord, thy Spirit's breath,
     And lo, by faith we live;
     Our twice-dead souls restor'd
     Discern Thee on the tree,
And I confess my God, my Lord,
     Who loved, and died for me.

II[83]

1.   O cou'd we with the Sign receive
     The spiritual, internal grace,
Power to repent, and to believe,
     And our dear, dying Lord embrace
Who bought our pardon with his blood,
And reconciled a world to God!

2.   Present if really Thou art,
     Now, Saviour, now the veil remove,
And sprinkling with thy blood my heart
     Fill all my sprinkled heart with love,
And conscious of my sins forgiven
O bid me go in peace to heaven.

82. [MS Misc. Hymns, p. 197.]
83. [MS Misc. Hymns, p. 197.]

III[84]

1. Set forth before our eyes,
       As fasten'd to the tree
    The Lord of earth and skies,
       Th'eternal God we see,
    God over all in form of man,
    Jehovah for his creatures slain!

2. Who call thy death to mind,
       Let us its virtues prove,
    The Lover of mankind,
       The Friend of sinners love,
    Whose death is immortality,
    Is glorious life, and Heaven to me.

V [85]

1. Come, Jesus, our peace,
       Whose death we record,
    Thy followers bless
       Obeying thy word;
    Thy blood we require,
       To save us from sin,
    From pride and desire
       To make our hearts clean.

2. If with us Thou art,
       Our burthen remove,
    And kindly impart
       The blessing of love,
    The fruit of thy passion
       Accomplish'd is this,
    'Tis present salvation,
       'Tis heavenly bliss.

84. [MS Misc. Hymns, p. 198.]
85. [MS Misc. Hymns, pp. 200–1.]

VIII[86]

1. 'Tis finish'd, He cries,
  While our Advocate dies!
  Thro' his prayer and his blood
 He hath brought us again to our pacified God:
  Our pardon he seals,
  While his love he reveals,
  And his Spirit imparts,
 And only requires us to give him our hearts.

2. Thro' the power of thy grace
  Thee, Lord, we embrace,
  With affectionate zeal
 The constraining effects of thy passion we feel:
  But we never can rest,
  Till, perfectly blest,
  We our gratitude prove,
 And ascend on thy cross, to embrace thee above.

IX[87]

AFTER SACRAMENT

1. Hosanna to God
  In his highest abode,
  Who to carry our cause
 Stoop'd down to our earth, & expir'd on a cross;
  Whose presence we find,
  While we call Him to mind,
  And the benefits prove
 Of his life-giving death, & his ransoming love.

2. Thro' faith in thy blood
  Our pardon bestow'd
  Exulting we feel;
 And the Spirit of love is the Witness & Seal,

86. [MS Misc. Hymns, pp. 202–3.]
87. [MS Misc. Hymns, p. 203.]

Is the Earnest, & more,
When our Lord we adore
Without shadow, or Sign,
And eternally feast on the fulness Divine.

[FATHER OF ALL, THE PRAYER ATTEND][88]

1. Father of all, the prayer attend
       Thro' my Advocate and Friend
           Presented at thy throne!
   The children Thou to me hast given
   Adopt, and claim as heirs of heaven,
           As members of thy Son.

2. In answer to my labouring heart,
       Now, ev'n now to each impart
           The seed of life within,
   The grace which sure salvation brings,
   And hide them underneath thy wings
           From hell, the world, and sin.

3. Before the inbred poison spread,
       Bruise in them the serpent's head,
           Thou Son of Man and God;
   Preserve in childlike innocence,
   And keep from every great offence
           By sprinkling them with blood.

4. Inspired with penitential fear,
       Let them shrink from evil near,
           Nor from thy sight remove,
   But worshipping a God unknown,
   Sincerely seek, and follow on
           To apprehend thy love.

88. [MS CW III(a) 4; MS Misc. Hymns, p. 254.]

5. Spirit of faith, to things divine
Still their tender hearts incline,
And stir them up to pray;
After an hidden God to feel,
Till Thou th'Incarnate Word reveal,
The Truth, the Life, the Way.

6. Shew them his blood and righteousness,
Blood that bought the sinners' peace,
Attests their sins forgiven,
For mercy and salvation cries,
Soul, body, spirit sancitifes
And speaks them up to heaven.

7. Come, Father, Son, and Holy Ghost,
Who thyself on man bestow'st,
To these thine image give,
And take the Vessels of thy grace
In Glory bursting from thy Face
Eternally to live.

HYMN FOR CHILDREN[89]

1. All Thanks and Praise to God belong
Our Father and Our Friend;
Let us with Life begin the Song,
Which never more shall end.

2. All Power and Majesty are His,
He ever reigns alone;
Our Souls He did in Mercy seize,
And He can keep His Own.

3. Unspotted from the World, and Sin,
In Innocence we live,
Before the Poison works within,
To GOD our Hearts we give.

---

89. [*Hymns and Sacred Poems* (1742), pp. 199–200. This poem was unaccountably omitted from *Poet. Works*, VI.]

4. Not to the vain Desires of Men
      We live, but to our GOD,
    Who died for us, and rose again,
      To wash us in His Blood.

5. To Him our earliest Fruits we bring,
      The Sacrifice of Praise;
    All our Diversion is to sing
      The dear Redeemer's Grace.

6. To Him we innocently live,
      Delight His Will to do;
    A Pattern to you Men we give,
      A Child may teach e'en You.

7. Children ye must be All again,
      Make Haste like us to be;
    Return ye wise, ye sinful Men
      To harmless Infancy.

8. Poor Men, acknowledge your Offence,
      And blush to hear our Song,
    And sigh to see the Innocence
      Ye have out-liv'd so long.

[WHAT IS THE GRACE I FAIN WOULD PROVE][90]

1. What is the grace I fain would prove
      When I for pardon pray?
    I want th'Omnipotence of Love
      To take my sins away;

2. I want a permanent release
      From sin's malignant power;
    I want in thy victorious peace
      To go, and sin no more.

90. [MS CW III(a) 12.]

3. Pardon itself would profit nought,
    (If pardon Thou impart)
  Unless the foul desire and thought
    Be chased out of my heart;

4. Unless Thou wash my heart with blood,
    And make my nature clean,
  And saved indeed, and born of God
    I can no longer sin.

5. Jesus, pronounce my spirit loosed
    From its infirmity!
  Now by thy love revealed, infused,
    Effect the change in me.

6. O cast not out my dying prayer,
    But now the curse remove,
  And from the gulph of sad despair
    Redeem me by thy love.

7. My fallen soul create anew,
    And principled[91] with grace
  Henceforth I loath, abhor, eschew
    My inbred wickedness.

FOR PRESERVING GRACE

I[92]

1.   Father, Son, and Holy Ghost,
      In thine almighty Name
    In thy love and truth I trust
      For evermore the same:
    Confident, Thou wilt protect
  Who hang upon thy faithful word,
    I abhor, renounce, reject,
      The thing by Thee abhor'd.

91. [The *Oxford English Dictionary* gives no example of this use of the word.]
92. [MS Misc. Hymns, pp. 289–91. Poem II under this title appears in *Poet. Works*, IX, p. 351.]

2.   On myself if I rely,
            Or trust an evil heart,
        Must I not with sin comply,
            And from my God depart?
        Free from sin to live below,
        The sin my nature loves so well,
            This I surely feel, and know
                With man impossible.

3.   In myself a feeble worm,
            From sin I cannot cease,
        In thy strength I can perform
            Impossibilities:
        My own evil to eschew
        Enabled by thy gracious power,
            I my covenant renew,
                And vow, to sin no more.

4.   With me, Lord, today abide,
            And kept by grace alone
        My own sin I lay aside,
            And all occasions shun,
        All that may to evil lead,
        So Thou my tempted soul secure,
            Every word, and every deed,
                And every thought impure.

5.   Thee the foe cannot surprize
            Whose eyelids never sleep,
        Thou my heart, my hands, my eyes,
            My soul and body keep,
        Every faculty, and power
        For thy most holy service claim,
            Shut me up in the strong tower
                Of thy almighty Name.

6.   There from sin preserv'd by Thee
            I shall today abide;
        If tomorrow's light I see,
            With equal grace supplied:

Shoud I see a thousand days,
I trust thy guardian power to prove,
Saved by all-sufficient grace,
And all-victorious love.

[O THE GRACE ON MAN BESTOW'D!][93]

1. O the Grace on Man bestow'd!
        We have a Great High-Priest,
    Jesus Christ, the Son of God,
        By Saints & Angels blest:
    Hold we then our Saviour fast,
        Him, whom GOD to All hath given,
    Him that thro' our Vale is past
        Up to the Highest Heaven.

2. Let us on his Faithful Love
        Unshaken stand & sure,
    True to our Profession prove
        And to the End endure;
    Trust in His sufficient Grace
        Who for helpless Sinners cares,
    For his weakest Members prays,
        And all our Burthens bears.

3. Our High-Priest in Heaven He lives,
        Yet still afflicted is,
    Touch'd most sensibly He grieves
        At our Infirmities,
    Still with sympathetic Woe
        Suffers in his Members' Pains:
    Let the Foot be crush'd below
        The Head above complains.

4. Draw we then with Boldness near
        Unto the Throne of Grace,
    Confident in Christ appear
        Before our Father's Face,

93. [MS Richmond Tracts, pp. 172–3.]

Come we now in Christ our Head
    Pardning Mercy to obtain,
Help in every Time of Need,
    And Grace, & Heaven to gain.

ADVICE TO ONE DEPRIVED OF THE MEANS OF GRACE[94]

1.   Turn again, thou trembling Reed
        To thine everlasting Rest,
    Lean on Him thy languid head,
        Sink on the Beloved breast;
    Lifting there thy streaming eye,
        Tell him all thy wants and fears:
    He shall all thy wants supply,
        He shall dry up all thy tears.

2.   Far, in body far remov'd
        From his instituted Ways,
    From the saints so dearly lov'd,
        Means, and Ministers of grace,
    Calmly at his feet forego;
        He doth to the desart call:
    Dwell with Christ alone, and know
        Christ alone is all in all.

[PRONE TO ILL, AVERSE FROM GOOD][95]

1.   Prone to ill, averse from good,
    Plagued by passions unsubdued,
    My continual want of grace
    Need I, Lord, to Thee confess?

2.   Grace, if Thou forbear to give,
    Me, if Thou one moment leave,
    Well Thou knowst I surely shall
    Into sin that moment fall.

94. [MS Misc. Hymns, p. 61.]
95. [MS Misc., 1786 (MS CW III[c]), p. 18.]

3. This, alas, I always feel,
   Till Thou dost the plague expel,
   Stay the foes Thou dost controul,
   Change the bias of my soul;

4. Make me thro' thy wondrous Name
   The reverse of what I am,
   Copy true of what Thou art,
   Lowly, meek, and pure in heart.

5. Mould me to thy will resign'd,
   One with Thee in heart and mind,
   Hide my life with God above
   Swallow up my soul in love!

6. Then, to terminate my race,
   Give me the last crowning grace,
   Wide display the heavenly scene,
   Take the heir of glory in!

BIRTH-DAY HYMN
DEC. 11, 1778[96]

1. God, in whom I move, and live,
       God who givst me still to be,
   Thankful I thy gifts receive,
       In the streams the Fountain see,
   See my natal day return,
   Bless Thee, that I e'er was born.

2. In the slippery paths of youth
       Led by all-preventing grace,
   Govern'd by the word of truth,
       Jesus, I thy hand confess,
   Wonderful in guardian power,
   Thee with all my soul adore.

96. [MS Misc. Hymns, pp. 247–8. There is room for one more verse at the foot of the page. Charles Wesley's birthday was actually on December 18.]

3. O beget my soul again,
   God of reconciling love,
That in a sublimer strain,
   Rival of the quires above,
I my Father may proclaim,
Shout my present Saviour's Name.

4. *With* me let thy Spirit dwell,
   Let him *in* my heart reside,
Teach, and sanctify, and seal,
   To that heavenly country guide,
Then I shall behold thy face,
Then I shall for ever praise.

THE COMMUNION OF SAINTS[97]

1. Jesus, we come to do thy Will,
   Our Faithfulness t'approve,
With all our joyful Hearts fulfil
   The new Command of Love.

2. By this we know our Passage here
   From Death to Life Divine,
Because we hold the Brethren dear,
   Our Brethren, Lord, & Thine.

3. By this the followers of our Lord
   We to the World are known,
Because we keep thy parting Word,
   And dearly love thine own.

4. This is the Proof, the Badge, the Seal,
   Our fervent Charity,
Lover of Souls, hereby we feel
   We still belong to Thee.

97. [MS Richmond, p. 37.]

5. This is the Bond of Perfectness
 Th'Anointing from above,
And all the Law of Life & Peace
 We find fulfil'd in Love.

AT THE MEETING OF MINISTER AND PEOPLE[98]

1. Glory, and power, and thanks, and praise
 To our divine Preserver give,
Who first united by his grace,
 Who bids us still united live,
Live, in one body call'd to prove
The fervor of primeval Love.

2. He made, He keeps us one in heart,
 In judgment, and in spirit one,
Baffles the fiend's malicious art,
 And casts the dire accuser down
Who never shall the flock divide,
Or tear us from each other's side.

3. The Lord is King! ye saints be glad,
 And joyful in his praises join;
He makes the sage diviners mad,
 He frustrates earth's and hell's design,
While all their efforts to remove
But root us more in Jesus' love.

4. In vain their malice hoped to see
 The sheep dispers'd, the shepherd flown;
Combin'd in stricter harmony
 We stand, more intimately one:
Let heathens part, and hirelings fly,
We all together live, and die!

98. [MS Misc. Hymns, pp. 1–2.]

MODERN CHRISTIANITY [99]

1. How vainly do the Heathen strive
       To falsify our Master's Word,
   Who teach us we may godly live,
       Yet never suffer for our Lord,
   In antient Times the Fact allow,
   But say, The World is *Christian* Now.

2. Christian the World of Drunkards is,
       The World of Whoremongers & Thieves,
   The Slaves of foul & fair Excess,
       Whoe'er the Christian Rite receives,
   Led from the Font at Satan's Will,
   Haters of Christ, & Christians still.

3. The Devilish, & the sensual Crowd,
       Who as brute Beasts their Lusts obey,
   Lovers of Pleasure more than GOD,
       Who dance, & curse, & fight, & play,
   Monsters of Vice, our Nature's Shame,
   All Hell assumes the Christian Name.

4. Yet still when Antichrist prevails,
       And Satan sits in Moses' Chair,
   The Gospel-Truths are idle Tales,
       No cross, no Holy Ghost is there,
   The Heathen World will Christian seem,
   And bid us take the Rule from them.

5. The Temple of the Lord are We,
       (The Synagogue of Satan cry)
   We need not persecuted be
       Or cruelly ourselves deny:
   Come see, ye Fools, who sigh & grieve,
   How much at Ease we Christians live.

99. [MS Richmond, pp. 70–1; *Rep. Verse,* No. 132, pp. 182–3.]

6. We are the Men—of Wealth & State,
    Of Pomp, & Fashionable Ease,
   Honour, & Power, & Pleasure wait
    The silken Sons of downy Peace,
   And lo! we glide secure & even
   Down a broad flowry Way—to Heav[e]n.

7. While House to House, & Field to Field,
    And Living we to Living join
   The gazing Crowd obeysance yield
    And praise the slick & smooth Divine
   Who saves them all the Madman's Care,
   The Drudgery of Faith, & Prayer.

8. No fanciful Enthusiasts we
    To look for Inspiration here,
   To dream from Sin to be set free
    Or hope to *feel* the Spirit near,
   Or *know* our Sins on Earth forgiven,
   Or madly give up all for Heaven!

AT THE HOUR OF RETIREMENT[100]

1. Again I come my friends to meet
    Around the throne of grace,
   I come to hold communion sweet
    With all the faithful race.

2. Swift on the wings of love & prayer
    To Jesus' saints I fly
   And on their GOD I cast my care,
    And on their Rock rely.

3. See, O thou Rock of Israel, see
    The Souls that ask thy aid,
   And still extend to them, to me,
    Thy love's almighty shade.

100. [MS Richmond, p. 112.]

4. Us in thy clefts vouchsafe to hide
        From earth & hell secure,
    Preserve us in thy wounded side,
        Till pure as GOD is pure.

[HAPPY THE SOULS WHO FEEL AND KNOW][101]

1. Happy the souls who feel and know
        The power of Jesus' name,
    Saved from their sins they live below,
        To praise and love the Lamb.

2. Salvation doth to God belong,
        Who bought them with his blood,
    Salvation is their endless song
        Who know the bleeding God.

[O HAPPY LIFE OF FAITH & LOVE!][102]

1. O happy Life of Faith & Love!
        Jeshurun's mighty God is mine,
    He comes All-glorious from above,
        He comes in Majesty Divine.

2. My God omnipotently nigh
        Rides on the Whirlwind's Rapid Wings,
    He hears my Look, & bows the Sky,
        My Helper is the King of Kings.

3. The Eternal God my Refuge is,
        And guards from all Impending Harms,
    And keeps my Soul in perfect Peace
        Clasp'd in his Everlasting Arms.

101. [MS Thirty, flyleaf i. The poem is transcribed from shorthand.]
102. [MS Thirty, pp. 4–5.]

4. He keeps my Sinfull Soul from Sin,
   Till I his Utmost Promise know,
Till I like God am pure within,
   And perfected in Love below.

5. He lifts me now to Pisgah's Top;
   He gives me now the Land to see,
He fills me now with Glorious Hope,
   And all the Promise is for me.

6. He shall in me himself reveal,
   And shine unto the Perfect Day,
He shall this Inbred Foe expell,
   And all my Sins for ever slay.

7. Sin shall not in my Flesh remain,
   The faithfull Saying I receive,
He gave me not this Faith in vain,
   And I a Sinless Life shall Live.

8. Love, perfect Love, shall cast out Sin,
   The Lord shall to his Temple come,
His endless Righteousness bring in,
   And make me his eternal Home.

9. Then, only then, when clean in Heart,
   An Israelite indeed I live,
I cannot from my Lord depart,
   I cannot for a Moment grieve.

10. From all Remains of self & Pride
    Secure, in Christ I dwell alone,
In Flesh & Spirit Sanctified,
    One with the Lord, for ever One.

11. In a Good Land of Corn and Wine
    I rest & Drink of Jacob's Well,
Th'Unfailing Well of Life Divine
    Fixt in my Inmost Soul I feel.

12. Jesus & Heaven is[103] all my Own,
        My Heav'n Drops Manna from above,
     And God into my Soul comes down
        In everlasting Streams of Love.

FOR ESTABLISHMENT [104]

1. Jesu, Shepherd of the Sheep,
       Pity my unsettled Soul,
    Guide, and nourish me, & keep
       Till thy Love hath made me whole;
    Give me, perfect Soundness give,
    Make me stedfastly believe.

2. Jesu, I believe Thee Now,
       But my ever-roving Eye
    Looses Thee, I know not how,
       Soon I faint, fall back, and die,
    Doubt again my Heart assails,
    Unbelief again prevails.

3. I am never at one Stay,
       Changing every Hour I am,
    But Thou art, as Yesterday
       Now, and evermore the same,
    Constancy to me Impart,
    Stablish with Thy Grace my Heart.

4. Lay thy mighty Cross on me,
       All my Unbelief controul,
    Till the Rebel cease to be,
       Keep him down within my Soul,
    That he never more may move,
    Root, & ground me fast in Love.

103. [Occasionally Wesley used a singular verb with a plural subject when the subjects for him were identical.]
104. [MS Thirty, pp. 175–7. Verses 1–5 appear in *Poet. Works*, IV, pp. 449–50.]

5.   Give me Faith to hold me up
      Walking over Life's rough Sea,
  Holy, purifying Hope
      Still my Soul's sure Anchor be,
  That I may be always Thine,
  Perfect me in Love Divine.

6.   This the high, the Heav'nly Prize,
      Perfect Love when I attain,
  I shall never quit the Skies,
      I shall never fall again,
  Pure as the Atoning Blood,
  Stedfast, as the Throne of God.

[O WHAT A STUBBORN HEART HAVE I][105]

1.   O What a stubborn Heart have I
      Which Nothing ere could move,
  Till God himself came down from high
      In all the Powers of Love!

2.   It would not be by Wrath compelled,
      His Threatnings it withstood,
  But Jesus made the Rebel yield
      By sprinkling me with Blood.

3.   Gladly I now to Love submit
      Unaw'd by slavish Fears,
  And lie, with Mary, at his Feet,
      And wash them with my Tears.

4.   His dear Redeeming Grace I prove
      That Antepast of Heaven,
  And much I weep, & much I love,
      For I have much forgiv'n.

105. [MS Thirty, p. 187.]

5. Humbly I lift my streaming Eye
       And to my Jesus pray,
    Still at thy Feet O let me lie
       And weep my Life away.

6. Thus let me All my Days, or Years
       Delightfully employ,
    And reap the Harvest of my Tears
       In Everlasting Joy.

AFTER A RECOVERY
HYMN III[106]

1. O Thou meek, and injur'd Dove,
       Wherefore dost Thou strive with me?
    Me, who still abuse thy Love,
       Me who grieve, and fly from Thee!
    Thee why should I longer grieve?
    Leave me Lord, thy Rebel leave.

2. Well Thou knowst, if now my Heart
       Melts to feel thy softning Grace,
    Ready am I to depart,
       Thine to quit for Sin's Embrace;
    Take thy Mercy back again,
    Wherefore shou'dst Thou strive in vain?

3. O that I might never feel
       One Desire or Drawing more;
    Rather than provoke Thee still,
       Now let all the Strife be o'er,
    Drive me from thy Blissful Face,
    Let me go to my own Place:

---

106. [MS Cheshunt, p. 76; MS Clarke, p. 84; *Hymns and Sacred Poems* (1749), I, p. 159. This hymn was unaccountably omitted from *Poet. Works*, IV.]

4. Or if thy unwearied Love
       Will not yet the Rebel leave,
    Stronger let thine Influence prove,
       Let me double Grace receive,
    Give me more, or give me less,
    Fix my Doom, or seal my Peace.

THE PRAYER OF ONE SEEKING THE TRUTH[107]

1. O Thou that dost in darkness shine,
    With clearest evidence divine
       Inform me who Thou art,
    Appear the true, and living Way,
    That Thee I simply may obey,
       And love with all my heart.

2. This earnest wish if Thou bestow
    Thy nature and thy will to know,
       With heavenly wisdom bless,
    That taught by thy unerring light
    To serve, and worship God aright,
       I may my Maker please.

3. A thousand different paths I view,
    But which to shun and which pursue
       Still unresolv'd I stand
    Till Thou thy secret counsel show,
    Direct me after Thee to go,
       And reach me out thy hand.

4. Thou know'st my feebleness of mind,
    My will perverse, my passions blind,
       My reason immature;
    But Thou, O God, if Thee alone
    My Guide infallible I own,
       Shalt make my footsteps sure.

107. [MS CW I(p) x. The poem is dated June 26, 1784.]

5. Wherefore in self-mistrust I flee,
   My Guide Infallible, to Thee,
      To Thee my soul resign,
   And while for light I humbly pray,
   Thou wilt not let me miss my way
      Who woud be led in thine.

6. Or if thro' self-presuming pride,
   I *have* mistook, and turn'd aside,
      Misled by my own will,
   I now thy Spirit's voice would hear
   Till following Him with faith sincere
      I reach the heavenly hill.

II^{108}

1. Father, that I thy child may be,
   That I may thy salvation see,
      Assist me to stand still,
   Thy kind instructions to receive,
   What to reject and what believe,
      And how perform thy will.

2. From Thee this good desire proceeds
   To follow Truth where'er it leads,
      While open to the light,
   All things impartially I weigh,
   Made willing God, not man, t'obey,
      And judge, and act aright.

3. I trust thy mercy to restrain
   My blind, implicit faith in man,
      My rash, prejudging haste,
   And every hindrance to remove,
   That fully I may all things prove,
      And find the Good at last.

108. [MS CW I(p) xi. There are two versions of this poem in MS CW I(p) but both are virtually the same.]

4. Fast let me hold the good I find,
    No longer tost by every wind,
        With every specious tale,
    But built on the Foundation sure,
    The WORD which always shall endure,
        The ROCK that cannot fail.

5. The word proceeding from that Rock
    Which Jesus, God incarnate, spoke
        And his Apostles too,
    Can it not save and sanctify
    If He th'ingrafted word apply
        And prove the record true?

6. The word in which I woud believe,
    Thou didst by inspiration give,[109]
        And if thy Spirit given
    Again, with faith inspires my heart,
    I know Thee, Saviour, who Thou art,
        And find my way to heaven.

[O FOR A SPARK OF HEAVENLY FIRE][110]

1. O for a spark of heavenly fire,
        From the Redeemer's throne,
    The pure and permanent desire
        Of loving Him alone!

2. The pure desire unquenchable
        Ev'n now I *seem* to prove,
    But only Thou, my God, canst tell
        If Thee I *wish* to love.

3. A stranger to the blisful grace
        I hitherto have been:
    But must I end my wretched race
        And die at last in sin?

109. [The MS has in error "given" instead of "give," no doubt a slip of the pen by Charles Wesley.]
    110. [MS CW IV, 76.]

4. A sinner hanging o're the grave,
   Assuredly I know
Thy grace alone my soul can save
   From everlasting woe.

5. When thou hast wrought a will in me
   The blessing to receive,
Thy hatred of iniquity,
   Thy sinless nature, give.

6. Partaker of my flesh, impart
   Thy Spirit from above,
And certify my happy heart
   That God in Thee is Love.

7. That I in Thee appeas'd might know
   The one eternal God,
Thou didst become a Man of woe,
   And pour out all thy blood.

8. Travail'd thy soul to ransom mine,
   To make me love again,
Nor woudst thou, Lord, thy life resign
   And bleed and die in vain.

9. Vouchsafe me then the wish sincere,
   The wish sincere fulfil,
And stamp me with thy character
   According to thy will:

10. Accomplish'd see thine own desires,
    And O! be satisfied,
When singing with th'immortal quires
    I triumph at thy side.

[O WHAT A MIGHTY CHANGE][111]

1. O what a Mighty Change
  Shall we thro' Jesus know;
When o're the Happy Plains we range
  Incapable of woe!
  No ill requited Love,
  Shall there our Spirits Wound;
No base Ingratitude above,
  No sin in Heaven is found.

2. Nor slightest Touch of blame,[112]
  Nor Sorrow's least Alloy,
Can violate our Rest, or stain
  Our Purity of Joy;
  In that Eternal Day,
  No Clouds of Tempests rise;
These gushing Tears are wip'd away,
  Forever from our Eyes.

3. This Languishing Desire,
  Which now for Heaven we feel,
Shall there Eternally expire,
  In Joy ineffable:
  That Weight of Glorious Bliss,
  That to our share shall fall;
Nor Angel Tongue can half express
  But we shall Have it all.

4. And tho' our Bodies part,
  To different Climes repair,
Inseparably Joyned in Heart,
  We still in Jesus are;
  Jesus the Corner Stone,
  Did first our Souls unite;
And still He holds and keeps us one,
  Who walk with him in white.

111. [MS CW IV, 67. With considerable alterations this poem forms part of two poems in *Poet. Works*, V, pp. 458–63. The latter half of this poem formed with alterations Hymn No. 521, p. 497 in the *1780 Collection.*]

112. [The rhyme is imperfect; "blame" is probably a slip for "pain" which appears in *Poet. Works.*]

5.   Then let our Heart, & Mind,
        Continually ascend,
That Heaven[113] of repose to find,
        Where all our Tryals end;
        Where all our Griefs are o're,
        Our sufferings and our Pain;
Who meet on that Eternal shore,
        Shall never part again.

6.   O Happy, happy Place,
        Where we shall shortly meet;
There we shall see each other's Face,
        And There each other Greet;
        The Church of the first born,
        We shall with them be Blesst,
And Crown'd with Endless Joy return
        To our Eternal Rest.

7.   With Joy we shall behold,
        In yonder blest abode,
The Patriarchs & Prophets old,
        And all the saints of GOD;
        Abraham, and Isaac there,
        And Jacob shall receive
The followers of their Faith & Prayer
        Who now in Bodies Live.

8.   We shall our Time beneath,
        Live out in Chearfull Hope;
And fearless pass the vale of Death,
        And gain the mountain Top,
        To gather Home his own,
        He shall His Angels send;
And bid our Bliss on Earth begun
        In endless Triumph End.

113. ["Heaven" is probably a slip for "Haven," which suits the context and appears in the *1780 Collection.*]

[TEACHER, GUIDE OF HELPLESS SINNERS][114]

1. Teacher, Guide of helpless Sinners,
       Us receive into thy School,
   Gently lead the young Beginners
       All our Works & Thoughts orerule;
   Every Appetite & Passion,
       Every Sense exalt, refine,
   Order all our Conversation,
       Seal our Souls forever Thine.

2. Choose for Us our whole Condition
       In our Pilgrimage below,
   All that stands in competition
       With thy blessed Will orethrow;
   Tear away the Rival Creature[115]
       Till we fully taste & see
   Good the Gift, but Thou art better,
       Happiness is all in Thee.

3. What we think woud bring us nigher
       To Thyself, we now submit,
   Every seeming good Desire
       Lo! we lay it at thy Feet:
   Lord, our Hearts no longer faulter,
       Take our costliest Sacrifice,
   See our Isaac on the Altar,
       At thy Word He bleeds & dies.

4. Standing to thy wise Decision
       Chuse we for Ourselves no more,
   With unfeign'd entire Submission
       We our darling Joy restore;
   Now to yonder fatal Mountain
       We our dearlov'd Isaac lead,
   Offering up, yet still accounting
       Thou canst raise Him from the Dead.

114. [MS Occasional, pp. 72–4.]
115. [Note the rhyme "Creature" and "better." Cf. the slang pronounciation "critter."]

5. From the Dead, if such thy Pleas[ur]e,
   We our Isaac shall receive,
   Find again our buried Treasure,
   Meet on Earth in Thee to live:
   Thee to taste in every Blessing,
   Joyfully on Thee to call,
   Sweetly at thy Feet confessing
   Thou, O GOD, art all in all!

PRAYER FOR RAIN[116]

1. A stupid nation doom'd
   To feel th'Almighty hand,
   Before we all are quite consum'd,
   O might we understand;
   In agony of fear
   Attend the threatning Rod,
   And conscious of his judgments near
   Prepare to meet our God!

2. God to chastise our sin
   The airy bottles stays,[117]
   And thro' a cloudless sky serene
   Frowns on our guilty race;
   Our sin has found us out:
   The messenger is sent,
   And by a long-continued drought
   He calls us to repent.

3. 'Tis not th'effect of chance,
   If second Causes join
   War, famine, pestilence, t'advance
   Jehovah's dread design:
   Destruction's baleful power
   We his strange work confess;
   O might we turn, that from this hour
   The plague of sin may cease!

116. [MS Misc. Hymns, pp. 85–6.]
117. [*Cf.* Job 38:37.]

4.   We from this moment vow
To put our sins away,
The rough east wind of judgments now,
   Merciful Father, stay:
Our wasted earth renew
With blessings from above,
Our gasping souls with gracious dew
And showers of Jesus' love.

HYMN FOR PEACE,
OCCASIONED BY SOME PUBLIC TROUBLES, FEB. 1766[118]

1.   While blackning clouds o'respread the sky,
And discord's turbid waves run high,
   Are Christians free from care?
Conscious our life is hid above,
Yet still we must our Country love,
   And all her troubles share.

2.   'Tis not for us to rule the state,
Or mingle in their high debate
   When Princes disagree:
Jehovah in their council stands,
And (for the Cause is in thy hands)
   We leave it, Lord, to Thee.

3.   Excus'd, our privilege we own,
We blame, arraign, and censure none
   That at the helm appear,
But quietly our souls possess,
Who worship Thee, the Prince of peace,
   Who God and Cesar fear.

4.   Yet danger national requires,
And draws out all our heart's desires
   For their prosperity;
Thy Church the common burthen feels,
Their present, and approaching ills
   With Jesus' eyes we see.

118. [MS Misc. Hymns, pp. 153–4; *Rep. Verse*, No. 272, pp. 308–9. The "troubles" resulted from the passing of the Stamp Act.]

5. With Jesus' sympathy we cry,
   Father of all, in trouble nigh
       Stir up thy helping power,
   Their violence curb, controul their rage,
   Nor let them war intestine wage,
       Each other to devour.

6. By whom Thou wilt the rescue send,
   But bid their fierce contentions end,
       But suddenly suppress
   And scatter who in war delight,
   And by thy Providential might
       Restore the public peace.

II^{119}

1. Jesus, assume thy right divine,
       Heir of an everlasting throne,
   The kingdoms of the earth are thine,
       Thy sovereign power in Ours make known,
   Exalted high at God's right-hand
       Thou dost, repos'd, in glory sit,
   Till all who now thy sway withstand
       Bow down subdued beneath thy feet.

2. The flouds, O God, lift up their voice,
       With discord horrible they roar,
   But Thou canst still their angry noise,
       The tempest chide, the calm restore.
   Master both of the ship, and storm
       Our Saviour at the helm we see:
   Tumults and hurricanes perform
       Thy will, and sink at thy decree.

3. The enemy of God and man
       His tares of civil strife hath sown;
   Jesus, the growing ill restrain
       And make our jarring Parties one:

119. [Misc. Hymns, pp. 154–6.]

All power is thine in earth and skies;
    Controuller of the creature's will,
Maker, and Lord of hearts, arise,
    And all our threatning breeches heal.

4.   To those who guide the tottering state
    Wisdom resolv'd, and temper give,
With strength to bear a Nation's weight,
    And Britain from the gulph retrieve;
On all an healing spirit bestow,
    And each to each as brethren join,
Let every heart with love o'reflow,
    Social, unanimous, divine.

5.   Our Monarch fill with inward peace,
    (The peace on faithful souls bestow'd)
Till all the storm dispers'd he sees,
    And glories in his people's good;
A Patriot-king, by special grace,
    A Father to his Country given,
Long may he guard thy chosen race,
    And late receive his crown in heaven.

THANKSGIVING FOR PEACE[120]

1.   O how ready is the Lord
    To help us from the sky!
While we speak th'inviting word,
    He answers, here am I!
Oft prevents the swiftest prayer,
More swift our heart's desire to grant,
Reading our intention there,
    He gives whate'er we want.

2.   Peace to ask we now design'd,
    To sue for public peace,
But He knew his Spirit's mind,
    And bad our discord cease,

120. [MS Misc. Hymns, pp. 156–8. As there is room at the bottom of p. 158 for one more verse, the hymn may not be complete.]

   Calm'd the angry hearts of men;
  And lo, they suddenly agree,
   Brethren, friends, embrace again
   In love, and unity.

3.   God omnipotent in grace,
    Thou hast thine arm reveal'd,
  Blest our highly favour'd race,
   And Britain's breeches heal'd,
  Baffled the malicious foe,
Who sow'd his hellish tares in vain:
  Check'd, he coud no farther go,
   Or break his straitned gain.

4.   Only Thou the work hast done,
    Whate'er the means employ'd,
  One in mind and spirit one,
   We see the present God!
  Jesus, his effectual Power,
The reconciling word is thine:
  O might all with us adore
   The Peacemaker Divine!

5.   Peace thro' Britain's happy Isle
    Thro' all its branches spread,
  God with sinners reconcile,
   And we are one indeed!
  Breathes as in us all one soul,
When rebegotten from above,
  Only love informs the whole,
   That[121] pure, primeval love!

PRAYER FOR PEACE & UNITY[122]

1. Author of everlasting peace,
   Lover of social harmony,
  Arise, and bid Contention cease,
   Rebuke the wind, and raging sea:

121. [In the margin "The" is written as an alternative to "That."]
122. [MS Misc. Hymns, pp. 170–1.]

Thou only canst our passions chide,
Our anger by a word remove:
Speak, and we suddenly subside,
And sink into the calm of love.

2. Thou whom the winds and seas obey,
The swelling waves of pride controul,
The gusts that hurry me away,
And shipwreck my impetuous soul:
Thou knowst I cannot, cannot rest,
Till Thou compose my stormy will,
Allay the tumult in my breast,
And bid this troubled heart be still.

3. Assume thy power, and reign below,
Peace inconceivable, divine,
Thy kingdom, Lord, on us bestow,
To keep my partner's heart, and mine:
Then shall we find the strength of grace
Display'd in our infirmity,
With love unanimous embrace,
And rest, for ever calm in Thee.

WRITTEN SEPT. 9, 1779
WHEN THE COMBINED FLEETS OF FRANCE
AND SPAIN WERE IN THE CHANNEL[123]

1. Supreme, Almighty Lord,
To whom in Christ we pray,
Tempests and storms fulfil thy word,
And winds and seas obey;
Thee King of kings we own,
Thee Lord of hosts confess,
And from thine outstretch'd arm alone
Expect our whole success.

123. [MS Misc. Hymns, pp. 239–40; *Rep. Verse*, No. 299, pp. 334–5, where the title is explained.]

2.   To save the faithful race
      From Rome and Satan near,
Appear as in the ancient days,
      On Britain's side appear;
      Thy wondrous works renew'd
      Let us exult to see,
And Fleets invincible subdued
      By one great word from Thee.

3.   Thou knowst the hellish aim
      Of our inveterate Foe,
Who Britain's rebel sons inflame
      Their country to o'rethrow:
      Defend the righteous cause,
      Thy needful help afford,
While urg'd, our injur'd Nation draws
      The slow, defensive sword.

4.   Dissolve their compact dire,
      Nor let their Counsel stand
Who vow to waste with sword and fire
      Our whole, devoted land:
      To lay their malice low,
      To end their furious boast,
Blow with thy wind tempestuous, blow
      And scatter all their host.

5.   By many, or by few
      Thou art not bound to save,
Whose arm th'Egyptian host o'rethrew,
      By the o'rewhelming wave:
      Extend that arm once more,
      And by a whirlwind driven
Compel our vanquish'd foes t'adore
      The Lord of earth and heaven.

6.　　So shall our lives declare
　　　　The Power who safely brings,
　　　The[124]

ON ENTRING A NEW HABITATION[125]

1.　Father, Son, and Spirit, come,
　　　　Manifest in grace and peace,
　　Consecrate this earthly home,
　　　　God of vital holiness,
　　Grace and peace to us impart,
　　Then reside in every heart.

2.　Not in temples made with hands
　　　　Doth the great Jehovah dwell;
　　Yet who keep thy dear commands
　　　　Shall thy constant presence feel,
　　Rais'd into a radiant shrine,
　　Fill'd with Majesty divine.

3.　Enter then thy mean abode,
　　　　Father, Son and Spirit of grace,
　　Holy, holy, holy God,
　　　　Fill the consecrated place,
　　Three in One, and One in Three,
　　God in us for ever be!

AT MEALS[126]

1.　Let us rejoice, give thanks, and sing
　　　　Our heavenly Father's praise;
　　Thankfulness is a pleasant thing,
　　　　And joy is happiness:

124. [The poem is incomplete. Wesley began the next page numbered 241 with a new pen and apparently forgot to transcribe the conclusion of the above poem on p. 240; hence, the incomplete verse 6.]
　　125. [MS Misc. Hymns, p. 171.]
　　126. [MS Misc. Hymns, p. 172.]

2. Blest be his Name, for ever blest!
    He smiles our joy to see,
    And the great God himself is pleas'd
    At our prosperity.

3. Still let us taste the grace of God
    Which doth his gifts impart,
    And glad from Him receive our food
    With singleness of heart:

4. Receive our every good from Him,
    Till call'd to joys above
    We find our happiness supreme
    In feasting on his Love.

HYMN FOR LOVE[127]

1. How can I hate what nature loves,
    And love what nature hates,
    Till in my soul Thy Spirit moves,
    And me anew creates?
    Till Thou out of a thing unclean
    An holy thing produce:
    I then shall loathe and fly from sin,
    And only goodness choose.

2. O that the miracle of grace
    Were now display'd on me,
    Renew'd in real holiness,
    Created after Thee!
    O might I now with joy perceive
    That, born of God above,
    I cannot sin, I cannot grieve
    Whom I intirely love.

127. [MS Death, p. 45. Verse 1, the first four lines of Verse 2 and the last four lines of
verse 3 appear in *Poet. Works*, VIII, p. 358.]

3. Lover of man's apostate kind,
        In me thyself reveal,
    Thy nature pure, thy heavenly mind,
        The Spirit impeccable:
    Satan, the world, and sin t'exclude,
        Thy matchless power exert,
    And dwell with all thy plenitude,
        Jehovah, in my heart.

MISCELLANEOUS,
OCT. 20, 1786[128]

1. Happy our highly favour'd Race
        Who saw the Man of woe,
    And brought to Him their last distress,
        When God appear'd below!
    Plagued by whate'er infirmity,
        Howe'er diseas'd and pain'd,
    Jesus, they all, by touching Thee,
        A perfect Cure obtain'd.

2. O had I lived, and languish'd then
        Under this sore Disease,
    Thou woudst not have despis'd my pain,
        Or scorn'd my soul to ease;
    Thou woudst not, sunk beneath my load,
        Have pass'd thy creature by,
    Or left me in my sins and blood
        To droop, despair, and die.

3. But art Thou not a Saviour still
        The same as heretofore?
    And is it not thy constant will
        To succour, and restore?
    Thy Spirit, Lord, is always nigh
        Incurables to heal,
    And could I but believe, ev'n I
        The balmy grace shoud feel.

128. [MS Misc., 1786 (MS CW III[c]), pp. 1–2. The title "Miscellaneous, Oct. 20, 1786," refers to the poems that follow in the MS.]

4. If Thou my unbelief remove,
      The virtuous energy,
    The emanation of thy love,
      Shall now proceed from Thee;
    The desperate evil of my heart,
      The plague which I confess,
    While Thee I touch, shall all depart,
      And sin for ever cease.

HYMN II[129]

1. Faith to be healed I surely have
      (And faith can all things do);
    Thou art Omnipotent to save,
      And Thou art willing too;
    The God who in thy feeble days
      Of flesh didst show thy power,
    The sick to cure, the dying raise,
      And bid the grave restore.

2. In these thy Spirit's days as near
      I trust my Lord to find,
    The Help of suppliants sincere,
      The Friend of human-kind:
    Thou canst root out this inbred Ill;
      And then the strife is o're,
    And sin I never more shall feel,
      Shall never find it more.

3. The thing I ask Thou wilt bestow,
      (The promise is for me);
    'Tis quite impossible, I know,
      And yet the thing shall be:
    Thy faithfulness is on my side,
      Thy truth which cannot move;
    For perfect Soundness I confide
      In thy almighty Love.

129. [MS Misc., 1786 (MS CW III[c]), pp. 2–4.]

4. For this continually I wait,
   After my God to rise,
   Restor'd to my unsinning state
   And love's sweet paradise;
   Thy word hath made the grace my own,
   And when the grace is given,
   Thy will by me on earth is done
   As by thy saints in heaven.

[THOU GOD OF FAITHFUL MERCIES, HEAR!][130]

1. Thou God of Faithful Mercies, hear!
   If plainly now begin t'appear
       The Tokens of thy Will,
   Our hearts prepare by just Degrees,
   With calm Delight & perfect Peace
       Thy Pleasure to fulfil.

2. Refrain[131] our Souls, & keep them low,
   In every State resolv'd to know
       Our Jesus Crucified;
   In simple childlike Purity,
   Preserve us, Lord, alive to Thee
       And dead to All beside.

3. Whene'er thy Providential Voice
   Confirms our long-suspended Choice,
       And fixes our Estate,
   Or let us *for the better* meet,
   And fall adoring at thy Feet,
       And there forever wait.

130. [MS CW III(a) 1. This would appear to come from a page torn off one of Charles Wesley's letters to his wife, Sarah.]
131. [This is a late example of the transitive use of the verb "refrain" in the sense of "to check." The last example in the *Oxford English Dictionary* is dated 1645.]

4. We would, Thou knowst, *we* would be Thine,
      In Jesus' Name & Spirit join
        Thy glory to display,
      To chear & help each other on
      Till Both appear before thy Throne
        Triumphant, at that Day!

FOR—[SOME CALLED FORTH TO EARN THEIR DAILY BREAD][132]

1. Call'd forth to earn my daily bread
        From those who know not God
      How shall I circumspectly tread
        Nor miss the heavenly road?

2. How shall I walk as in thy sight,
        And keep my conscience clean,
      And minister to their delight
        Yet never to their sin?

3. Who gavest me my work to do,
        Do Thou point out[133] my way,
      And while my calling I pursue,
        Thy Order I obey;

4. Perform the task thy laws ordain
        As govern'd by thy word,
      And whatsoe'er I do for man,
        I do unto the Lord.

132. [MS CW III(a) 3.]
133. [In the margin "direct" is written as an alternative to "point out."]

INTERCESSORY
HYMNS AND POEMS

I
FOR THE UNAWAKENED[1]

1. Eternal Son of God most high,
    Whose only voice can wake the dead,
  Speak to the souls, for whom we cry,
    For whom we in thy Spirit plead,
  And bring them up from Nature's grave
  And *now* stretch out thine arm to save.

2. The dead in trespasses convince,
    And turn from Satan's power to God,
  Reveal thy wrath against their sins,
    Orewhelm them with the mountain-load,
  Till all that load of guilt and fear
  Rolls off—into thy sepulchre.

II
FOR THE AWAKENED[2]

Where'er Thou hast thy work begun
  And shew'd a soul its want of thee,
Carry the gracious wonder on,
  Set every strugling sinner free,
And bid them feel thy blood applied,
And add them to the Justified.

1. [MS Misc. Hymns, p. 173; MS Intercession (MS CW IV), 68.]
2. [MS Misc. Hymns, p. 173; MS Intercession (MS CW IV), 68.]

III
FOR ONE UNDER THE LAW [3]

1. Eternal Sun of righteousness,
       Arise, with healing in thy wings,
    On Him, who feels his sore disease,
       Yet, when thy grace salvation brings,
    With abject fear rejects his cure
    Nor dares believe his pardon sure.

2. Lift the dejected sinner up
       Who only canst the valley raise,
    Begotten to that gospel-hope,
       That sense of free forgiving grace;
    In peace dismiss the prostrate soul,
    Assur'd his faith hath made him whole.

IV
FOR THE TEMPTED [4]

1. O most compassionate High Priest
       Thy days of flesh recall to mind,
    Tempted like us, aggriev'd, opprest,
       To all thy tempted Members join'd,
    Support them, while they drink thy cup
    And fill thine after-sufferings up. [5]

2. Sustain'd by Thy sufficient grace
       Preserv'd by Thy or'eshadowing power,
    Let them the hallow'd cross embrace
       And, brought thro' the Satanic hour,
    Out of the fiery furnace rise,
    To share thy glory in the skies.

3. [MS Misc. Hymns, p. 174; MS Intercession (MS CW IV), 68.]
4. [MS Misc. Hymns, p. 174; MS Intercession (MS CW IV), 68.]
5. [*Cf.* Colossians 1:24.]

V
HYMN FOR THOSE IN DOUBT [6]

1.   O God, our refuge in distress,
     Most present when we need Thee most,
  Thy pitying eye the sinner sees,
     Who dares not in thy mercy trust,
  Tortur'd with doubts, and torn with fears,
  And dying—till thy blood appears.

2.   Thy death to every heart reveal,
     That trembles at a God unknown,
  Make manifest thy gracious will,
     The servant change into a Son,
  Chase all the clouds of sin away
  And shine unto the perfect day.

VI
FOR ONE TEMPTED TO DESPAIR [7]

1.   Jesus, thy vengeful power exert,
     The foul Blasphemer to confound,
  Who tells a drooping sinner's heart
     That sin doth more than grace abound,
  Threatens, out of thy hands to tear,
  And seal him up in sad despair.

2.   Lion of Judah's tribe, arise,
     Thy foe to spoil, thy prey to seize,
  Display before the captive's eyes
     The blood that signs his soul's release,
  And speaks the Penitent forgiven,
  A child of God, an heir of heaven.

6. [MS Misc. Hymns, p. 175; MS Intercession (MS CW IV), 68.]
7. [MS Misc. Hymns, p. 175; MS Intercession (MS CW IV), 68.]

VII
FOR THE BACKSLIDERS[8]

1. Thou sinners' Advocate with God,
       The poor backsliding children save,
    Who wand'ring down the spatious road
       Must sink into that hellish grave,
    Unless the blood of sprinkling cry,
    Unless thy Father's heart reply.

2. Bowels of pitying Love divine,
       From Adam's fall in Jesus mov'd,
    Yearn or'e the souls Thou callest thine,
       Sound, and declare their guilt remov'd,
    Their sickness heal'd, their sin forgiven,
    And speak them back from hell to heaven.

VIII
FOR THOSE THAT ARE SHUT UP[9]

1. Jesus, our absent Brethren bless,
       Absent in body not in heart,
    Kept from the channels of thy grace,
       Shut up with Thee who pray apart,
    And let that Spirit obtain'd for all
    On Eldad & on Medad fall.[10]

2. O might they now the blessing find,
       The grace on this assembly shed,
    While to the living members join'd,
       And close united to our Head,
    One body & one church we rise,
    And greet our brethren in the skies.

8. [MS Misc. Hymns, p. 176; MS Intercession (MS CW IV), 68.]
9. [MS Misc. Hymns, p. 177; MS Intercession (MS CW IV), 68.]
10. [*Cf.* Numbers 11:26–7.]

IX
FOR A DISOBEDIENT CHILD[11]

Jesus, th'essential Power divine,
    Thy virtue on this Rebel shew,
His iron-sinew'd neck incline,
    His stubborn heart by love subdue,
And glad all heaven with the sound,
"The dead's alive, the lost is found!"

X
FOR MEN IN A STORM[12]

1. O Thou, whom winds and seas obey,
        Sole Potentate in earth and heaven,
    Thy power in their behalf display,
        The men by furious tempests driven,
    And give the Christless souls to cry,
    "Save, Lord, or we for ever die!"

2. Soon as to Thee for help they look,
        Thy help to the distrest afford,
    Silence the winds, the flouds rebuke,
        That all may own their GOD and Lord,
    And find the calm of faith within,
    And rest from all the storms of sin.

3. Or if Thou hast the sentence seal'd,
        And doom'd them to the wat'ry grave,
    O let thy love be first reveal'd,
        O let them feel thy power to save,
    Sink calmly down, and find in death
    The everlasting Arms beneath.

11. [MS Misc. Hymns, p. 177; MS Intercession (MS CW IV), 68.]
12. [MS Misc. Hymns, p. 177; MS Intercession (MS CW IV), 69.]

XI
FOR THOSE IN THE WILDERNESS[13]

1. Jesus, with thy disciples stay,
        Allur'd into the wilderness,
    Led thro' a strait unbeaten way
        To pleasant paths of lasting peace;
    Their former fervent zeal restore,
    And fix them that they rove no more.[14]

2. Beneath the hidings of thy face
        With languishing desire they mourn:
    The rapt'rous tokens of thy grace,
        O might they, Lord, with Thee return!
    Bright Sun of souls, the clouds remove,
    Shine out, & perfect them in love.

XII
FOR ONE UNDER PERSECUTION[15]

Jesus of Nazareth, appear
    To take thy suffering Servant's part,
To scatter all his grief and fear,
    To comfort his believing heart,
And let thy glorious Spirit rest
Forever in his peaceful breast.

XIII
FOR A BELIEVER IN PAIN[16]

O Saviour, sanctify this pain,
    And join these sufferings to thine own,
The Partner of thy griefs sustain
    And deeply in thy member groan,
Till on thy cross transfixt & dead,
He lives, he rises with his Head.

13. [MS Misc. Hymns, p. 178; MS Intercession (MS CW IV), 69.]
14. [This line is found in shorthand in the margin of MS Intercession, as well as in MS Misc. Hymns (p.178), as an alternative to: "And make their hearts with joy run o're."]
15. [MS Misc. Hymns, p. 179; MS Intercession (MS CW IV), 69.]
16. [MS Misc. Hymns, p. 179; MS Intercession (MS CW IV), 69.]

XIV
FOR A DYING UNBELIEVER[17]

The sinner sad, who void of Thee
  Is turning to the wall his face,
Save as the Felon on the tree,
  To shew forth all thy power of grace,
And bid him from thy cross, arise,
And reign with Thee in paradise.

XV
FOR A DYING BELIEVER[18]

1. Father, into thy hands receive
      An happy Spirit on the wing
    Who now exults his clay to leave,
      To hear the heavenly Convoy sing
    Mixt with the Ministerial Quire,
    Just mounting in his Car of fire.

2. Fill up, and change his faith to sight,
      And when the spotless Soul departs,
    Shine, O Thou everlasting Light,
      To chear his old Companions' hearts,
    Prepare us all thy face to see,
    And send the chariot next—for me!

XVI
FOR THE SELF-RIGHTEOUS[19]

1. Saviour, Thou readst what is in man,
      Thine eyes his inmost substance see:
    Wrapt up in forms and shadows vain
      He cannot hide himself from Thee,
    Who knowst his deep, serpentine art,
    And all the windings of his heart.

17. [MS Misc. Hymns, p. 179; MS Intercession (MS CW IV), 69.]
18. [MS Misc. Hymns, p. 179; MS Intercession (MS CW IV), 69.]
19. [MS Misc. Hymns, pp. 180–1; MS Intercession (MS CW IV), 69; *Rep. Verse*, No. 227, pp. 249–50.]

2. Ev'n now thy searching eye perceives
    Thy fugitives among the trees,
Veiling their shame with virtuous leaves,
    (The fig-leaves of self-righteousness)
Willing themselves to justify
And Thee with thy own gifts to buy.

3. Tear from them, Lord, their figleaves tear,
    Themselves let the deceivers know,
Wretched, & poor, & blind, & bare,
    Consign'd to everlasting woe,
Unless thy mercy step between
And freely save them from all sin.

4. Stop Thou their mouths, confound their pride,
    Their souls to endless woe condemn;
Then point them to thine open side
    Then plunge them in that purple stream,
Which only can for sin atone,
And wafts the Pardon'd to thy Throne.

XVII
FOR THE PRETENDERS TO FORGIVENESS[20]

1. With pity, Lord, the men behold
    Lull'd in a false presumptuous peace,
Thro' pride secure, thro' error bold
    To claim thy unfelt promises,
To boast of grace they have not known,
As God, and heaven were all their own.

2. The foretast[e]s of alluring love
    If for *the* gospel-faith they take,
Their hearts of unbelief reprove,
    Their fond deluded souls awake,
Where in the mouth of hell they lie,
The fancied portal of the sky.

20. [MS Misc. Hymns, p. 182; MS Intercession (MS CW IV), 70.]

3. When wounded by thy Spirit's sword
    Their vain pretensions they forego,
Jesus, pronounce the healing word,
    The true substantial faith bestow,
The evidence of things unseen,
The power divine, that saves from sin.

4. Strength from the Lord, & righteousness
    The proof of their acceptance be,
And lowly fear, and ruling peace
    And restless hungring after Thee,
Declare thy dying love reveal'd
And clearly speak their pardon seal'd!

XVIII
FOR THE PRETENDERS TO PERFECTION[21]

1. Arise, Thou jealous God, arise
    Whose word doth soul and body part,
Look with thy all-discerning eyes
    And sound the most deceitful heart
Of those whom erring men approve
As witnesses of perfect love.

2. Thou knowst, the fiend hath set them up,
    Hath on the sacred summit placed,
That falling from their towering hope,
    From highest heaven to hell debas'd,
Their souls may prove his wretched thrall,
And stumble thousands by their fall.

21. [MS Misc. Hymns, pp. 183–4; MS Intercession (MS CW IV), 70.; *Rep. Verse*, No. 228, pp. 250–1.]

3.   Ah, do not, Lord, the tempted leave
      A prey to Luciferian pride,
  Ah, do not let the foe deceive
      The souls for whom thyself hast died,
  Or shake our faith who dare profess
  Our faith in finish'd[22] holiness.

4.   Whoever stands or falls, the word
      The one Foundation, must endure,
  Sure is the promise of our Lord,
      The oath divine hath made it sure,
  And *we*, when Christ the power imparts,
  Shall love our GOD with all our hearts.

5.   Now, Saviour, now our hearts prepare
      Thy gracious fulness to receive:
  But pluck our brethren from the snare
      Beguil'd like vain, aspiring Eve,
  Deliverance to the captives send,
  And let the strong Delusion end.

6.   Gently into the valley lead
      And give them then themselves to know,
  Till to themselves intirely dead
      Their grace they by their *silence shew*,
  Thee only good & perfect *call*
  And sink, and into nothing fall.

FOR ONE IN A DECLINE[23]

1.   Physician, Friend of sinsick man,
      Our weak declining Brother save,
  Broken by sickness, shook by Pain
      Whose Flesh is hastening to the grave:
  His Spirit of thy Love assure
  And keep, till Thou compleat the Cure.

---

22. [MS Intercession reads: "Our faith in perfect holiness," with the alternative "hope of finish'd" in the margin.]
23. [MS Misc. Hymns, p. 185; MS Intercession (MS CW IV), 70.]

2. The more his outward man decays
   His inward by thy Love renew,
   And perfected in a short space
   Admit Him to the Blisful View,
   The grace to saints triumphant given,
   The sign that makes an heaven of heaven.

FOR THE PRIME MINISTER[24]

1. O that we coud obtain by prayer
   A Man by special grace bestowed
   (Brittania's Refuge in despair)
   A man to seek our nation's good,
   Resolved our sinking land to save,
   Or rush into his Country's grave.

2. His Talents take into thy hand,
   And bless them for the public weal,
   His spirit bow to thy command,
   His heart with heavenly fervor fill,
   And fix the patriot's noblest aim,
   To act for God in Jesus' name.

3. As One whom heaven delights to bless,
   As Daniel prosperous and wise,
   Restorer of true righteousness
   By Him, by Him let Jacob rise,
   Virtue revisit Albion's coast,
   And Piety for ages lost.

---

24. [MS Misc. Hymns, pp. 185–6; MS Intercession (MS CW IV), 70.; *Rep. Verse*, No. 317, p. 361. The opening lines of the poem in MS Intercession read:
   Father, we praise thy guardian care,
   Which hath on Us a Man bestow'd.
The Prime Minister is Lord North who served from 1770–82.]

FOR ONE UNDER A PROSPECT OF WANT—JAN. 1753[25]

1.   The Lord, the wise, almighty Lord
      Hath given, and resum'd the grace:
  For ever be his Name ador'd!
      His name with all my heart I praise,
  And cry, surrendring up his own,
  Father, thy only will be done.

2.   Hath not the heavenly Potter power
      To mould at will the passive clay?
  To raise, or sink his creature lower?
      To give, or take his gifts away?
  And who shall daringly reprove
  The just decrees of Sovereign Love?

3.   LOVE only doth the loss ordain,
      Whate'er inferior Causes join,
  Female revenge, or fraud in man:
      To God, not Them, I all resign:
  Let rapine seize, or avarice crave,
  Or envy cruel as the grave.

4.   I meet the Providential blow,
      Whoe'er fulfils my God's command,
  A seeming friend, or open foe,
      A stranger's, or a brother's hand,
  The fire from heaven, the spoiler's sword,
  Whate'er afflicts—It is the Lord!

5.   On Him I fix my faithful eye,
      The baser instrument look thro',
  On Him in all events rely;
      The Lord his utmost pleasure show,
  His Name be own'd, his goodness blest;
  Whatever is from God is best!

25. [MS Misc. Hymns, pp. 141–2.]

$$II^{26}$$

1.   Jesus, thy faithful love I praise,
      Accept the answer of my prayer,
  If honour'd by peculiar grace
      Thy sacred poverty to share,
  Thy state of indigence to know,
  And live as Thou didst live below.

2.   Oft hast Thou seen my soul aspire
      And gasp for full conformity,
  Oft hast Thou seen my heart's desire
      Impatient to be all like Thee,
  To tread the path my Pattern trod,
  One with th'afflicted Son of God.

3.   And shall I not with thanks receive
      The scanty portion of my Lord,
  To sovereign Love the matter leave
      And bless the kind, revoking word,
  If poor, and destitute of bread
  I want a place to lay my head?

4.   Yes, Lord; I will, I do embrace
      The lot on earth for me design'd:
  But fill me with thy patient grace,
      But arm me with thy suffering mind,
  And make thy Servant as Thou art
  Lowly, and meek, and pure in heart.

5.   Inur'd to want, in spirit poor,
      Still may I with my Master stay,
  All things, like Thee, thro' life endure,
      And calmly wait the welcome day
  That brings the heavenly kingdom down,
  And decks me with a glorious crown.[27]

26. [MS Misc. Hymns, pp. 142–4.]
27. [Space is left for two more verses.]

FOR MISS DURBIN[28]

III

1. O might the prayer of faith prevail
   T'effect the thing impossible!
   O might thy grace her heart incline
   To give up her own will to Thine!

2. Who can against thy counsel stand?
   Lay on her soul thy mighty hand,
   Bend by resistless love, or break
   The iron sinew in her neck.

3. Then let her, conscious of her fall,
   Out of the deep for mercy call,
   From every fond attachment free,
   And yield her heart intire to Thee.

4. But when she wakes in dread surprize
   And sees her state with open eyes,
   And faints beneath the tort'ring pain,
   Do Thou her fainting soul sustain.

5. Do Thou restrain the baffled Foe,
   Nor let him deal a parting blow,
   Or drive her, scap'd out [of] his snare,
   To death, distraction, or despair.

6. Her danger *past* O may she see
   With thanks, and deep humility,
   And meek in all thy footsteps move
   Or'whelm'd with shame, & lost in love.

28. [MS CW I(p) xii, pp. 5–6; MS Misc. 1786 (MS CW III[c]), pp. 24–5.]

IV[29]

1.   Israel's God & strength, arise
To scatter all thy foes,
Human, hellish enemies
Who Thee & Thine oppose!
Blast the world's malicious aim,
Who watch to see us halt, or fall,
For the sin of One to blame
And pour reproach on all.

2.   Shall the haters of the Lord
Thy hallow'd Name prophane?
No: the honor of thy word
And Church Thou wilt maintain;
God of truth and jealousy,
Thou wilt thy righteous Cause defend:
Sure of this, we trust in Thee
And calm expect the end.

3.   Pity to the Tempted show
Who wanders far from home:
Save her from the threaten'd woe,
Nor let the scandal come:
Lest from Thee she farther stray,
And fall the Tempter's easy prize,
Hide her from the evil day
Secure in paradise.

4.   But Thou canst redeem her here
From sin & Satan's wiles,
Ignorant, yet still sincere,
And strugling in the toils:
Speak, and she shall now be freed
From passion's fascinating power,
Saints shall wonder at the deed,
And all thy hosts adore!

29. [MS CW I(p) xii, pp. 6–7.]

V[30]

1. Lord, we will not let thee go,
   Till thine Arm, reveal'd below,
   Captive leads captivity,
   Sets the ransom'd prisoner free.

2. Tho' she takes the Tempter's part,
   Well Thou knowst, her simple heart
   Doth no evil thing intend,
   Woud not wilfully offend.

3. By thy Spirit's power convince
   One who ignorantly sins,
   Darkness still mistakes for light,
   Fondly thinks that Wrong is Right.

4. Willing made her God t'obey
   Bring her back into thy way:
   Thine the pleasant way of peace,
   Duty, love, and happiness.

5. Now avenge her of her Foe,
   Now release, and let her go,
   Free indeed, renew'd, restor'd,
   All devoted to the Lord.

6. Let her, as thy laws require,
   Wait on her respected Sire,
   Cherish him with pious care,
   Gladly all his burthens bear:

7. Staff of his declining age
   Sent, his sufferings to assuage,
   Aid to minister, and ease,
   God, by pleasing Him, to please.

30. [MS CW I(p) xii, pp. 7–8. Verse 6 suggests the nature of the fault that is implied in the previous poem. John Wesley married Miss Helen (Nellie) Durbin to John Horton in 1780. She died in 1788.]

8. Make her Duty her delight,
    Acceptable in thy sight,
    That she may thy glory see
    Find her full reward in Thee.

WRITTEN IN JULY, 1786[31]

1. Jesus, we thy promise claim,
        We who touching this agree,
    Grace to challenge in thy Name,
        Peace, and perfect liberty,
    Life for One Insensible,
    Life for One Thou lov'st so well.

2. By the smooth Seducer's skill,
        By the cunning of the Foe,
    Drawn to follow her own will,
        Urged in nature's paths to go,
    Her we mourn, a Captive blind,
    Casting all thy words behind.

3. Pains which might a father aid,
        Pains which first to Him she owes,
    Corban[32] call'd, with-held, delay'd,
        Lo, on Others she bestows,
    Comfort to his age denies,
    Till he gives her up—and dies!

4. Deaf to his expiring prayers,
        Unconcern'd his grief she sees,
    Thus repays a Father's cares,
        Thus relieves his last distress,
    Fixt to please herself alone,
    Thus she hastes to be undone!

31. [MS Misc. Hymns, 1786 (MS CW III[c]), pp. 21–3; MS CW I(p) xii. Sally Wesley notes: "For Miss H.D. when she refused to return to her Father and was said to be attached to Mr. Horton." In MS CW I(p) xii, she notes: "On Miss Nelly Durbin when forming an attachment contrary to her Father's wish." However, see previous footnote.]
32. [*Cf.* Mark 7:10ff.]

243

5.   Who can stay her violence? who
        Can arrest her as she flies?
     Lord, we know not what to do,
        But to Thee we lift our eyes:
     Love, almighty Love Thou art;
     Turn her disobedient heart.

6.   Now with thorns hedge up her way,
        From her fatal purpose hide,
     Stop the unsuspicious Stray,
        By thine eye the Wanderer guide,
     Without pain (if that can be)
     Bring her gently back to Thee.

7.   From her eyes the Scales remove,
        From her stubborn heart this Stone,
     Taught by wisdom from above,
        That she may thy counsel own,
     See the depths of hell laid bare
     Scape the fiend's [   ]^{33} snare!

8.   Jesus, spoil him of his prey,
        Her thy lawful Captive claim,
     That with all thy Church we may
        Magnify thy saving Name;
     Purchase dear of blood divine
     Seal her now for ever thine.

9.   To a father's fond embrace
        Both his Fugitives restore,
     Wipe the sorrow from his face,
        That he may thy hand adore;
     That he may thy goodness prove,
     Give him back his former love.

10. Quench not the last spark of hope
        In thine aged Servant's heart,
     But whene'er Thou cal'st him up,
        Bid him, Lord, in peace depart;
     Bid his children *live* forgiven,
     Live, and follow him to heaven!

33. [The missing word is not supplied by either manuscript.]

II[34]

1. Besieging still thy gracious throne
   For our deluded Friend,
   We pray, and plead, and wrestle on
   Till Thou deliverance send:

2. Beguil'd like poor, unwary Eve,
   By the old serpent's art,
   No more permit him to deceive
   Or blind her simple heart.

3. Dissolve the charm which long hath held
   A soul that woud do right,
   Disperse the cloud which hath conceal'd
   Her Duty from her sight.

4. Duty and inclination, Lord,
   Must struggle in her breast,
   Till Thou pronounce the powerful word
   Which turns her to her Rest.

5. O woudst Thou now thine arm display
   On which our hopes depend,
   The strong Delusion chase away,
   The hour of darkness end!

6. Her sins of ignorance forgive,
   That, when thy mind is known,
   She may to Thee entirely live,
   And serve thy will alone.

FOR MRS. G.[35]

1. Christ the Lord, the woman's Seed,
   Bruiser of the serpent's head,
   Swift Avenger of thine own,
   Listen to thy Spirit's groan.

34. [MS Misc. 1786 (MS CW III[c]), pp. 23–4; MS CW I(p) xii.]
35. [MS Preachers (MS CW I[q]) xxxi. The poem is incomplete.]

245

2. Hear us for a chosen child,
    Long by Satan's art beguil'd,
    Fallen, yet insensible,
    Easy in the toils of hell.

3. Wandring o're inchanted ground,
    By a strong delusion bound,
    Taking the Deceiver's part,
    Left to trust her own weak heart.

4. Jesus, to her help descend,
    Let the hour of darkness end,
    Brought by faith's effectual prayer
    Come, and break the hellish snare.

5. Lull'd in a Satanic dream,
    While our common foes blaspheme,
    While the sacrilegious croud
    Scoff the truths and sons of God.

6. [unfinished]

**PRAYER FOR THE CONVERSION OF A MURTHERER,
THE E[AR]L OF FER[RER]S[36]**

1. Come, let us join the wrestling race
        With Jacob's faith endued,
    And all besiege the throne of grace,
        And prove our power with God:
    Whoe'er in Jesus' merits trust
        In Jesus' strength arise,
    To snatch from hell a sinner lost,
        And bear him to the skies.

2. Father, in the prevailing name
        We urge our faithful plea,
    Repentance for an outcast claim,
        Who hates thy Son and Thee;

36. [MS Misc. Hymns, pp. 17–20. The Earl of Ferrers, cousin of Lady Huntingdon, was executed on May 5, 1759 for the murder of his land steward.]

By the old murtherer possest
   Who eyes the gulph beneath,
Affecting on its verge to rest,
   And scorn eternal death.

3. God of resistless power and love,
       In answer to our cry,
   Appear the mountains to remove,
       Appear the Lord most high;
   Thy wrath against thy foe reveal,
       Confound his wickedness,
   And let the pangs of inbred hell
       His waken'd conscience seize.

4. Now thy convincing work begin,
       In terrible array
   Th'exceeding sinfulness of sin
       Of his own sin display:
   Give him to feel his guilty load,
       His long-dissembled wound,
   And hear the voice of innocent blood
       Cry *vengeance* from the ground!

5. While yet we call, his spirit arrest,
       And stop his flight from Thee,
   With *horror fill his flinty breast,*
       Stir up the troubled sea:
   Till Thou the keen conviction dart,
       All his strong-holds o'rethrow,
   And break his adamantine heart,
       We will not let thee go.

6. Put him in fear; this moment, Lord,
       Abase his sullen pride,
   And let thy Spirit's two-edg'd sword
       Marrow and joints divide;
   Or'eturn by one resistless frown,
       Compel him to submit,
   And bring the stubborn rebel down,
       Down, down beneath thy feet.

7. Great God of all-victorious Love,
        The work is worthy Thee
    Such guilty mountains to remove,
        Such hellish enmity:
    Forgive him at the point to die,
        And speak his soul renew'd,
    That all thine enemies may cry
        "This is the hand of God!"

8. To Jesus' name if all things bow
        In heaven, and earth, and hell,
    If praying by his Spirit now
        Our hearts his presence feel;
    We now on Thee may cast our care,
        And say, thy will be done,
    But have respect to Jesus' prayer,
        But glorify thy Son!

HYMN II[37]

1. Father, whose goodness knows no bound,
    If now in us thy bowels sound,
        With yearning pity see
    A ruffian stain'd with guiltless blood,
    A murtherer both of man and God,
        A wretch as lost—as me!

2. In Jesus found, for Him we cry,
    Whose heart doth all thy wrath defy,
        And all thy patience scorn:
    Who but our Advocate above
    With all his power of dying love
        The stone to flesh can turn?

3. Father, regard the sprinkled blood,
    Which from the wounds of Jesus flow'd,
        Accepted sacrifice!
    It did for all mankind atone,
    And now it speaks before the throne
        And fills both earth and skies.

37. [MS Misc. Hymns, pp. 20–21.]

4. Louder than that his hands have shed,
    Thou hearst it for the murtherer plead
        Whom on our hearts we bear;
    The blood doth mercy, mercy sound,
    And every drop a voice has found,
        And swells into a prayer.

5. To that almighty prayer divine
    Thou must thy gracious ear incline,
        While Jesus gasps "Forgive!"
    He cannot ask, and bleed in vain;
    He died for this lost child of man,
        And prays that he may live.

6. O for his prayer and passion sake,
    This brand out of the burning take,
        A present for thy Son,
    Implunge in his Redeemer's side,
    And bear him thro' the crimson tide
        To thy eternal throne.

HYMN III[38]

1. Poor guilty worm, or'ewhelm'd with fear
    Before an earthly judge t'appear,
        And meet thy lighter doom,
    How wilt thou meet that fiery hour,
    When arm'd with glorious, vengeful power
        The Judge from heaven shall come?

2. Heir of that everlasting curse,
    Canst thou depart without remorse
        Or one relenting sigh,
    So daunted at a moment's pain,
    So bold, and harden'd to sustain
        The death that cannot die?

38. [MS Misc. Hymns, pp. 22–3.]

3. Tremendous God, in mercy frown,
    Cast all his hellish courage down,
        Which Satan's breath inspires,
    Make this incarnate fiend submit,
    And shake him o're the burning pit,
        And scorch him with the fires.

4. Now, Father, now thy terrors dart,
    And pierce, and fill his stubborn heart
        With horrid pangs unknown:
    Justice divine, thy prisoner seize,
    Compel'd by torture to confess
        The murther of thy Son.

5. Before he sinks among the dead,
    O may he guilty, guilty plead,
        And justify our God:
    Then, Jesus, then step in between,
    To part the punishment and sin,
        To save him by thy blood.

6. Thy blood alone can purge his guilt,
    Can expiate that his hands have spilt,
        And all his crimes efface:
    Get thyself honor on thy foe,
    Wash the foul monster white as snow,
        And show forth all thy grace.

7. Or if thy wise and righteous will
    Its counsels deep from us conceal,
        We bless th'award divine,
    We leave him in a state unknown,
    And let him die to God alone,
        And die—without a Sign!

8. But while he yields his parting breath,
    And swim his closing eyes in death,
        Before his closing eyes
    Show Thyself bleeding on the tree—
    Then let him gasp, Remember me—
        And wake in paradise!

FOR ONE GROWN SLACK[39]

1. And is it come to this at last
        With one that did run well,
    Arrested is my rapid haste,
        And quench'd my flaming zeal?
    Nothing at last for me remains
        But to lament my case,
    And sadly count my mournful gains,
        And muse on what I was.

2. I was (himself can tell) sincere
        To seek the God unknown,
    When, only influenc'd by fear,
        I blindly labour'd on;
    To stablish my own righteousness
        In ignorance I strove,
    Nor knew the way of gospel-peace,
        The freeness of his love.

3. I hid me in the secret shade
        With solitary care,
    And oft implor'd my Maker's aid,
        And found his comforts there:
    His transient comforts but increas'd
        My wounded spirit's smart,
    The mountain still my soul oppress'd,
        The vail was on my heart.

39. [MS Misc. Hymns, pp. 27–33.]

4. I fasted, read, and wept, and cried
   For permanent relief,
   Nor yet in Jesus' blood espied
   The balm of all my grief.
   Weary and faint, beneath my load,
   I at his altar lay,
   But fear'd t'approach an angry God,
   Yet dared not disobey.

5. I wanted still I knew not what,
   Or how the grace t'obtain:
   The children to the birth were brought,
   But all my pangs were vain:
   Myself I coud not shun, nor bear,
   I coud not fight nor fly,
   And sunk o'rewhelm'd with just despair,
   And wish'd, and fear'd to die.

PART II

1. Ev'n then, while in my sins and blood
   I heard the welcome sound,
   "Sinner, behold the Lamb of God,
   "Who hath the ransom found!
   "The ransom found, the debt is paid
   "In precious blood divine:
   "Believe thy sins on Him were laid,
   "And all his grace is thine."

2. With eager joy I ran, I flew
   To my Redeemer's side,
   And long'd to prove the tidings true,
   To feel the blood applied;
   I flew to catch the pardning word,
   The messengers to greet,
   And wash'd, in honor of their Lord,
   His dear disciples' feet.

3.   O who can paint the joy that blest
      My simple soul so long!
  It glow'd, and panted in my breast,
      And warbled on my tongue;
  It knit my heart to all that fear
      The Name of the Most high,
  And made me at his altar swear
      With them to live, and die.

4.   My Saviour's friends by men despis'd
      I gloried to embrace,
  And more than life, like them, I priz'd
      The channels of his grace;
  There with his saints communion sweet
      I held in praise and prayer,
  Nor ever failed my wish to meet,
      For God and heaven were there.

5.   Athirst for Jesus and the word,
      I urg'd my one request,
  To see the beauty of my Lord,
      And in his temple rest:
  For this obedient to his call,
      I coud no longer stay,
  But gave my friends, my life, my all,
      But gave myself away.

6.   Witness the listning quire above,
      Who clapp'd their wings, and spread
  The volume of our plighted love,
      Recording what we said!
  Witness the Searcher of my heart,
      And all his chosen race,
  I languish'd then for Mary's part,
      I pin'd for Jesus' grace.

PART III

1. O where is now my hunger gone,
     My soul's awaken'd sense,
    How am I sunk supinely down
     In listless indolence!
    How have I set[t]led on my lees,
     And closed mine eyes again!
    My slumbring soul is now at ease,
     As Christ had died in vain.

2. The fatal cause I see not yet,
     The dire effects I feel,
    Extinguish'd all my sacred heat,
     And quench'd my flaming zeal:
    Th'immortal bread no more I seek,
     But loath so light a food,
    Nor covet with his saints to speak
     Nor love to talk with God.

3. Vanish'd my last attempt to pray,
     My last desire is fled,
    The morning cloud is past away,
     And all my hopes are dead:
    Devoid of power and will to rise,
     Devoid of love and fear,
    I see my state with stony eyes
     Which cannot drop a tear.

PART IV

1. What is it then which now constrains
     My hardness to lament?
    Why do I *miss* my former pains,
     And wish I coud relent?

It is my Advocate above,
  Who forces me to hope,
It is the voice of bleeding LOVE,
  "How shall I give thee up?"

2. Lord, if thy love doth still abound
      Above my sin's excess,
    If still Thou art my Spokesman found
      Before the throne of grace;
    If one so doubly dead to God
      Thou canst revive again,
    Revive me now; restore my load,
      And give me back my pain.

3. Giver of power to them that faint,
      Thy power to me impart,
    Thy whole omnipotence I want
      To rouse my languid heart:
    I want the voice that wakes the dead,
      To bid my soul arise,
    And follow where my Captain led,
      And labour up the skies.

4. O for the strength of fervent zeal,
      The faith in Jesus' Name,
    Which dares the floud, & scales the hill,
      And rushes thro' the flame;
    Which wrestles on, divinely bold,
      The secret Name to know,
    With violent faith on God lays hold,
      And will not let him go!

5. Spirit of power and life, inspire
      This faint and feeble breast
    With even, infinite desire
      Of my eternal rest:
    Stir up my soul its strength t'exert,
      With never-slackning care,
    And groan Thyself within my heart
      Th'unutterable prayer.

6. I woud be govern'd by thy will,
 I woud be wholly thine:
Now, Lord, my gasping spirit fill
 With energy divine;
And that my zeal no more may cool,
 Come, heavenly Comforter,
Take full posession of my soul,
 And dwell for ever here!

FOR A BACKSLIDER[40]

1. Sinner's Advocate, again
 I must to Thee apply,
Vilest of the sons of men,
 The worst of rebels, I
To thy mercy-seat draw near,
Yet hardly dare thy grace implore:
 Bleeding Lamb, my conscience clear,
 And bid me sin no more.

2. As the caught adulteress,
 Confounded in thy sight,
Guilty, guilty I confess
 Eternal death my right;
Swallow'd up in shame and fear,
I deprecate thine anger's power:
 Bleeding Lamb, my conscience clear,
 And bid me sin no more.

3. While the guilt of sin remains,
 The strength must still abide,
Therefore purge my crimson stains,
 Pronounce me justified:
That I may with heart sincere
With all my life my Lord adore,
 Bleeding Lamb, my conscience clear,
 And bid me sin no more.

40. [MS Misc. Hymns, pp. 34–6.]

4.   Well Thou knowst, I chiefly woud
Thy pardning grace receive,
That my most indulgent God
I may no longer grieve,
Never from thy statutes err,
Or thwart thy will, as heretofore:
Bleeding Lamb, my conscience clear,
And bid me sin no more.

5.   Happy they whoe'er obtain
The sense of sin forgiven,
Peace and joy with faith they gain,
They live the life of heaven:
But I want the Comforter
To make me meek, & chast, & poor:
Bleeding Lamb, my conscience clear,
And bid me sin no more.

6.   Pardon less than power I want,
Than purity within:
Holy God, thy nature plant,
The antidote of sin;
By thy hallowing spirit chear,
Thy kingdom to my soul restore;
Bleeding Lamb, my conscience clear,
And bid me sin no more.

7.   If the strength and joy of grace
Can ever parted be,
Still with-hold the happinéss,
But give the power to me:
Let me mourn, and suffer here,
Till pain and life at once are o're:
Bleeding Lamb, my conscience clear[41]
And bid me sin no more.

8.   Tost on life's tempestuous wave,
I ever cry to Thee,
Ready if Thou art to save,
Rebuke the winds and sea;

41. [In verses 7 and 8 the last two lines are abbreviated to "Bleeding Lamb, &c." in the MS.]

Thou this shatter'd vessel steer
In safety to th'eternal shore,
 Bleeding Lamb, my conscience clear,
 And bid me sin no more.

9.   Might I now to heaven repair,
    Thy face I coud not see,
Heaven, if sin pursued me there,
    Woud be no heaven to me;
Sinai's trump I there shoud hear,
And tremble, while its thunders roar:
    Bleeding Lamb, my conscience clear,
    And bid me sin no more.

10.   Lord, I will not let thee rest,
    Till I the blessing find,
Of the precious pearl possest,
    The pure, unsinning mind:
Author, End of faith appear,
And bless me with the perfect power,
    Bleeding Lamb, my nature clear,
    And bid me live no more.

FOR ONE IN THE WILDERNESS[42]

1.   Jesus, help as weak a soul
    As ever hoped in Thee,
Longing still to be made whole,
    And perfectly set free:
Lo, I at thy feet remain,
And groan in exquisite distress
    Turn, and look me out of pain,
    And look[43] me back my peace.

42. [MS Misc. Hymns, pp. 40–42. Frank Baker thinks that this poem may arise out of Charles Wesley's unhappiness at his brother's marriage.]

43. [This transitive use of the verb "to look" is not quoted in the *Oxford English Dictionary*. *Cf.* Luke 22:61.]

2.   Once in a new world of light
        On eagles' wings I rode,
      Long convers'd in Tabor's height
        With Thee my friend, my God:
      Now I droop, and mourn again,
    Along the dreary wilderness:
        Turn, and look me out of pain,
        And look me back my peace.

3.   Strong I seem'd, and rich in grace,
        When first I lisp'd thy name,
      But the hidings of thy face
        Have show'd me what I am:
      Yes, I know myself but man,
    I feel my utter helplessness:
        Turn, and look me out of pain,
        And look me back my peace.

4.   Sinks my weary, feeble mind
        Beneath its weight of care,
      Labouring thro' the fire to find
        Its old relief in prayer;
      Labouring on, yet still in vain,
    While horrid doubts my spirit seize:
        Turn, and look me out of pain,
        And look me back my peace.

5.   Faintly hoping against hope,
        Devoid of life and power,
      Now I woud decline the cup
        I gladly drank before;
      Now I shun my former gain,
    And fears of death my heart oppress:
        Turn, and look me out of pain,
        And look me back my peace.

6.   Once I knew the Master's mind,
        Which now I cannot know,
      Doubly dead to God, and blind
        To all his ways below:

Who his counsel can explain,
Or trace him thro' the dark abyss:
Turn, and look me out of pain,
And look me back my peace.

7.   O for one kind, pitying ray
To chear me in the gloom,
Till the long-expected day
Of my deliverance come!
Till that heavenly port I gain,
Emerging from these stormy seas,
Turn, and look me out of pain,
And look me back my peace.

HYMNS FOR THE USE OF A BACKSLIDER, J. H[UTCHINSON][44]

I

1.   Whither, ah, whither shall I go,
I who my Lord no longer know,
No longer feel the sprinkled blood,
Or find my happiness in God!

2.   Back to the world shall I return,
Or court the objects of my scorn,
Again for sensual pleasures pine,
That sordid happiness of swine?

3.   Will a good name, or fortune fair
The life-imbittering loss repair,
Allay this tumult in my breast,
Or give my troubled conscience rest?

4.   Can I the perfect beauties trace
Of Jesus in an human face?
Can all the creature's boasted art
Supply his absence in my heart?

---

44. [MS Misc. Hymns, pp. 44–5. John Hutchinson of Leeds, an erratic Methodist, devoted to the Wesleys, died July 23, 1754.]

5. No, Saviour, no: it cannot be
   That I shoud rest, bereav'd of Thee,
   Shoud sooth with toys this aching breast,
   Or e'er forget that I was blest.

6. Here then I all my hopes forego
   Of comfort, or repose below.
   I yield my punishment to bear,
   I sink in calmness of despair.

7. Away, ye dreams of vain relief,
   Nor once disturb my sacred grief,
   Or hope t'assuage my misery,
   For God alone shall comfort me.

8. Till then I hug my load of pain,
   And meekly sad thro' life remain;
   And if at last his mercy save,
   I drop my burthen in the grave.

II[45]

1. When will the pardning God appear
   A poor, desponding soul to chear,
      Who once rejoic'd to prove
   His people's rest, his saints' delight,
   And fed on Jesus day and night,
      And gloried in his love?

2. His love was once my daily bread,
   His love refresh'd me on my bed,
      And bless'd my every dream:
   In Him my whole of bliss I sought,
   In every work, and word, and thought
      I only lived for Him.

45. [MS Misc. Hymns, pp. 45–7.]

3. Where'er I turn'd my willing feet,
   The tokens of his grace I met,
       And blessings without end:
   In every field, in every grove
   I found the Object of my love,
       And talk'd with God my Friend.

4. Witness, ye echoing hills and dales,
   Ye conscious streams & secret vales:
       When I my Saviour found,
   How have I shouted forth his praise,
   How have I fell before his face,
       And kiss'd the sacred ground!

5. I heard his voice among the trees,
   The ghastly uncouth wilderness
       At Jesus' Presence smiled:
   I saw the new creation rise,
   And lo, a beauteous paradise
       Was open'd in the wild!

6. But I have lost my bower again,
   An outcast wretch, a banish'd man
       From Jesus' presence driven,
   Pain'd with the sense of what I was,
   I mourn the life-imbittering loss,
       I wander unforgiven.

7. O woud my God return at last,
   When all my penal woes are past,
       To save me as by fire;
   O might I, Lord, thy love retrieve,
   And happy in thy favor live
       One moment, and expire!

III[46]

1. Father, thy speaking rod I hear,
   Thy judgments graciously severe
       With deepest reverence meet,
   Unworthy to be called thy Son,
   Thou seest the Prodigal brought down,
       And weeping at thy feet.

2. If justice shoud abridge my days,
   Yet O, thy more surpassing grace
       My latest breath shall tell:
   Thou mightst have left me to sin on,
   Thou mightst have suddenly cut down
       And swept me into hell.

3. The tokens of paternal love
   In all thy sharp rebukes I prove,
       The warnings of a Friend:
   I know the meaning of this pain;
   It tells me I shall turn again,
       And hope is in my end.

4. Stupendous height of love divine!
   It bids me leizurely decline
       By sensible degrees,
   Wills me a dying life to live,
   Till Thou my sinsick soul retrieve,
       And give me back my peace.

5. I now discern thy gracious aim,
   Thy mercy shook this feeble frame,
       To rouse my slumbring soul:
   Thee, Lord, I in the sickness see,
   It comes a messenger from thee,
       To make my spirit whole.

46. [MS Misc. Hymns, pp. 47–9.]

6. For this the kind, angelic bands
   Have gently borne me in their hands
      To the sequester'd shade;
   For this the servants of my Lord
   With softest sympathy afford
      Their ministerial aid.

7. Those objects of my former love,
   With whom I peevishly have strove
      With causeless enmity,
   How have they all my burthen borne,
   How have they wept for my return,
      And pray'd me back to Thee!

8. Ev'n now their powerful prayer I feel
   And yield me, Father, to thy will
      And bless thy chastning rod;
   For neither life nor death I pray,
   But let me all thy will obey,
      And live, and die to God.

IV
HYMN FOR HIM BY A FRIEND[47]

1. God of love, who hearst the prayer,
   Mark the object of my care,
   See, with bleeding pity see,
   One who once was blest in Thee.

2. Stranger now to thee, and peace,
   Stript of all his happiness,
   Sad he wanders up and down,
   Droops beneath thine angry frown.

3. Help him in his greatest need
   Catching at a broken reed,
   Till thy love his wandrings end,
   Pining for an earthly friend.

47. [MS Misc. Hymns, pp. 49–50.]

4. O that his afflicted mind
Might its wonted comfort find,
Turn again to his true Rest,
Sink on his Redeemer's breast!

5. Jesus, now his heart inspire,
Dart a ray of pure desire
From thy gracious throne above;
Give him back his former love.

6. All thy benefits restore,
Faith, and zeal, and life, and power,
Power to pray, and never cease,
Power to go in perfect peace.

7. Give him, Saviour, above all
Power on Thee his God to call,
Till thy goodness Thou proclaim,
Tell him all thy glorious Name:

8. Then, when all his heart is prayer,
Let him *my* affliction share,
Pay me back my sympathy,
Wrestle, and prevail for me!

HYMN V
FOR THE SAME
WRITTEN ON THE ROAD TO [A FRIEND] FROM LEEDS, SEPT. 21[48]

1. My leader, my Lord,
    Thy call I obey,
   Come forth at thy word,
    I go on my way;
   In mercy's direction
    I heavenward move,
   And bless the protection
    Of ransoming Love.

48. [Wesley Family Letters, IV, 84; MS Misc. Hymns, pp. 50–2. We have printed the eight
verses of the Wesley Family Letters. The other MS contains verses 1–5 and 7 with variations,
and is entitled, "Written by his friend on the road."]

2. On God I attend
        My strength to renew,
    On God I depend
        To carry me thro':
    My gracious Creator
        In Jesus I see;
    The weakness of nature
        He felt it for me.

3. His spiritual want,
        His hunger I feel,
    When weary, and faint
        He dropt on the well:
    The drink He required
        I eagerly crave;
    He only desired
        A sinner to save.

4. O Jesus, Thou knowst
        My thirst is the same,
    To save what is lost
        Impatient I am;
    Thou readst the strong passion
        That burns in my breast:
    Without *his* salvation
        I never can rest.

5. But canst Thou impart
        What is not in Thee?
    All pity Thou art
        To sinners like me:
    Ah, lighten the burthen
        Of him I bemoan,
    And chear by a pardon
        Thy sorrowful Son.

6. His forfeited peace
        In mercy restore,
    His comforts increase
        Abundantly more:

Pronounce the glad Sentence
And give him to prove
The Life of Repentance,
The Heaven of Love.

7. O make on his soul
Thy countenance shine,
And he shall be whole,
And he shall be thine,
Restor'd to thy favor
He with his last breath
Shall sing of his Saviour
In life, and in death.

8. His Sickness to heal
Thy Servant prevent,
And now let him feel
The Spirit's Descent:
Come kindly to give him
His Pasport of Love,
And then to receive him
Triumphant above.

HYMN VI[49]

1. While hovering on the brink of fate,
The margin of the tomb,
In awful doubt I humbly wait
To know my instant doom,
Help me, great God of truth and love,
To wisely weigh my end,
And rightly use, and well improve
The talent of a Friend.

2. The Giver of my faithful guide
Thee in my friend I see,
And beg I never may confide
In him, instead of Thee,

49. [MS Misc. Hymns, pp. 52–4.]

May never rob Thee of thy due,
    But thankfully embrace
The instrument, whom I look Thro'
    And give Thee all the praise.

3. I woud not vex thy glorious eyes
    Whose grace I wait to feel,
Or make thy jealous anger rise
    By loving him too well:
I woud not place him in thy stead,
    Or, making him my stay,
Compel Thee to remove my reed,
    And take my friend away.

4. But what my Lord is pleas'd t'impart
    May I not safely take,
And clasp the comfort to my heart,
    And love him for thy sake?
I *shoud* injoy the boon bestow'd,
    While ready to restore,
Shoud prize my friend, but prize my God
    Incomparably more.

5. O woudst Thou by thy special grace
    My fallen soul redeem,
And guard me from the fond excess,
    Th'idolatrous extream!
O that the Sea might drown the drop
    Descending from above,
While both our souls are swallow'd up
    In all the depths of love!

HYMN VII[50]

1. To Thee, great Friend of helpless man,
    Doubly oppress'd by sin and pain,
        For aid I feebly cry:
O might I but thy grace retrieve,
One moment in thine image Live,
        And in thine image die!

50. [MS Misc. Hymns, pp. 54–5.]

2. I cannot live, or die in peace,
   Till Thou my strugling soul release
       From passion's tyranny:
   My spirit, and my flesh it tears,
   And shakes my faith, & damps my prayers
       And drives me back from Thee.

3. I reason, and resolve in vain,
   I weep, and rise, and fall again
       By furious wrath subdued;
   Life's latest, golden sands I lose,
   The patience of my friends abuse,
       And weary out my God.

4. Nor generous hope, nor servile fear,
   Nor death with hasty strides drawn near
       And brandishing his dart,
   This proud, impetuous spirit can tame,
   Or sink the leopard to a lamb,
       Or make me meek in heart.

5. Tormentor of myself I rove,
   Tormentor of the man I love,
       Or seem to love so well,
   Rest I pursue with vehemence vain,
   Relief I seek by giving pain,
       And spreading my own hell.

6. A sinner tottering o're the grave,
   What shall I do myself to save,
       Or how for death prepare?
   As weak in body as in mind,
   No succour in myself I find,
       No fitness but despair.

7. Then let thy own compassions plead,
   Then let the cry that woke the dead
       And rent the rocks in twain,
   My stubborn soul and spirit part,
   And break my adamantine heart,
       And bind it up again.

PRAYERS FOR SOME IN A FOREIGN LAND[51]

1.   Thou never-failing Friend
       Of all that want thy grace,
    Stir up thy power, and now defend
       An Orphan in distress;
          Thy great, unshorten'd arm
          Make bare in her defence,
    And rescue from th'intended harm
       Her heedless innocence.

2.   Thou seest their dark design
       The simple to betray,
    Infidels and apostates join
       To swallow up their prey:
          Her wealth their hopes devour,
          Her soul their mercies doom,
    A victim to the cruel power
       Of Antichristian Rome.

3.   Cut off from all retreat,
       Her soul is in the snare,
    And lo, where Satan keeps his seat
       Their thoughtless Prize they bear!
          The Romish wolves surround,
          The fiends their Captive seize,
    And shouts of hellish joy resound
       Their prosperous wickedness.

4.   Who can deliver, who
       Defeat their surest plan?
    Alas, we know not what to do,
       There is no help in man:
          Wherefore into thy hand,
          Great God, the matter take,
    And heaven, and earth, and hell command
       To bring the Captive back.

51. [MS Misc. Hymns, pp. 61–6. Part III appears in a letter dated 1753, as well as in MS Misc. Hymns, so all three poems are probably of the same date, and possibly refer to a Miss D. who was being pressed heavily by Roman Catholics.]

5.   The succour we desire,
          For Her in faith we claim,
      Faith, which can quench the burning fire,
          The furious lion tame,
          Which calls th'Almighty down
          To vindicate his power,
      Arrests the sea, drives back the sun,
          And bids the grave restore.

6.   Believing against hope,
          Till Thou thy power declare,
      Into thy hands we give her up
          In confidence of prayer:
          Her innocence secure
          From Rome's destructive zeal,
      And keep her heart & conscience pure
          Midst all the filth of hell.

                    II

1.   Jesus, with pity see,
          And succour from above
      The captives, hastning to be free,
          The objects of thy love;
          Thy tyrant's aim defeat,
          The plots of earth and hell,
      Nor let them perish in the pit,
          Nor let the foe prevail.

2.   In chains of conscious fear
          The persecutor bind,
      And when his surest wish is near,
          Thy bridle let him find;
          In that determin'd hour
          Thy mighty arm display,
      And far beyond his cruel power
          Transport the lawful prey.

                    271

3.   Till then with Thee conceal'd
         Their pretious lives defend,
From secret fraud, and violence shield,
         And save them to the end;
         Their fainting flesh sustain,
         Their wasted strength repair,
And far from sin, and far from pain
         Their ransom'd spirits bear.

4.   Happy in Thee alone
         O may they ever dwell,
Meekly beneath thy cross go on,
         And heavenly comforts feel:
         In banishment, debar'd
         The channels of thy grace,
Thyself from sin, and error guard,
         And shine on all their ways.

5.   Into their longing hearts
         With beams of mercy shine,
And write it on their inward parts,
         The law of love divine;
         The true essential Word
         Let them with joy receive,
And know their dear redeeming Lord,
         And sensibly believe.

6.   According to thy will
         If now, O God, we pray,
The answer on their conscience seal,
         And take their sins away;
         Thy banish'd ones assure
         Their sins are all forgiven,
And keep them in thy wounds secure,
         Till we all meet in heaven.

III [52]

1. Thou most compassionate High-priest,
   Thou Helper of the poor distrest,
      Behold with melting eye,
   With bleeding sympathy behold
   Our exil'd Friend to evil sold,
      And at the point to die.

2. Is there no medicine for her wound,
   Is there no good Physician found
      To mitigate her smart?
   Answer, thou heavenly Comforter,
   If now thy balmy blood is near
      To cure her broken heart.

3. Her hunted life in mercy spare,
   And let our faithful, fervent prayer
      Both soul and body heal,
   Arrest the spirit in its flight,
   And sweetly to Thyself unite
      In love ineffable.

4. The sweetness of thy pardning love
   Shall all her griefs at once remove,
      And soften every pain,
   Shall sanctify the heaviest cross,
   And turn her momentary loss
      Into eternal gain.

PRAYER FOR AN UNBORN CHILD [53]

1. Fountain of life and happiness,
      Jesus, sent the world to bless
         With true felicity,
   My infant yet unborn receive,
   And let it for thy glory live
         A sacrifice to Thee.

52. [Misc. Hymns, pp. 65–6; MS Letters, p. 219.]
53. [MS Misc. Hymns, p. 71.]

2. Before it sees this outward light,
   Claim it, Saviour, as thy right,
       Thy purchas'd Creature claim,
   Before it draws this[54] tainted air,
   Adopt for thy peculiar care,
       And mark it with thy Name.

PRAYER FOR A SICK CHILD[55]

1. God of love, incline thine ear,
   Hear a cry of grief and fear,
   Hear an anxious Parent's cry,
   Help, before my Isaac die.

2. All my comfort in distress,
   All my earthly happiness,
   Spare him still, the precious Loan;
   Is he not my only Son?

3. Whom I did from Thee obtain
   Must I give him back again?
   Can I with the blessing part?
   Lord, Thou know'st a Mother's heart:

4. All its passionate excess,
   All its yearning tenderness,
   Nature's soft infirmity
   Is it not a drop from Thee?

5. For thy own compassion's sake,
   Give me then my Darling back,
   Rais'd as from the dead, to praise,
   Love, and serve Thee all his days.

54. [In the margin "our" is written as an alternative to "this."]
55. [MS Misc. Hymns, pp. 71–2; *Rep. Verse*, No. 251, pp. 279. If this refers to Charles Wesley's firstborn son, it is John, who died of smallpox in January, 1754, at the age of sixteen months.]

6.   Speak, and at the powerful word,
      Lo, the witness for his Lord,
      Monument of grace divine,
      Isaac lives, for ever thine!

HYMNS FOR A BLIND MAN[56]

[HYMN I]

1.   Jesus, Thou Son of David, hear,
      And help a beggar to draw near;
          A poor, blind beggar, I
      Sit languishing by the way-side,
      And cry for a celestial Guide,
          And for salvation cry.

2.   These sightless orbs on Thee I turn,
      And wrapt in double darkness mourn
          To see thee as Thou art:
      Jesus, thy heavenly face reveal,
      Shine, everlasting Light, and heal
          The blindness of my heart.

3.   Thou knowst what I woud have thee do:
      To me thy pardning mercy show,
          These scales of sin remove,
      This burthen of Egyptian night,
      Restore in faith my inward sight,
          And manifest thy love.

4.   Come then, thou great Messiah, come,
      Of unbelief dispel the gloom,
          Declare my sins forgiven,
      So shall my soul exult to see
      The living Way to God, in Thee,
          And walk in Thee to heaven.

56. [MS Misc. Hymns, pp. 105–6.]

HYMN II[57]

1. O Thou, whose wise mysterious love
       Hath darkned my corporeal Sight,
   My mind irradiate from above
       With beams of uncreated light,
   The glories of thy face display,
   The brightness of eternal day.

2. Open my faith's interior eye
       To see Thee full of truth and grace,
   Th'almighty God who bow'd the sky
       To ransom our devoted race,
   Who bought my pardon on the tree,
   Who pour'd out all his blood for me.

3. O coud I now discern thee near,
       Conspicuous with thy garments died!
   In my dark, drooping heart apppear
       The slaughter'd Lamb, the Crucified,
   Who once for all the winepress trod,
   Who died for me—my Lord, my God.

[HYMN]III[58]

1. Sun of righteousness, arise,
       Light of life, thy beams impart,
   Pouring eye-sight on my eyes,
       Pouring faith into my heart,
   Faith, to see my sins forgiven,
   Love, to taste my present heaven.

2. Dark, I mourn, till Thou appear,
       Bound in chains of unbelief,
   Till the heavenly Comforter
       Chase away my sin and grief,
   Make my soul his hallow'd shrine,
   Change my human to divine.

57. [MS Misc. Hymns, pp. 106–7.]
58. [MS Misc. Hymns, pp. 107–8. The poem is perhaps incomplete, as there is room for two more verses.]

3. Give me an inlighten'd mind,
    O thou great Unsearchable,
Senses spiritual to find
    Him for whom I blindly feel,
Him I know not how t'adore,
Him I never miss'd before.

4. But I now my want bemoan;
    God of love, restore my sight,
Only by thy Spirit known,
    Visible by thy own light,
Give me eyes of faith to see
Him who loved, and died for me.

PRAYER FOR THE CHURCH OF ENGLAND—III[59]

1.   Jesus, behold the men
        Who thy designs oppose,
And hope by Sion's loss to gain,
        Her sworn, but secret, foes;
        Who wait with spiteful eyes
        To see our Church o'rethrown,
That they may on her ruins rise
        And stand, and reign alone.

2.   To gain the multitude,
        Their counsel deep they hide,
And cloak, with specious shows of good,
        Their selfishness and pride:
        But vain their closest art,
        And hellish subtlety,
When every thought of every heart
        Is manifest to Thee.

3.   With strength of guardian grace
        The little flock surround,
Our foes' malicious pride abase,
        And all their plots confound,

59. [MS Misc. Hymns, pp. 139–40. Poems numbered I and II appear in *Poet. Works,* VIII, pp. 417ff.]

That not one sheep may fall,
To grievous wolves a prey,
Preserv'd, till on the Right they all
Are found in that great day.

4. Now, Lord, we have made known
To Thee our joint request,
And on thy faithful word alone
With calm affiance[60] rest,
Assur'd thy Spirit shall guide,
And still our Church defend,
Till Thou return, to fetch the Bride,
And all to heaven ascend.

FOR THE PRINCESS OF WALES[61]

1. O Thou, who dost in secret see,
Regard the hearts bowed down to Thee
And labouring unto prayer:
For One distinguish'd Soul we cry
And bear her burthen to the sky,
And to thy bosom bear.

2. If Thou hast call'd her by her name,
Thy nature in her soul proclaim,
And tell her who thou art:
Appear her bleeding Sacrifice,
And now her inward Saviour rise
Victorious in her heart.

3. Her in affliction's furnace chuse,
And fit the vessel for thy use
By deep humility,
By sacred grief, and godly fear,
By faith unfeign'd, and love sincere,
The mind which was in Thee.

60. ["Affiance" is a rare word. The *Oxford English Dictionary* quotes only one example of
its use between 1741 and 1858.]
61. [MS Misc. Hymns, pp. 145–6.]

4. Detain'd in the Refiner's fire,
   Exalt her every virtue higher,
      Her every grace improve;
   In wisdom train thy servant up,
   In all the patient toils of hope,
      And all the works of love.

5. Then, Lord, in thine appointed hour,
   Call forth the witness of thy power,
      To answer thy design,
   To feed thy Lambs with softest care,
   The ruins of thy Church repair,
      And build the house Divine.

PRAYER FOR MISS HOTHAM
APRIL, 1768[62]

1. Jesus, God of love, appear!
      Whom we to thy grace commend,
   Show thyself her Comforter,
      Visit our afflicted Friend
   By a world of woes opprest,
      Ever pining to depart,
   Languishing for endless rest,
      Dying of a broken heart.

2. Dying, while in pain she lives
      Sad, disconsolate, alone,
   For her old Companion grieves,
      Grieves for all her comforts gone;
   Faints beneath thy heaviest load,
      Dark, and crucified with Thee,
   Cries in death, My God, My God,
      Why hast Thou forsaken me!

3. Saviour, on the cross forsook,
      Hear thy own repeated cry,
   Drawn by her imploring look
      Haste thy precious blood t'apply,

62. [MS Misc. Hymns, pp. 149–50.]

Pour the balm into her soul,
    Balm that bids her anguish cease,
Makes a wounded spirit whole,
    Seals her sure, eternal peace.

4.   Answering to thy Spirit's groan
    In thy suffering members here,
Speak the final word, 'Tis done,
    Faith's almighty Finisher!
When she hath thy griefs fill'd up,
    Perfected thro' patient grace,
Then remove the mortal cup,
    Then reveal thy heavenly Face!

A WIDOW'S PRAYER FOR HER SICK SON (SR. C. H[OTHAM?])[63]

1.   Jesus, friend of the distrest,
    Grant my sorrowful request,
    Melting at a Widow's moan,
    Give me back my only Son:

2.   Snatch'd so often from the grave,
    Him vouchsafe again to save,
    By the prayer of faith restor'd,
    Bid him rise, to serve his Lord;

3.   Willing made for Thee alone
    Still to live, and suffer on,
    Still to droop beneath the skies,
    Still to want his paradise,

4.   Thou in life his soul detain
    Blest with consecrated pain,
    Fill'd with comforts from above,
    Swallow'd up in heavenly love.

63. [MS Misc. Hymns, pp. 150–2. Sir Charles Hotham was seriously ill on a number of occasions. On one of them (before 1756, in which year Sir Charles's wife died) Charles Wesley wrote to his wife Sally telling of his visit to Sir Charles, "just snatched from the brink of the grave. . . . Young Lady Hotham . . . joined me in fervent prayer and love." *Journal of the Rev. Charles Wesley* (London, n.d.), II, p. 259.]

5. By the feeble flesh opprest
    Hide his spirit in thy breast,
    Clothe his soul with vigour new,
    Raise his mortal body too.

6. Nothing is too hard for Thee,
    Thou in our infirmity
    Dost thy perfect strength reveal,
    Heal whom medicine cannot heal.

7. Thou canst animate the dead,
    Grant the weak a stronger thread.
    Nature's wither'd powers repair,
    All thy Name in man declare.

8. God of all-sufficient love,
    On my Son thy nature prove;
    Jesus, evermore the same,
    Mark him with thy saving Name.

9. Kindly minding my request,
    Thou wilt grant whate'er is best,
    Still preserve, and bless thine own,
    Till our earthly work is done.

10. Then Thou wilt thine own receive,
    Happy in thy sight to live,
    Numbred with the Glorified,
    Throned for ever at thy side.

HYMN FOR AN HUSBAND AND WIFE[64]

1. Author, Prince of lasting Peace,
    Us thy ransom'd spirits bless,
    Make us thro' thy grace alone
    One of twain, for ever One.

64. [MS Misc. Hymns, p. 169.]

2. One in will, and heart, and mind,
   Each for each by heaven design'd,
   One with perfect harmony,
   Spiritually one in Thee.

3. Take us both into thy hand
   Subjected to thy command,
   Pleas'd thy easy yoke to prove,
   Happy in our Saviour's love.

4. Shed it in our hearts abroad,
   Speak us reconciled to God,
   Then we to each other cleave,
   Then in heaven on earth we live.

5. Happy in each other then
   We shall by our lives explain
   Love's sublimest mystery,
   Union of thy Church, and Thee:

6. Every word and act shall show
   How Thou lovst thy Church below,
   Folded in thy kind embrace
   How the Church her Head obeys.

WRITTEN IN JULY, 1784
FOR A FRIEND, NEARLY RUINED[65]

1. It is the Lord, whose sovereign will
       Appoints our sanctified distress,
   Employs the instrument of ill
       To circumvent, and spoil, and seize,
   Chaldean, or Sabean bands,
   They execute Divine commands.

65. [MS Misc. Hymns, pp. 205–6. *Cf.* Job. 1:15–17 for verse 1 line 5.]

2. Injur'd, bereav'd—what shall we say?
       He justly doth his own require,
    If what he gave, he takes away
       By fraud, or violence, or fire;
    Whate'er the means, It is the Lord,
    His will be done, his Name ador'd!

3. Not out of earth the trouble springs,
       But comes in mercy from above,
    An heavenly messenger, it brings
       The tokens of a Father's love,
    Who thus his dearest children tries,
    And fits, and takes them to the skies.

4. We know not what estate is best,
       But his unerring goodness knows:
    We might forget, with riches blest,
       From whom our every blessing flows,
    We might to earthly objects cleave,
    And all our comfort here receive.*[66]

5. But God, the jealous God of love,
       Who claims our undivided heart,
    Hath pleas'd our danger to remove,
       And blest with Mary's better part,
    Possessing Him, we still possess
    Our souls in patience, and in peace.

6. Still, gracious Lord, our portion be,
       Be Thou our wealth, we ask no more,
    Happy to know, and worship thee;
       And when the storms of life are o're,
    To find in our Redeemer's breast
    The haven of eternal rest.

66.   *And while to earthly things we cleave
               Our consolation *here* receive.
[Wesley adds these alternative lines to the last two of verse 4 in a footnote.]

II^{67}

1. Searcher of the deceitful heart,
      My heart shall I from Thee disguise,
   Or cloak with false, serpentine art
      What cannot 'scape thy glorious eyes?
   Thine eyes mine inmost substance see,
   Thou knowst, O God, what is in me.

2. Me, Father, to myself make known,
      Reflecting on this evil day,
   That when my follies I bemoan,
      A stragler from the narrow way,
   Thou mayst thy humbled son restore,
   And never let me wander more.

3. Who *will* be rich, (thy word declares,)
      They sorrow for themselves require,
   They fall into temptations, snares,
      And many an hurtful, vile desire,
   Which sink them in th'abyss profound,
   In bottomless perdition drown'd.

4. But who thy warning voice attend,
      Or dare the gilded bait refuse?
   Did I my danger apprehend
      By gain my deathless soul to lose?
   Losing my soul, what shoud I gain,
   But sad remorse, and endless pain!

5. Yet hasting riches to acquire,
      I *have* the giddy chase pursued,
   With eagerness of keen desire
      Join'd the deluded multitude,
   Who headlong to destruction run,
   And die, eternally undone.

67. [MS Misc. Hymns, pp. 206–10.]

6. With sinners I cast in my lot,
       As in a common Cause combin'd,
    Riches, and precious substance sought,
       One with the world in heart, and mind,
    Nor ill, nor harm from Thee I fear'd
    Who neither God nor man rever'd.

7. As beasts that on each other prey,
       By rapine, wiles, and plunder live,
    They dragg'd me down the beaten way,
       With them my portion to receive,
    The fruits of our united toils,
    To gather, and divide the spoils.

8. Pitch coud I touch, and yet be clean,
       In filth and in infection pure?
    Partaker of their sordid sin,
       Yet still insensible, secure,
    I shut my eyes, nor cared to know
    My heart, and treasure were below.

9. But by a Providential stroke
       The Lord hath slain my comforts here,
    Out of my golden dream awoke,
       And stopt me in my mad career,
    Blasted my sure, pernicious aim,
    And pluck'd the brand out of the flame.

10. Arrested, seiz'd by mercy's power,
       The prisoner of the Lord I stand:
    He woud not let the gulph devour,
       But saved me with an outstretch'd hand,
    As in affliction's fire refin'd,
    And glad to leave my dross behind.

11. My wealth, my friends, my plans I leave,
       And looking up for daily bread,
    From a kind Father's love receive
       Whate'er his wisdom knows I need,
    Comforts that from his presence flow,
    And peace which earth cannot bestow.

12.   O God, who hast my manners borne,
          Nor quite exil'd me from thy face,
      Thy Son made willing to return,
          Thy pardon'd Prodigal embrace,
      Again into thy house receive,
      And let me there for ever live.

FOR MISS A. D. (SEPTEMBER, 1784)[68]

1.   Jesus, The promise made by Thee
     We plead, and touching this agree
         To ask it for our friend,
     The help Thou only canst bestow,
     Deliverance from her hellish foe,
         A swift deliverance, send.

2.   The virtues of Thy balmy name,
     Today as yesterday the same,
         In her relief exert;
     The fiend who dares Thy temple seize,
     No longer suffer him to oppress,
         But bid him now depart,

3.   Thou canst with equal ease make whole
     The body, and the sinsick soul,
         Physician of mankind;
     Thy patient, Lord, at once restore,
     Fill'd with the spirit of love and power,
         And of a healthful mind.

4.   Clothed with humility and grace,
     Thy ransom'd, happy handmaid place
         Attentive at Thy feet;
     And never may she thence remove,
     Till spotless in Thy sight above
         She finds her joy complete.

68. [MS Misc. Hymns, pp. 210–11. The poem is found in *Poet. Works*, VIII, p. 421, but is included here as the following poem is incomplete without it.]

[*II*] [69]

1. Or if, our humble faith to try,
   Thy wisdom lingers to comply
     With our too bold request,
   Give us with patience to submit,
   And own, expecting at thy feet,
     Thy time, O God, is best.

2. While mercy wills the kind delay,
   We dare not murmur at thy stay,
     Or faint, and let thee go,
   But wrestle on in ceaseless prayer,
   Till Thou thy mighty arm make bare,
     T'avenge her of her foe.

3. Point out the means if means there be
   Requir'd, to second thy decree;
     But thine it is, to bless;
   The help which upon earth is done,
   Thou dost it, Lord, and Thou alone,
     And givst the whole success.

4. Wherefore to Thee alone we look,
   Stir up thy power, the fiend rebuke,
     Vex the tormenting foe,
   Buffett the buffetter, and chase
   Th'accuser foul to his own place
     Of punishment below.

5. Daughter of Abraham, and Thine,
   The purchase dear of blood Divine
     Command her to be free,
   By Satan's tyranny opprest,
   O speak her suddenly release
     From her infirmity.

69. [MS Misc. Hymns, pp. 211–12.]

6. Manner and time to Thee we leave,
    Only do Thou her sins forgive,
       Her soul with strength supply,
    Upright to walk in all thy ways,
    And live a Vessel of thy grace,
       And for thy glory die.

FOR TWO FRIENDS[70]

1. Agreed, and meeting in thy Name,
       Confiding in thy word,
    We Two thy promis'd Presence claim;
       Jesus, be Thou the Third!

2. Appear, the true eternal Light,
       The Wisdom from above,
    And each to each our hearts unite,
       And mould us into Love.

3. To ask the Grace we humbly join,
       Which Thou art bound to give,
    Let both receive the Love divine,
       Let both Thyself receive.

4. If now thy time be fully come
       The Spirit now impart,
    And give us in our heavenly home
       To see thee as Thou art.

70. [MS Misc. Hymns, pp. 246–7; MS CW III(a) No. 3. In the latter it appears in the form of two eight-lined verses.]

HYMNS FOR SOME CALLED TO EARN THEIR BREAD

II[71]

1.   Come, let us away,
        And his summons obey,
        Who justly demands
    The sweat of our brows, and the work of our hands;
        His acceptable will
        Let us gladly fulfil,
        And rejoice in the Lord,
    Whose service on earth is our present reward.

2.   None on earth can conceive
        How happy we live,
        Who our labour pursue,
    And do unto the Lord whatsoever we do:
        Whene'er with a smile
        He repays all our toil,
        Of his favor possest,
    We an earnest obtain of our heavenly rest.

3.   While earning our bread,
        On the mercy we feed
        Of a God reconcil'd,
    The Father of Mercies in Jesus the Child;
        While he deigns to approve
        Our service of love,
        At his glory we aim,
    And present our Oblations in Jesus's Name.

4.   O Father, impart
        His grace to my heart,
        To the heart of my friends
    And companions in toil, till our pilgrimage ends,

---

71. [MS Misc. Hymns, pp. 274–5; *Rep. Verse*, No. 112, pp. 149–50. There is a draft of the poem in MS CW IV, 74. The first hymn under this title in MS Misc. Hymns also appears in MS Preachers and is printed above on p. 70 with other poems from that MS. The opening verses contain recognizable echoes of the well-known hymn, "Come, let us anew," (*Hymns for New Year's Day* [1750], No. 5), especially lines five and six. See also the poem above on p. 224.]

Till our work is all done,
And receiv'd to thy Throne
Our Redeemer we see
And inherit our heaven of heavens in thee.

III[72]

1. The foe is as a floud come in,
   The world their flattering favors pour!
   To save me from the gainful sin
   To guard me from the prosperous hour,
   Lift up, eternal Spirit of God,
   The Standard stain'd with Jesus' blood.

2. Thro' Thee, superior to their frown,
   Superior to their smile thro' Thee,
   If Thou his dying love make known
   Who bare my sorrows on the tree,
   If Thou the conquering Sign impart,
   And stamp his cross upon my heart,

3. Soon as the slaughter'd Lamb appears,
   Sensible of his blood applied,
   Redeem'd from earthly hopes and fears
   I to the world am crucified,
   The world is crucified to me,
   And Christ, and only Christ, I see.

4. Come then, dear Lord, the love declare
   Which sin, and earth, and hell o'recame,
   That I thy victory may share,
   And kept by thy almighty Name,
   And mounted on thy cross, may rise,
   To see thy glory in the skies.

72. [MS Misc. Hymns, pp. 275–6.]

IV[73]

1. Jesus, if by thy light I see
   That all on earth is vanity,
       And in a moment gone,
   Let me, in outward things employ'd,
   Look thro' the universal void,
       To thy eternal throne.

2. O that redeem'd from worldly cares,
   Superior to my calling's snares
       I might my God pursue,
   Might every nerve and sinew strain,
   Thy grace, and image to regain,
       And keep my End in view.

3. This earth, I know, is not my place,
   And travel thro' the wilderness,
       To fairer worlds on high,
   I seek a permanent abode,
   The city of the living God,
       My mansion in the sky.

4. My one, momentous business here,
   To wait, till Thou with clouds appear,
       And bid thy saints ascend,
   Boldly to stand before thy face,
   And find the Judge of human race
       My Saviour, and my Friend.

5. Saviour and Friend, my soul prepare
   To mount, and meet Thee in the air,
       With all the sons of light,
   To see my bliss-inspiring Lord,
   And gain my infinite reward
       In that transporting Sight.

73. [MS Misc. Hymns, pp. 277–8.]

V[74]

1. While they their calling here pursue,
   Nor keep eternity in view,
   How many to destruction run
   By lawful things alas, undone!

2. They make themselves, not God, their End,
   Themselves, not Him, to serve intend,
   They do not seek his will alone,
   But live, to gratify their own.

3. Intangled in their calling's snares,
   In vain desires, and hurtful cares,
   For wealth's, or pleasure's husks they pine,
   The sordid happiness of swine.

4. They *will* be rich, whate'er betide,
   And Wisdom's warning voice deride,
   Their hope, by toils that never cease,
   To riot in luxurious ease.

5. What are their dreams of bliss below?
   Shadows of joy, and solid woe;
   What is their miserable hire
   When justice doth their souls require?

6. When cited at the bar t'appear
   Whose treasure, & whose hearts were here,
   They wake out of their sleep profound,
   In bottomless perdition drown'd.

VI[75]

1. Warn'd by their fall, we wou'd be wise,
   The world, and all therein despise,
   Things temporal by faith look thro'
   And do for God whate'er we do.

74. [MS Misc. Hymns, pp. 278–9.]
75. [MS Misc. Hymns, pp. 279–80.]

2. Then hear us, O thou gracious God,
Us in external works employ'd.
Into thy kind protection take,
And vessels of thy mercy make.

3. Still let us labour to fulfil
The orders of thy sovereign will,
In all our ways thy guidance own,
And seek to please our God alone.

4. Then may we ever keep in mind
Our six days' work by Thee injoin'd,
Performing with a single eye,
The wants of nature to supply:

5. Not artifical wants to feed,
But earn by toil our daily bread,
Our daily bread from Thee receive,
Not live to eat, but, eat to live:[76]

6. Happy, might we at last obtain
The bread that always doth remain,
And keep at that celestial feast
A sabbath of eternal rest!

VII[77]

1. Father, let thy will be done,
Thine alone I come to do,
(Providentially made known)
Nature's leading I pursue,
Labour for my daily meat,
Earn it from the rich, and great.

---

76. [This saying goes back to classical times. It is attributed to Cicero, *ad Herennium: edere oportet ut vivas, non vivere ut edas.* Socrates is alleged by Athenaeus to have said, "Some live to eat, but I myself eat to live." The editors owe this identification to the kindness of the Rt. Hon. J. Enoch Powell, P.C.]

77. [MS Misc. Hymns, pp. 281–2.]

2. Me if Thou vouchsafe to give
        Grace and favor in their sight,
    Shoud I not with joy receive,
        Thankful in the gift delight,
    Pleas'd my Father's hand to see,
    Happy, that it comes from Thee?

3. Only Thou thy blessing guard,
        Lest I in myself confide,
    While my foolish heart insnar'd
        Yields to self-important pride,
    Lest I swell with vanity,
    Boast of gifts—receiv'd from Thee.

4. Nature's talents to improve,
        Bless me with sufficient grace
    That in wisdom from above
        Humbly I may pass my days,
    Answer the whole will divine,
    Live and die intirely Thine.

FOR ONE SEEKING THE TRUTH [78]

1. God, whom all are bound to fear,
        God, who dost in secret see,
    See thy feeblest worshipper,
        One that woud be led by Thee;
    In the morning of my day,
        Teach me by thy Spirit's light,
    How to find the heavenly way,
        How to worship Thee aright.

2. More inclin'd to ill than good,
        More to error than to truth,
    While my heart is unrenew'd,
        Guide my inexperienc'd youth;
    All the adverse powers controul;
        By thy secret hand restrain,
    Lover of my ransom'd soul,
        Safely lead me up to man.

78. [MS Misc. Hymns, pp. 285–6.]

3. Who thy doctrine woud obey,
        Shall, Thou say'st, thy doctrine know:
    Leave me not to go astray
        Willing in thy paths to go,
    If thy pleasure Thou reveal,
        Light, and strength, if Thou supply,
    Lo, I come to do thy will,
        Come in Thee to live, or die.

4. Help me then to search the word
        Which doth all thy mind contain;
    All thy mind and counsel, Lord,
        To my simple heart explain;
    Small, and mean, in my own eyes,
        Fitted by humility
    Make me to salvation wise,
        Then receive me up to Thee.

ANOTHER[79]

1. Father of light, & God of grace,
    Who woudst that all our ruin'd race
        Shoud know the truth and live,
    A fallen child of Adam, I
    To Thee for saving knowle[d]ge cry,
        Which Thou alone canst give.

2. All we, like sheep, have gone astray,
    Nor can we find the living way,
        Without celestial light:
    Thy Spirit, Lord, vouchsafe to me,
    That I the shining path may see,
        And serve my God aright.

79. [MS Misc. Hymns, pp. 286–7. The poem may be incomplete as the next page is
blank.]

3. Which of a thousand different roads
   Will lead me to those bright abodes,
       Where my Redeemer dwells?
   Father, I woud thy word receive;
   The answer unambiguous give
       From thy own oracles.

4. Thy Spirit doth thy mind explain:
   I ask, and cannot ask in vain,
       That sure, unerring Guide:
   O might that Unction from above
   Inspire with humble faith and love,
       And in my heart reside!

5. Spirit of truth, thy mind he knows,
   Thy mind benevolent he shows
       To humble sinners given,
   He searches the deep things of God,
   And sprinkles that atoning blood
       Which bought my place in heaven.

FOR A SICK FRIEND, (MRS. H.)
APRIL 2, 1786[80]

1. See, Lord, the Cause of our distress,
   Sick of a languishing disease,
       And drawing towards her end,
   Unless thy timely succours come,
   To snatch her from the greedy tomb,
       And give us back our Friend.

2. Convinc'd that thy great will is done,
   We dare not clamour for our own,
       Impatient for her stay:
   But till Thou manifest thy will,
   May we not urge our suit, and still
       For her recovery pray?

80. [MS Misc. Hymns, pp. 313–14. The poem may be incomplete, as space is left for three more verses on the rest of the page.]

3.   Nature in vain woud hide its fears;
    Our sorrows, & too tender tears,
      Our silence speaks to Thee:
    O let thy pleading Spirit explain
    (Who only knowst what is in man)
      This soft infirmity.

4.   This soft infirmity forgive,
    Which asks, that here she still may live,
      May toil, and suffer on,
    Walk in the works for her prepar'd,
    Inhance her infinite reward,
      And win a brighter crown.

THE PRAYER OF A DAUGHTER FOR HER FATHER[81]

1.   Father, accept my fervent prayer,
    While to thy throne of grace I bear
      A much respected Sire;
    Life, endless life for Him I claim,
    And what I ask in Jesus' Name
      With all my soul require.

2.   O for my dear Redeemer's sake
    Let Him the precious faith partake
      Which Thou to me hast given,
    The mountain-obstacles remove,
    And bless him with a taste of love,
      The antepast of heaven.

3.   Thou knowst the burthen of my heart:
    Shall I be blest with Mary's part,
      The meanest handmaid I,
    And shall the man who gave me birth
    Affect the world, and cleave to earth,
      And unconverted die?

81. [MS Misc., 1786 (MS CW III[c]), pp. 5–7.]

4. Forbid it, gracious God, forbid!
    And let th'Incorruptible Seed
        This moment stir within;
    And never suffer him to rest,
    Till of thy pardning love possest
        He lives redeem'd from sin.

5. Still will I wrestle on with Thee,
    With violent importunity
        My instant suit repeat,
    Till thou in mercy cast him down,
    And own him for a pleasant Son
        When weeping at thy feet.

6. Fain woud I weep my life away,
    My life for his a ransom pay;
        But mine cannot suffice;
    More than a thousand worlds it cost
    To save a single sinner lost,
        And bid his soul arise.

7. O might the blood that flow'd for him,
    For me, for all, our souls redeem,
        And speak us up to Thee.
    As vessels of peculiar grace
    To bless thy name and sing thy praise,
        Thro' all eternity.

II^{82}

1. Instruct me, Lord, with tenderest zeal
    Another's weaknesses to feel,
        With wisdom from above,
    A Father, for his good, to please,
    By duty's kindest services
        By all the toils of love.

82. [MS Misc., 1786 (MS CW III[c]), pp. 7–8.]

2. My will I woud to his resign,
In things not contrary to thine,
    And run without delay,
And fly, preventing his desires,
To do whate'er his heart requires,
    And Thee in Him obey.

3. I woud not in a Parent see
Frailties, or faults, which Thou in me
    Dost every day forgive,
But walk (if Thou the grace bestow)
And by my fair example show
    How real Christians live.

4. If Thou my loving labour speed,
I prosper in the pious deed;
    Commission'd by my Lord,
A soul redeem'd from death and sin,
A precious Soul for Thee I win
    And win without the word.

FOR ONE IN A DECLINE (MRS. BULGIN)[83]

1. Lord, in whom I fain woud trust,
Nearest them who need Thee most,
See, the helpless Creature see,
Touch'd with my infirmity.

---

83. [MS Misc., 1786 (MS CW III[c]), pp. 8–9; MS CW I(p) x. The latter has variant readings in shorthand in verses 2, 3, and 6.
Verse 2, lines 3 and 4:

    Let me feel my present aid,
    Lean on Thee my languid head.

Verse 3, line 1: (three alternatives)

    (a) Calmly in thy bosom mourn
    (b) Calmly and resign'd I mourn
    (c) Calmly and submissive mourn

Verse 3, line 2:

    For my loving Lord's return

Verse 6, line 2:

    Thee my only Lord I own.]

2. While I sensibly decline,
    Unassur'd that Thou art mine
    Tired with life, of death afraid,
    Let me feel thy present aid.

3. Calm with meek submission mourn
    For the Comforter's return,
    For the Reconciling Kiss
    Seal of my eternal bliss.

4. When his Coming from above
    Re-assures me of thy love,
    Stamps thine image in my heart,
    Ready am I to depart.

5. Or, if so my Lord ordain,
    Still I in the flesh remain,
    Neither life nor death request,
    Sure whate'er Thou wilt is best.

6. Till thy welcome will is done,
    Hang I on my Lord alone,
    Happy Thine in life to be,
    Happier still to die in Thee.

FOR PATTY TOMS[84]

1. Jesus, help the Woman's Seed,
    Bruiser of the Serpent's Head,
    Help a Soul belov'd by Thee,
    Hated by thine Enemy.

2. Thou hast broke his deadly blow,
    Soul and body to o'rethrow,
    Baffled his malicious will,
    Sinking both at once to kill.

84. [MS Misc. 1786 (MS CW III[c]), pp. 9–11; MS CW I(p) x, and MS CW I(q) xv.]

3. Straitning the old Felon's chain,
   Thou his violence didst restrain,
   Stop the murder-loving Fiend,
   Bid his fierce temptation end.

4. Send the Angels now to chear
   One who cost her Lord so dear,
   One, the Property of God,
   Bought with all her Saviour's blood.

5. Come Thyself, her soul to raise,
   Minister of balmy grace,
   Grace (if Thou Thyself reveal)
   Shall both soul and body heal.

6. Come, and bring her pardon back,
   Whom Thou never wilt forsake,
   Never to the Tempter leave,
   Her into thy arms receive.

7. Make her thy peculiar care,
   Scaped out of the fowler's snare,
   Let him not, approaching nigh,
   Touch the apple of thine eye.

8. With Thyself her life conceal,
   Till Thou dost thy wrath reveal,
   Power omnipotent assume,
   In the clouds to judgment come.

9. Righteous Judge, Thou wilt, we know,
   Soon avenge us of our foe,
   Bruise him underneath our feet,
   Chase to hell, & seal the pit.

10. Then we shall triumphant stand
    With the Sheep on thy right-hand,
    Give the victory to Thee,
    Sing thro' all eternity.

A PRAYER FOR THE REVD. MR. LA-TROBE
GIVEN OVER BY THE PHYSICIANS[85]

1. Lord of life, thy people hear
   For our dying Minister,
   If he is not yet at rest,
   Is not numbred with the Blest;

2. If his soul is on the wing,
   Listning, as the Angels sing,
   Mounting to the realms of light
   Stop the Prophet in his flight:

3. Still his ready soul detain,
   Bring him back to earth again,
   Here to find his works prepar'd
   Gain a more than full reward.

4. If Thou mayst intreated be,
   Hast not fixt the firm decree,
   Let the prayer of faith prevail,
   Turn for life the hovering scale.

5. Wait we now, resign'd and still,
   Till Thou dost declare thy will:
   Lord, not ours be done, but thine,
   Execute thy own design:

6. But when Him Thou dost remove
   Follow'd by his works of love,
   Let the children Thou hast given,
   All pursue their Guide to heaven.

85. [MS Misc., 1786 (MS CW III[c]), pp. 11–12. Benjamin La Trobe, who started out as a Baptist but became a Moravian under the influence of John Cennick, was the minister of a Moravian congregation in Dublin, and died on November 29, 1786. He remained always friendly with Charles Wesley.]

THE PEOPLE'S SALUTATION
OF THEIR MINISTER ESCAPED SHIPWRECK[86]

1.   Welcome from the Rocks and Waves!
     Welcome from the Winds and Seas!
Jesus, who his servant saves,
     Bids us meet again in peace;
Bids us still in Him confide,
     Held in his almighty hand
Till we every storm outride,
     Reach with shouts the heavenly land.

2.   Who his truth and mercy know,
     Passing thro' the watry deep,
Us the flouds cannot or'eflow,
     Safe with Jesus in the ship:
Passing thro' the harmless flame
     We the fiery Test endure,
Triumph in our Saviour's name,
     Make the Prize thro' sufferings sure.

3.   Jesus, dear redeeming Lord,
     On thy Promise we depend,
True and faithful to thy Word,
     Thou shalt save us to the end,
Raise our bodies from the tomb,
     Raise our souls with glory crown'd—
Worthy Judge eternal, come,
     Come, and bid the Trumpet sound!

86. [MS Misc., 1786 (MS CW III[c]), p. 35.]

SUNG FOR THE REVD. J[OHN] W[ESLEY]
AT THE SOCIETY IN BRISTOL
SUNDAY DECEMBER 5, 1779[87]

1. Jesus, thy hated Servant own,
   And send thy glorious Spirit down,
      In answer to our prayers,
   While others curse, & wish him dead,
   Do Thou thy choicest blessings shed,
      And crown his hoary hairs.

2. Not for his death, but life, we pray:
   In mercy lengthen out his day,
      Our venerable Guide;
   LONG MAY HE LIVE, thy flock to keep,
   Protect from wolves the lambs & sheep,
      And in his bosom hide.

3. LONG MAY HE LIVE, for England's Good,
   The Church redeem'd by thy own blood,
      And thro' thy Spirit turn
   Sinners from sin to righteousness,
   While thousands & ten thousands bless
      The day that he was born.

4. LONG MAY HE LIVE, to serve thy cause
   To spread the victory of thy cross,
      To minister thy grace,
   And late, t'augment the Church in heaven,
   With all the Children Thou hast given,
      Appear before thy face.

5. Thou God that answerest by fire,
   With fervent faith & strong desire
      Whom we present to Thee
   Fill with pure love his ravish'd breast,
   And let the Spirit of glory rest
      On all thy Church—& me!

87. [MS CW III(e) 1–2 and MS CW III(a), No.8; MS CW Letters, p. 499, and a broadsheet of The Methodist Archives (Manchester). Verses 1–2 and 4–6 appear in *Poet. Works*, VIII, pp. 415–16, and in Jackson's *Life of Charles Wesley* (1841), II, p. 317. *Cf.* the poems on pp. 443ff., 451ff.]

6. Me, Me, thy meanest Messenger
    Admit his happiness to share;
    And intimately One
    Thro' life, thro' death together guide
    To sing with all the sanctified
    Before thy azure throne!

FOR THE CHURCH OF ENGLAND

III[88]

1.   Founder of thy Church, and Lord
        Of all in earth and heaven,
      Plead we thy unchanging word
        To thy Apostles given.
      We thy constant promise claim
        Thy continual aid implore,
      Lo! with you I always am
        Till time shall be no more.

2.   Still with us of England's Pale
        Thy Presence we confess,
      Never, never can it fail,
        Thy truth and faithfulness:
      Earth and heaven may pass away,
        Firm thy word remains and sure,
      Longer than the night and day
        The Sun & Moon indure.

3.   Our Particular Church contain'd
        We in the General see,
      Challenging, with faith unfeign'd,
        Her Perpetuity:
      In thy mercy's arms embrace
      And bless her children from above
        With the permanence of grace,
        Th'eternity of love.

88. [MS CW III(a) 3–4; MS CW III(c) 36–9. Note the change of metre in verse 3, which is most unusual for Charles Wesley.]

WRITTEN AUGUST 1, 1779[89]

1. God of all grace and patience, hear
   The few that still thy rod revere
      And stoop beneath thy hand,
   Hear, and revoke the dreadful word,
   Nor let the desolating sword
      Go through our sinful land.

2. In haste their measure to fulfil,
   The multitude, mature in ill,
      Mock at Destruction nigh;
   Thy lingring plagues and judgments dare,
   The waste and grievousness of war,
      And all thy threats defy.

3. But chiefly *we* the Scourge require
   And raise thine indignation higher
      Than all the ungodly crowd,
   We who have truly call'd thee Lord,
   And heard the reconciling word,
      And felt the sprinkled blood.

4. What are their sins compared to Ours,
   Who tasted once the heavenly powers
      Begotten from above,
   But did not in thy grace remain?
   Thy grace we have receiv'd in vain,
      And spurned thy richest love.

5. Numbers have left the narrow way
   Regardless of their faith's decay,
      Willing the cross to shun:
   Numbers have lost their single eye
   And sought themselves to magnify
      And not their Lord alone.

---

89. [MS Misc. Hymns, p. 235; MS CW I(s); MS CW III(a) 9. An earlier draft has the title "For the Fast Day, July 30, 1779."]

6. Raised from the people's lowest lees,
    They blush their Master to confess
        By patient poverty,
    No longer small in their own eyes;
    But each above the rest would rise,
        But each would greatest be.

7. Our wine with water mixt, our gold
    Is dim, our charity grown cold;
        The world that loves its own,
    No more as hereticks reject,
    Or brand us, as an odious sect;
        The world and we are One.

8. How can we 'scape the curse extreme
    Unless we all ourselves condemn
        And to our Smiter turn?
    Judgment must at thy house begin,
    Unless our aggravated sin
        With contrite hearts we mourn.

9. Saviour and Prince, enthron'd on high,
    To Thee, our last resource, we cry
        And sue to be forgiven,
    We join our weak desires to Theirs
    Whose prevalent effectual prayers
        Can shut and open heaven.

10. Since Thou hast left thyself a seed
    Who ceaseless for our Sodom plead
        With Abraham's faith endued,
    Hear Thy own Spirit's cry in Them
    And from a double death redeem
        The guilty multitude.

11. Our prayers presenting with thine own,
    Our Advocate before the throne,
        Obtain for us the grace,
    Bid a rebellious nation live,
    And to the righteous remnant give
        Our whole devoted race.

12. So will we praise and magnify
    The Lord of Hosts, the Lord most high,
        Our Saviour-Prince above,
    Extol thy glorious majesty
    And give our hearts entire to Thee,
        Th'Almighty God of love.

II[90]

1. Jesus, believing in thy Name,
   May we not now the Promise claim
       For One so justly dear,
   So greatly by thyself belov'd
   By twice ten thousand Seals approv'd
       Thy honour'd Messenger?

2. Permit him not to start aside,
   Nor let his latest footsteps slide
       By men, or fiends o'rethrown:
   Screen him from every fiery dart,
   And guard his unsuspicious heart
       Till all his work is done.

3. Thro' life the Servant of thy will,
   He cannot knowingly do ill,
       In heart he cannot err,
   But flatter'd, and surpriz'd may be,
   And drawn by fond Credulity
       Into the Fowler's snare.

4. The Foe in an unguarded hour
   May urge him thro' the love of power
       At higher things to aim,
   A Croud of Followers to collect,
   And form[91] into a purer Sect
       And call them by his Name.

90. [MS CW III(a) 11; MS CW III(e) 9. The poem is clearly for Charles's brother John.
See especially verse 4.]
    91. [In the margin "mould" is written as an alternative to "form."]

5. Has Satan the advantage got?
    The Servant by the Tempter caught
        Thou only canst set free,
    Canst strip the Fiend of his disguise,
    Open our Guide's unwitting eyes,
        And force the Blind to see.

6. This moment put him, Lord, in fear
    Of danger, & Destruction near,
        (If prosper'd Saints presume,)
    Of pride that swells aspiring worms,
    Of Error in a thousand forms,
        And endless ills to come.

7. Show him the Enemy's Design,
    An hoary minister of thine
        Against his God t'employ,
    As Author of a causeless Rent
    To make thy gracious Instrument
        Thy gracious work destroy.

8. Convinc'd his foot hath slipt, uphold,
    And bring him back into the Fold,
        The Shepherd and the Sheep;
    And safe within thy arms of Love
    One with thy Family above
        Our Church for ever keep.

A MIN[ISTE]R'S PRAYER[92]

1. Shepherd of Souls, for whom alone
        I spend my happy Days,
    To make thy faithful mercies known,
        And minister thy grace;

92. [MS Richmond, pp. 102–3. Verses 2 and 7 were never written.]

2.

3.   The little flock of feeble sheep,
      Thou hast by me brought in,
   Out of the reach of Satan keep,
      Out of the reach of sin.

4.   I ask thee not to take them hence
      But keep them safe from harms,
   And still extend for their defence
      Thine everlasting arms.

5.   The stumbling block of self & pride
      Far from their path remove,
   Their souls from every idol hide,
      From every creature-love.

6.   Ah! leave them not in error's maze
      Far from thy paths to rove,
   Thou GOD of all-redeeming grace,
      Of all-renewing love.

7.

8.   O might I all present to Thee
      With that triumphant boast,
   The children these thou gav'st to me,
      And not a soul is lost.

[O MAY I NEVER TAKE THE PRAISE][93]

O may I never take the praise
    Or my own glory spread,
If made thy instrument to raise
    A sinner from the dead.
O may I never boast my own
    Successful ministry,
But sink forgotten and unknown
    And swallow'd up in Thee.

FOR ONE IMPRISONED FOR RIGHTEOUSN[ES]S' SAKE[94]

1.   Father of everlasting grace,
     Thy awful Providence we own,
    Holy & just are all thy ways,
     Thy name be prais'd, thy will be done.

2.   Thy wise permissive will be bliss
     Which lets the sons of night succeed,
    With lawless might thy serv[an]t seize
     And trample on his guiltless head.

3.   By Satan into prison cast,
     His bonds thy gospel shall proclaim,
    And thou shalt bring him forth at last,
     In honour of thy glorious name.

4.   Lord, we believe against his foes,
     Thou soon shalt laugh their rage to scorn,
    Confound who thee & thine oppose,
     And all their hellish strength o'return.

93. [The MS is found in a scrap book of the Rev. A. E. Farrar at The Methodist Archives (Manchester), p. 111. This poem appears in *Short Hymns*, II, p. 218, based on Luke 8:56 with one minor variant in line three: "thine" for "thy." In *Poet. Works*, XI, p. 178, however, Osborn printed a version in a different metre; therefore, the above version is included here.]

94. [MS Richmond, pp. 114–15. The poem appears to be incomplete, as the remainder of p. 115 is blank to the bottom with space for four verses.]

FOR A BACKSLIDER[95]

1. O helper of sinners distrest,
   To thee in a moment of hope
   I make my imperfect request,
   And feebly for mercy look up;
   I live, to recover thy grace,
   Thy favour & mercy to meet,
   To see the bright beams of thy face,
   And joyfully die at thy feet.

2. Ah! look not at what I have done,
   Remember offences no more,
   But send me the Comforter down
   My forfeited peace to restore.
   The pardon I once had in thee,
   O write it again on my heart,
   And then from my prison set free,
   And bid me in triumph depart.

FOR OUR ENEMIES[96]

1. Let GOD arise & let his foes
   Who fiercely Him & His oppose
   Be scatter'd far away!
   Thou, Jesus, on our side appear
   And bring thy great salvation near,
   And answer, while we pray.

2. Rebuke their proud tyrannic boast,
   Who vaunting ag[ains]t Israel's host
   Do Israel's GOD defy;
   Thee in thy people they reproach,
   And touching us, presume to touch
   The Apple of thine eye.

95. [MS Richmond, p. 120.]

96. [MS Richmond, p. 125. The poem is incomplete as indicated by Wesley's number 5 for an additional verse which he did not write.]

3. Who persecute the sons of light,
    And kick against the pricks, & fight
        Against their Maker-GOD,
    Bow down beneath thine Anger's Wei[gh]t,
    Convince them of their lost Estate,
        And shew them to thy Blood.

4. No farther let their Rage proceed,
    Arise, & bruise the Serpent's Head,
        Who bruises now thy Heel;
    Thou knowst thy feeble Followers' Pain,
    For Thou dost all our Griefs sustain,
        And all our Sorrows feel.

5.

FOR THE TRAVELLER[97]

Beneath thy kind protection keep
    Whoe'er by land their way pursue,
Or tempt the dangers of the deep,
    O let them there thy wonders view,
Held in the hollow of thy hand,
Brought thro' a thousand deaths to land.

FOR THE FATHERLESS AND WIDOWS[98]

1. Relieve whoe'er thy succour need,
        A father to the orphans be,
    Who dost the hungry ravens feed,
        Provide for all that cry to thee,
    The poor and fatherless defend,
    Their sure, their everlasting friend.

97. [MS Drew.]
98. [MS Drew, the page is numbered 26.]

2. The widows desolate, distrest,
        Into thine arms of mercy take,
    And tell them leaning on thy breast
        Thou never wilt the soul forsake
    Whose humble faith in thee receives
    An husband that forever lives.

FOR A SLUGGARD[99]

1. 'A little more delicious sleep,'
        The self-indulgent Sluggard cries,
    'Mine eyes I cannot open keep,
        I cannot find the heart to rise.'

2. He folds his arms to rest again,
        Talents, and life he thus employs,
    And sinking into endless pain,
        Body, estate, and soul destroys.

3. His slumbers loth to discompose
        He rests secure, insensible
    (As if to God he nothing owes)
        Sleeps out his time, and wakes in hell!

4. But here Thou mayst awake, and call,
        Sleeper, upon the pardning God,
    Who died, and offers life to all,
        Who pitying sees thee in thy blood.

5. Now, Saviour, now thy latest cries
        Repeat; thy quickning word, Forgive,
    And bid the slumbring soul arise,
        And bid the twice-bad sinner live;

6. Live to employ thy gifts aright,
        His precious moments to improve,
    Blameless to walk before thy sight,
        And pay Thee back thy dying love.

99. [MS Misc., 1786 (MS CW III[g]), p. 16.]

HYMNS FOR MALEFACTORS

FIRST
HYMN FOR A CONDEMNED MALEFACTOR[1]

1. Suffer'd a few more hours to live,
   Before I my deserts receive,
     And justice satisfy,
   Unless my stubborn heart relent,
   Dying, unless I first repent,
     I must for ever die.

2. Yet careless on the brink of hell,
   I no remorse, or sorrow feel,
     No fear or guilty shame;
   Stupid to my own place I go
   To lift my haggard eyes below
     In that tormenting flame,

3. Devils my parting soul surround,
   To plunge me in the gulph profound,
     The bottomless abyss,
   And the great God's eternal Son,
   A Prince and Saviour on his throne,
     My lost condition sees.

4. He sees, and if he pities too
   He can incarnate fiends subdue,
     The fiends of Adam's race,
   He surely can show forth on me
   Whose all is sin and misery
     Th'omnipotence of grace.

5. His heart, constrain'd by love divine,
   To touch, and turn, and soften mine
     Was ready long ago:
   And if his love *my* heart constrain,
   I, after death may live again,
     And my Redeemer know.

1. [MS Malefactors (MS CW I[h]), pp. 1–2.]

6.   Here then I at his footstool lie,
    To catch the influence of his eye,
      His blessing to partake,
    If in himself a Cause he find
    To save the basest of mankind
      For his own mercy sake.

FOR CONDEMNED MAL[EFACTO]RS[2]

1.   Jesus, to Thee in faith we cry
    For sinners justly doom'd to die;
    Wisdom and Power Divine Thou art
    And greater than their stubborn heart.

2.   Author of penitential woe
    That These the contrite grace may know,
    Thy wrath against their sin reveal,
    Thy wrath, the Antepast of hell.

3.   Now let them feel the torturing fear
    And tremble at damnation near,
    O'rewhelm'd with horrible affright
    And plunging in eternal night.

4.   With grief their flinty bosoms tear,
    With hate of sin, & just despair,
    Which calls on rocks to hide their shame
    And screen them from the Angry Lamb.

5.   While wounded by thy Spirit's sword,
    They sink into the pit abhor'd,
    One ray of hope, in pity, dart
    And chear in death the broken heart:[3]

2. [MS Malefactors (MS CW I[h]), p. 12.]
3. [As the poem ends with a colon, it is apparently incomplete.]

FOR CONDEMNED MALEFACTORS[4]

1. Jesus, the Crucified for all,
      Thy followers, on thy Name we call,
        Thy mercy we implore,
      For These our guilty brethren plead,
      So soon to sink among the dead,
        And to be seen no more.

2. Made, and redeem'd by Love divine,
      Their precious Souls are doubly Thine,
        Originally good;
      And shall their precious souls be lost?
      More than a thous[an]d worlds they cost,
        They cost Thee all thy blood.

3. Wilt Thou thy Property forego,
      And leave them to thy ancient Foe,
        Who waits to seize his prize,
      And torture them in his own hell,
      Doom'd to the fire unquenchable,
        The worm that never dies!

4. They have his faithful Servants been
      And claim the wages of their sin,
        Yet still belong to Thee;
      Thou hast a ransom found & paid,
      For all their sins atonement made
        And bought them on that tree!

5. That tree Thou never ca[n]st forget
      Where, loaded with the general debt,
        Thou didst our sorrows bear,
      That These, the Outcasts of mankind,
      The gracious benefits might find
        Of thy expiring prayer.

4. [MS Malefactors (MS CW I[h]), pp. 14–15.]

6. Then help them with their parting breath
   To plead the meritorious death
      That a dead world might live:
   O let thy Spirit take their part
   And cry in every broken heart,
      'My Lord and God, forgive!'

FOR A CONDEMNED MALEFACTOR[5]

1. By violence from the body driven,
      Where shall my naked soul appear?
   A sinner, dying unforgiven,
      I but begin my sufferings here.

2. Soon as I take my gloomy flight
      Vengeance will seize its destin'd prey,
   And bound in chains of darkest night
      Reserve me to that dreadful day.

3. All the foul secrets of my heart
      And life that dreadful day shall show,
   And God condemn me to depart
      Accurst into eternal woe.

4. A moment here I still remain
      (Before the Judge hath sentence past,)
   T'escape th'intolerable pain,
      The pain which shall for ever last.

5. They tell me, who the Judge have known,
      Divinely good, humanely kind,
   If I my sins and merits own,
      Mercy ev'n I may hope to find.

6. They tell me, that my dying cry
      For mercy He this moment hears,
   And at the throne of God most high
      The sinner's Advocate appears.

5. [MS Malefactors (MS CW I[h]), pp. 16–17.]

7. Jesus, Jehovah, God supreme,
       I all my crimes to Thee confess,
    From sin and endless death redeem,
       Forgive, & bid me die in peace.

8. My trust is in thy blood alone,
       Whom I my Lord and God adore:
    Thy will concerning me be done:
       In life & death I ask no more.

EPITAPHS
AND OTHER
POEMS ON DEATH

AN EPITAPH ON EDWARD HEARNE OF MONMOUTH, WHO DIED APRIL 28, 1776[1]

Stranger to Vice, with early grace imbued,
The pious youth his Saviour's steps pursued:
Pursued, a zealous Follower of his Lord,
A mother labouring for her full reward:
Traced her from earth, by lawless violence driven,
And found the martyred Saint enshrined in heaven.

EPITAPH TO MRS. LINNELL OF WHITTLEBURY, THEN OF BRAMPTON, CUMB[ERLAND][2]

This silent grave, it doth embrace
A virtuous wife with Rachel's comely face,
Sarah's obedience, Lydia's open heart,
Martha's good care, and Mary's better part.

Adieu! dear Linnell! from the shades of night
Thy passage swift into the realms of light.
Hard was thy conflict, but thy pains are o'er
And trouble never shall oppress thee more.

---

1. [*Arminian Magazine* (1781), p. 344; MS Death, p. 111. MS Death has the title: "Epitaph (at Monmouth), Here rest the Ashes of Edward Hearne who finished his Christian course Apr. . . ." The grave of Edward Hearne is no longer to be found in St. Mary's churchyard, Monmouth, but W. E. Welch in his *History of Monmouth Methodism* (1891) quotes this epitaph (with variants) as being on a stone which "formerly stood in the east end of the churchyard." In the 1770's there was no law for Methodists in Monmouth. In 1780 Zachariah Yewdall commented, "When I returned to Monmouth at one month's end one of our friends was almost killed by a stone from the rioters which struck him on the head."]

2. [This epitaph is really two: the second "Adieu, dear Linnell!" is on the headstone of the grave of William Linnell in Brampton Old Churchyard, Cumberland. William Linnell of Crow Hall, who died on February 23, 1779 at age 36, served for a time as one of Wesley's preachers. The first verse is for his wife Eleanor, but it must have been composed before her death, as she died in 1791. Charles Wesley died in 1788. The Rev. Colin D. Harbach has kindly verified that the second verse is no longer to be seen.]

AN EPITAPH ON THE DEATH OF MR. CHARLES PERRONET[3]

Here lies, who late a living emblem lay
Of human greatness, in a tent of clay;
A pilgrim, wandring through this desart wild,
Weak as a Reed, and helpless as a Child: *4*
Whose strengthen'd arm by Faith untaught to yield,
Oft foil'd the Tempter, and maintain'd the field.
In wars without, in warring fears within,
He conquer'd Terror as he conquer'd Sin;   *8*
Look'd for himself to Him, whose potent breath
Can light up Darkness, or extinguish Death:
Dart from his eye destruction on the foe,
And make hell tremble as she hears the blow: *12*
He look'd, and found what all who look receive,
Strength to resist, and Virtue to believe;
Meek, to endure and suffer from his God
The tender chast'nings of a Father's rod: *16*
While thus corrected, as by Pain refin'd
His spirit groan'd to leave its dross behind:
The dross is left—no more his spirit mourns,
But spreads her wings, and to her Ark returns: *20*
Great Ark of Rest—the sufferer's bright abode;
The Arms of Jesus, and the Ark of God!

IN MEMORY OF MR. CHARLES PERRONET, WHO DIED ON MONDAY, AUGUST 12, 1776, AGED 53[4]

Farewell! thou Man of complicated strife,
Thou heir immortal of immortal life!
Protracted years of long protracted pain
Were *here* thy portion—but are *now* thy gain.

3. [*Arminian Magazine* (1783), p. 336. This text appears in the *Gospel Magazine*, edited by A. Toplady, for September, 1776, p. 434 with the heading "The Epitaph" and concluding with the benediction, "Blessed are the dead that die in the Lord." In the *Gospel Magazine* version there is a variant reading in line nine: from himself. Did both this and the following poem circulate in manuscript form so that a copy reached Toplady quite early?]

4. [*Arminian Magazine* (1783), p. 224. This text also appears in the *Gospel Magazine*, for September, 1776, p. 434, with the heading, "In the midst of life we are in death." How did Toplady come across it so soon after Perronet's death on Aug. 12?]

Who tried thy patience has refined its dross,
To bear his image as it bore his cross.

Yet not thy hope of pardon, or its crown,
From sorrows suffered, or from duties done:
This all from Him—whose everlasting grace
Became thy ransom, as it bought thy peace.

This all thy life, this all thy death confest,
That 'Christ was all—and Refuse all the rest:'
Even Him—on whom as *first* and *last* depend,
Where grace shall work, and how that work shall end.

EPITAPH FOR MR. THOMAS GARFORTH[5]

Lover of every Sect, attach'd to none,
But Those in all who clave to Christ alone,
For more than thirty years his even race
He ran, a witness of redeeming grace: 4
For twenty more intrusted with the word
He preach'd, and liv'd the doctrine of his Lord,
His loving faith by works of mercy show'd,
By giving all his time, and goods to God: 8
But lo, in perfect peace, meet for the skies,
An hoary Saint, he bows his head and dies,
In Christ he dies, a full reward receives,
And in his Saviour's Sight the life of glory lives!   12

ON THE DEATH OF PRUDENCE BOX, JAN. 9, 1777[6]

1.   HE's come!—to set the prisoner free,
        The dear Redeemer's come!
     To give the final victory,
        And take his Servant home;
     To wipe the sorrow from her eyes,
        To end her mourning days,
     And shew her soul the glorious prize,
        In his unclouded Face.

---

5. [MS Death, p. 113. Is this perhaps Mr. Thomas Garforth of Skipton?]
  6. [MW CW I(p) ii; MS Death, p. 89. Verses 1–4 and 6–8 appear with variations in *Poet. Works* VI, pp. 399ff. Verse 6 would appear to be a later version of verse 5.]

2. Long in the toils of death she lay,
      Nor fear'd the ghastly king,
    When Christ had borne her sins away,
      And spoil'd him of his sting:
    Ling'ring she drank the bitter cup
      Of grief and pain extreme,
    And fill'd his after-passion[7] up
      And *tasted* death with Him.

3. Seeing the great Invisible
      Her Saviour and her Friend,
    She suffer'd all his righteous will,
      And suffer'd to the end:
    Thro' a long vale of misery
      She walk'd with Christ her Guide,
    And bleeding on the sacred tree
      Confess'd the Crucified.

4. With all the Spirit's powers she pray'd
      With infinite desire,
    To bow her weary, fainting head,
      And on his cross expire:
    The agonizing prayer was heard,
      For everlasting peace:
    While yet her gracious Lord defer'd
      To sign her soul's release.

5. She languishes, in life detain'd,
      Superior grace to prove,
    Unshaken hope and faith unfeign'd,
      And all-victorious love.
    Love, heavenly love, her heart o'reflows
      Immense and unconfin'd
    To friends & relatives & foes
      Imbracing all mankind.

6. He holds her, still in life detain'd,
      Her ripen'd grace to prove
    Her stedfast hope and faith unfeign'd,
      And all-victorious love:

7. [*Cf.* Colossians 1:24.]

To emulate his sacrifice,
    Obtain a richer crown,
And point us to the opening skies,
    And pray the Saviour down.

7. "Unutterable things I see—
        The purchase of his blood,
    The place He hath reserv'd for me,
        Come, O my Lord, my God!
    I dare not murmur at thy stay;
        But to depart is best:
    Come, O my Jesus, come away,
        And take me into rest.

8. "Into thy hands my soul receive,
        That Thee my soul may bless,
    May Thee entirely love, and live
        To thine eternal praise."
    She speaks, and hears the joyful word,
        "Come up, my ready bride,"
    And angels waft her to her Lord
        And seat her at his side!

ON THE DEATH OF MRS. GWYNNE[8]

1. Rejoice, ye happy spirits above,
    Another thro' the Saviour's love
        Is added to your quire:
    Redeem'd from earth, and great distress,
    She comes t'inhance your happiness
        And raise your raptures higher.

2. Detain'd in a long vale of tears,
    She suffer'd out her seventy years
        With patient grace indued,
    Servant of all, for others liv'd,
    And no reward from man receiv'd
        But black ingratitude.

8. [MS CW Letters, I, 65, p. 107. After the title is added in another hand, "of Garth, Mother of Mrs. S. Wesley." Another MS of this poem is at Drew University in Charles Wesley's handwriting. Mrs. Gwynne died on January 3, 1770.]

3. All her delight and joy below
    Requir'd by Mercy to forego,
        With her last hope to part,
    Father, she cried, thy will be done,
    And urg'd by a beloved Son*[9]
        The dagger reach'd her heart!

[HAIL THE SAD MEMORABLE DAY][10]

1. Hail the sad[11] memorable day
        On which my Isaac's soul took wing!
    With us he *would* no longer stay,
        But soaring where Archangels sing,
    Join'd the Congratulating Quire,
    And swell'd their highest Raptures higher.

2. His soul, attun'd to heavenly Praise,
        Its strong, celestial Bias shew'd,
    And fluttering to regain its place,
        He broke the Cage, & reach'd his GOD.
    He pitch'd in yon bright realms above,
    Where all is Harmony & Love.   &c.

FOR MYSELF[12]

1. 'Tis finished! O Almighty Love,
        Accept our everlasting praise!
    Our friend is safe arrived above,
        Hath hardly won the doubtful race;
    But all his toils at last are o're,
    And sorrow's Son shall weep no more.

9. *The Death of her Son Roderick, Governor of Tobago.
10. [MS CW Letters, I, p. 232, and in Jackson's *Life of Charles Wesley* (1841), vol. II, p. 60. The poem was written on the first anniversary of the death of their firstborn son, aged one year, four months, and seven days, in a letter from Brecon dated Jan. 7, 1754/5. The poem is incomplete as indicated by "&c" at the end of line 6, verse 2.]
11. [In the margin "glad" is written as an alternative to "sad."]
12. [MS Wesley Family Papers. The poem is not in Charles Wesley's handwriting but by the mother of G. Howden, copied from a paper in Wesley's writing found in Miss Sally Wesley's pocketbook. The poem is incomplete.]

2. He is, he is at last possest
    Of that for which so long he pin'd;
The happy soul hath found its Rest,
    Left all its Tears and Griefs behind,
Weather'd the Storm, escaped the wave,
And dropped his Burden in the Grave.

ON THE DEATH OF ALEXANDER HARFORD, WHO DEPARTED THIS LIFE JANUARY 24, 1783[13]

1. And is the happy moment come,
    When Jesus hath recalled thee home,
        And wiped off every tear?
And must we part, no more to join,
Till all who tread the path divine
        Shall with their Lord appear?

2. Go, happy saint, by Jesus blessed,
Of all That happiness possessed
    Thy Saviour hath in store;
Thy conflicts now for ever past,
And thou from earth escaped at last
    Hast reached the heavenly shore.

3. A blessing to the church below,
He longed that all the truth might know,
    And all its sweetness prove;
He by example spread around
The precious faith himself had found,
    The faith that works by love.

4. Long in affliction's furnace tried,
But still with heavenly grace supplied,
    He bowed beneath the rod;
Resigned to his Redeemer's will,
Desirous always to fulfil
    The pleasure of his God.

13. [*Arminian Magazine* (1784), p. 59.]

5. He testified to all around
   The happiness in Jesus found,
       And praised his loving Lord;
   While in excruciating pain,
   Did heavenly consolation gain,
       Relying on his word.

6. Thus longing for the welcome word,
   And wishing to behold his Lord,
       The happy prisoner lay;
   Till Jesus did his convoy send,
   Who bore the spirit of our friend,
       To realms of endless day.

7. Supported by the power of grace,
   May we behold the Saviour's face,
       To wonder and adore;
   From him receive the glorious prize,
   And claim our mansion in the skies,
       Where parting is no more.

ON THE DEATH OF DR. [JOHN] MIDDLETON, DEC. 16, 1760[14]

1. Glory to the Redeemer give,
       The glory of a soul brought home;
   Our friend, for whom we joy and grieve,
       Is to th'eternal garner come.
   Like a ripe shock of corn laid up,
       In season due, for God mature,
   He kept the faith, held fast his hope,
       And made his crown through sufferings sure.

2. Let infidels and heathen mourn,
       Hopeless to see their dead restor'd;
   We *feel* him from our bosom torn,
       But calmly say, "It is the Lord!"

14. [MS Death, p. 12. Verses 1–6 and 10–12 appear in *Poet. Works*, VI, pp. 300–2.]

In pity of His creature's pain,
  Whom God hath to th'afflicted given,
He justly claims His own again,
  And takes to his reward in heaven.

3. Let us the shining path pursue,
      And, following him, to God ascend,
    His bright example keep in view,
      His useful life and blessed end.
    He lived a life of faith unfeign'd,
      His rigid virtue unsubdued,
    His strict integrity maintain'd,
      And boldly own'd—he fear'd a God.

4. O when shall we his equal find,
      To all so just, to all so dear!
    The pious son, the husband kind,
      The father good, the friend sincere!
    Not David lov'd his friend so well,
      Loath from his Jonathan to part,
    Or serv'd him with so warm a zeal,
      Or held him in so fond a heart.

5. Yet in no narrow bounds confin'd,
      His undisguis'd affection flow'd:
    His heart, enlarg'd to all mankind,
      Render'd to all the love he ow'd:
    But chiefly those who lov'd his Lord,
      Who most of Jesu's mind express'd,
    Won by their lives without the word,
      He cherish'd in his generous breast.

6. Cover'd with honourable shame,
      He mark'd the poor, afflicted few,
    The faithful followers of the Lamb,
      In life and death to Jesus true:
    Rejected and despis'd of men,
      He heard the saints departing sing;
    He saw them smile in mortal pain,
      And trample on the grisly king.

7. Not biass'd by a party zeal,
        Their unsought advocate he stood,
    "The men who live and die so well,
        Howe'er decried, they must be good:"
    Happy his tenderest help t'afford,
        A servant of salvation's heirs,
    He look'd on earth for no reward,
        And ask'd no payment "but their prayers."

8. In part, before he reach'd the sky
        He found his loving labour *paid*,
    He found their prayers return from high
        In blessings on his hoary head:
    Warn'd of his dissolution near,
        He miss'd that Witness from above
    Or felt him in distrusting fear
        And not in sweet forgiving love.

9. The God unknown his Servant knew
        Long in the school of *Moses* tried;
    The sin-convincing Spirit blew,
        And wither'd all his virtuous pride:
    With publicans and harlots now
        He comes, the sinner's Friend to meet,
    By grace subdued, and taught to bow
        A leper poor at Jesu's feet.

10. While weeping there the sinner lay,
        Asunder sawn by hopes and fears,
    He cast, as filthy rags, away,
        The righteousness of seventy years:
    Loathsome, and foul, and self-abhorr'd,
        Full of all sin, void of all good,
    His soul at the last gasp implor'd
        One drop of that atoning blood.

11. Nor yet the peaceful answer came;
        His spirit, to the utmost tried,
    Must suffer all his guilty shame,
        Condemn'd, and scourg'd, and crucified;

Must all his Saviour's sorrows share,
    And cry, as bleeding on the tree,
As in the depths of self-despair,
    "My God hath quite forsaken me!"

12.   "Not so," replied the Father's love,
    And Jesus in his heart reveal'd;
He felt the comfort from above,
    The gospel-grace, the pardon seal'd:
How strange that instantaneous bliss,
    While to the brink of *Tophet* driven,
Caught up, as from the dark abyss,
    He mounted to the highest heaven!

III
ON THE DEATH OF MR. JOHN MATTHEWS, DEC. 28, 1764[15]

1.   Blessing, and thanks, and power, and praise,
    Jesus is worthy to receive,
Who keeps His saints throughout their days,
    And doth the final victory give!
He hath his faithful mercies shown
    To him whose loss we now deplore,
Safe enter'd on that land unknown,
    To weep, and fret, and die no more.

2.   A servant in his earliest years,
    After the hidden God he griev'd,
Till from his Saviour's messengers
    The welcome tidings he receiv'd.
His alms and prayers were not in vain,
    But rose acceptable to heaven;
And God assur'd the pious man
    His sins were all through Christ forgiven.

15. [MS Death, p. 21; MS CW I(p) vi. Verses 1–7 appear in *Poet. Works,* VI, pp. 308–10. Parts II and III follow on pp. 310–15.]

3. O what a mighty change was wrought,
      By Jesus in his heart reveal'd!
    'Tis past the reach of human thought,
      That peace which spake his pardon seal'd:
    As quite exempt from sin and care,
      He feasted with the saints above;
    And all his life was praise and prayer,
      And all his soul was joy and love.

4. Long he on Tabor's top abode,
      His Pattern there, and patient Head
    The perfect way through sufferings show'd,
      And to the cross His follower led:
    'Twas there he learn'd with Christ to die,
      And daily languish'd on the tree,
    And echoed back the plaintive cry,
      "Why hath my God forsaken me?"

5. Yet not forsook, but sorely tried,
      But pain'd throughout the evil day,
    And fashion'd like the Crucified,
      He never cast his shield away:
    Chose in the furnace of distress,
      Kept by the power of Jesu's name,
    He highly priz'd the passive grace,
      And prais'd his Saviour in the flame.

6. Witness his old companions there,
      How close in Jesu's steps he trod,
    The man of diffidence and prayer,
      The humble, upright man of God!
    Happy if all their faith could prove
      Like him, like him their Lord confess,
    By every work of genuine love,
      By mercy, truth, and righteousness!

7. A doer of the word he heard,
      He *liv'd* an *Israelite* unseen,
    And always bless'd, who always fear'd,
      Not the reproach, but praise, of men:

Not all the visits from his Lord,
 The favours or the grace bestowed,
Could tempt to one vainglorious word,
 Or make him witness, "I am good!"

8. Five hundred witnesses arose,
 In proof of instantaneous grace,
And each his own perfection *knows*,
 And *simply* utters his own praise!
Th'impeccable, immortal band
 Intirely pure, intirely new,
His sudden, full assent demand
 "And he shall then be perfect too!"

9. Cautious their sayings he receiv'd,
 Nor fondly fed their secret pride,
Nor weakly every spirit believ'd,
 Till in the sacred balance tried:
The language of their lives he heard,
 Their sufferings, and their tempers *prov'd*,
And waiting till the fruit appear'd,
 He saw them short; yet still he lov'd.

10. His wary, quick, judicious eye
 Look'd every self-deceiver thro',
But pass'd the imperfections by
 Of people, and of preachers too:
Paternal faults he woud not see;
 O'er failings in a saint indeed,
O'er wrinkles of infirmity
 His pious love the mantle spred.

IV
ON THE DEATH OF MRS. HANNAH BUTTS[16]

PART II

1. Sinners she with pity saw
     Of their own perfection proud,
   Pleas'd the public eye to draw,
     Forward, turbulent, and loud,
   Witnesses of their own grace,
     "Instantaneously secure,
   "Choicest of the chosen race,
     "Pure at once, intirely pure!"

2. Calm from such she turn'd away
     Left them to their God unknown,
   Them to judge she coud not stay,
     Busied with herself alone;
   Free from proud, or bitter zeal,
     Nature's wild or fierce excess,
   Studying to be quiet, still,
     Still she kept her love and peace.

3. Walking in her house with God,
     Portion'd with the better part,
   She her faith by actions show'd,
     Martha's hand and *Mary's* heart:
   Labouring on from morn to night,
     Still she offer'd up her care,
   Pleasing in her Saviour's sight,
     Sanctified by faith and prayer.

4. Taught of God Himself to please,
     Daily she fulfill'd His word,
   In her meanest services
     Ministering unto the Lord:
   Happy if her constant smile
     Might but ease the sufferer's load,
   Soften a companion's toil,
     Win her little ones to good.

16. [MS Death, pp. 35–6; MS CW I(o) xviii-xxiv. Verses 4–6 appear in *Poet. Works*, VI, pp. 335–6. Part I is found on pp. 333–5 and Part III on pp. 336–8.]

5.   Gently she their will inclin'd,
          Diligent her house to build,
     Wisely, rationally kind,
          With Divine discretion fill'd:
     Far remov'd from each extreme,
          Conscious why her babes were giv'n,
     Heirs of bliss, she liv'd for them,
          Liv'd to train them up for heaven.

6.   Principled with faith unfeign'd,
          Bless'd with Jesu's quiet mind,
     Every part she well sustain'd,
          Bright in every function shin'd:
     Simple love, with lowly fear,
          Kept possession of her breast,
     Made her every act appear
          Wisest, virtuousest, best.

X
ON THE DEATH OF THE PRINCESS DOWAGER[17]

1.   Glory to God above,
          Whose mercy's arms receive
     The Object of his constant love
          With Him inthron'd to live,
     Beyond our world of care,
          In mansions of the blest:
     The wicked cease from troubling there,
          The weary are at rest.

2.   Long in the conflict, long
          Appointed to sustain
     With meekest awe th'outrageous wrong,
          The soul-afflicting pain,
     She drank the hallow'd cup
          Which Jesus once desir'd,
     And fill'd his mournful measure up
          And on his cross expir'd.

17. [MS Death, p. 69. The Princess Dowager was Princess Augusta of Saxe-Gotha who died February 8, 1772.]

3.   What tho' she daily died
        A follower of her Lord,
    Faith in the fiery furnace tried
        Inhances her reward;
        What tho' she languish'd on,
        Tormented more and more,
    A jewel added to her crown
        Was every pang she bore.

4.   For now the Prize is gain'd,
        The Lord delights t'approve
    Her works of piety unfeign'd,
        Her patient hope and love,
        Her faithfulness to death:
        And lo, the spotless bride
    From Jesus' hand receive[s] the wreath
        And triumphs at his side!

ON THE DEATH OF W. HITCHIN
OCT. 29, 1773[18]

1. Rejoice, who bow to Jesus' Name!
        The righteous man by God approv'd,
    Meek follower of the patient Lamb
        If from our Vale of tears remov'd;
    His days of pain & grief are o're:
    Rejoice for Him who weeps no more.

2. Void of offence tow[ard] God & man
        With care he kept his con[science] here,
    Good works industrious to maintain,
        A simple Israelite sincere
    Thro' life he Israel's King conf[ess']d,
    God over all for ever blest.

18. [MS Preachers (MS CW I[q]) i. Space is left at the end for two or three more verses.
The last line of verse 5 is incomplete.]

3. Faithful to death he own'd his Lord,
   An heir of sure salvation seal'd,
The kingdom to his soul restor'd
   The earnest in his heart reveal'd
By more than works he testifies,
And gasps for Jesus in the skies.

4. Come, my beloved Saviour, come,
   Thou seest me to thy will resign'd,
Made ready for my heavenly home,
   Lover of Thee & all mankind,
Conqueror of hell & death & sin,
Open thine arms & take me in.

5. Bright kindred saints around his bed
   To catch his parting spirit stay,
Angels their golden pinions spread
   And Jesus beckons him away:
I come, I come, with smiles he cries
[   ] dies!

6. He lives to God, he greatly lives,
   And thro' the merits of his Lord
According to his works receives
   The labourer's hire, the full reward,
The promis'd crown, the purchas'd grace,
The heaven of heavens—in Jesus' face.

II
FOR HIS MAJESTY[19]

1. O God, who dost for ever live,
   Yet suffer'st mortal man to grieve
      When bosom-friends depart,
   Us for a royal Mourner hear,
   And shew Thyself the Comforter
      Of his afflicted heart.

19. [MS Death, p. 71. The grief referred to in this hymn was at the death of the Princess Dowager, George III's mother.]

2. A soul detatch'd from all below
   By sad variety of woe
       Thou only canst relieve.
   Into his heart the peace convey
   Which death can never take away,
       Which life can never give.

3. His troubled breast, and tearful eyes
   The best of Parents justifies:
       Yet let the pious Son
   Thy mercy's kindest act approve
   Who from the arms of filial love
       Hast caught her to thine own.

4. Inspire his soul with faith to soar
   Where safe on the celestial shore
       Her raptur'd Spirit sings,
   Welcom'd by all those angel-quires,
   Who shout, and strike their plausive lyres,
       And clap their golden wings.

5. His grief be lost in joy's excess,
   In her consummate happiness
       His every care and pain:
   Jesus, to him thy goodness show,
   Earnest of heaven thy love bestow,
       And let his joy remain.

6. Still may he hold the earnest fast,
   Till all his suffering days are past,
       His race of glory run;
   Then, then our hoary king remove,
   To find his full reward above
       In an immortal Crown.

XVII
ON THE MURDER OF MISS RAY[20]

1.   Bleeding Tenderness, farewell
      Hurried in a moment hence,
  (Thy sad, unexampled tale
      Shocks the tingling, tortur'd sense)
  Pitied and deplor'd by all!
      Virtue's self, no more severe,
  Grieves at thy untimely fall,
      Drops the soft, forgiving tear!

2.   Martyr of fidelity,
      Fatally, alas, belov'd!
  Brutal Appetite to Thee
      Crueller than hatred prov'd:
  By the dire Assassin's hand
      Torn from all thou lov'st below—
  Who the deed can understand,
      Who the ways of heaven can know?

3.   Wherefore was she form'd to please,
      Gentlest of the gentle kind?
  Why were want and wretchedness
      Sure in her a friend to find?
  Lo, the pleasing form appears
      Mangled, weltring in her gore!
  Misery's sons, indulge your tears,
      Misery's Friend is now no more!

4.   Dare we hope her safe above,
      Snatch'd from the infernal grave?
  Who shall bound Almighty LOVE,
      Teach his God *how far* to save?
  MERCY's thoughts are not as ours:
      He who bought her with his blood,
  Conqueror of all adverse Powers,
      Jesus claims her soul for God!

20. [MS Death, p. 81. The poem was written about April, 1779. It is found with variants on the leaf of a book with the name and book plate of The Rev. J. Reighton and entitled "On the Death of a lady who was murdered." For a hymn on the murderer, *cf. Rep. Verse*, No. 298, p. 334.]

FOR JOHN HENDERSON
APRIL 8, 1787[21]

1. Lover of Lazarus, and Friend
   Of all that on thy love depend,
      With yearning bowels see
   A chosen Vessel of thy grace
   Who only for thy Coming stays,
      And gasps to die in Thee.

2. His precious soul in life detain,
   And raise him from a bed of pain
      To minister thy word,
   To spread the wonders of thy Name,
   And thro' a listning world proclaim
      His dear, redeeming Lord.

3. Why were thy Gifts on him bestow'd
   But that the Messenger of God,
      Preacher of righteousness,
   His various Talents might improve,
   By labours of unwearied love,
      And show forth all thy praise?

4. If hitherto, intirely Thine,
   He has not answer'd thy Design,
      Or liv'd for God alone,
   But stoop'd, admiring crouds to please;
   Thy Servant, Lord, this moment seize,
      And seal him all thine own.

5. The virtue of thy hallowing blood,
   Thy Spirit's power, in strength renew'd,
      This moment may he feel,
   Body and soul to Thee present,
   Strain up the steep of Excellent
      And scale the heavenly hill.

21. [MS Henderson (MS CW III[f]), No. 1, p. 2; MS Drew, The Methodist Archives (Madison), with two or three minor variants and entitled "For J. H."]

6. Wise to redeem the time below
   Close in thy steps resolv'd to go,
       Support and lead him on
   From all the *arts of hell* secure,
   To make his glorious calling sure,
       And win a brighter crown.

7. Point out the works for him prepar'd,
   Till ready for a full reward
       Thy hoary labourer prove,
   Thy character and mind express
   Mature in finish'd holiness
       And pure, consummate love.

8. Then let the gates be open'd wide
   Then let him, with the Sanctified,
       Find his allotted place,
   Enter into his Master's joy
   And all eternity employ
       In rapt'rous hymns of praise.

II[22]

1. Jesus, thro' every age the same,
   The virtues of thy Saving Name
       With thankful joy I own:
   Thou hast, for thy own mercy sake,
   Snatch'd him from death, and giv'n me back
       My Son, my darling Son!

2. Accept from me the cordial praise
   From my Companions in distress
       Who did his burthen bear,
   Who still, around thy gracious seat
   Their suit importunate repeat,
       And wrestle on in prayer.

22. [MS Henderson (MS CW III[f]), p. 2.]

3. Thy healing work in him begun
    We ask Thee, Lord, to carry on,
        Commanding him to live;
    Fill with abundant life his soul,
    Make his distemper'd body whole,
        And perfect soundness give.

4. O let him by thy quickning word,
    In thy appointed time, restor'd
        To double health, arise,
    Walk after Thee in all thy ways,
    Take up his cross, his Lord confess,
        And labour up the skies.

5. The Fever, which rebuk'd by Thee
    Has left him weak as infancy,
        Prohibit its return,
    And still thy messenger supply
    With strength to walk, to run, to fly
        On wings of eagles borne.

6. So shall he magnify thy Name,
    His Saviour, & the World's proclaim
        To all so freely given,
    Whose word both soul and body heals,
    Whose blood the general pardon seals,
        And speaks us up to heaven.

III [23]

1. And am I in the body still?
    Reserv'd to know the Master's will,
        And govern'd by his word,
    To do whate'er his love ordains,
    To suffer, and fill up the pains
        Of my expiring Lord!

23. [MS Henderson (MS CW III[f]), p. 4.]

2. Saviour, who liftest up my head,
    And call'st me back as from the dead
        A witness of thy grace,
    To Thee, who bidst my soul arise,
    My life be all a sacrifice
        And every breath be praise.

3. But let me first with tears lament
    My talents buried, or misspent,
        My too obsequious mind,
    My love of indolence and ease,
    My nature's fond desire to please
        Not benefit mankind.

4. When half my course, alas, is run
    A single soul I have not won,
        Or *strove* my God t'obey,
    But careless to perform thy will,
    Irresolute I linger'd still
        And threw my life away.

5. Idle I in the vineyard stood,
    Or vain philosophy pursued
        Eager, athirst to know
    The mysteries of earth and sky,
    And skill'd in *curious arts* to pry
        Into the depths below.

6. But lo! I from this moment turn
    To Thee whom I have pierc'd, & mourn
        My sins & wandrings past,
    And offering up my ministry
    (If Thou vouchsafe to send by me)
        I yield, I yield at last.

7. All other gain I count but loss,
    Study the mysteries of thy cross
        And in thy love abide,
    (If Thou the constant mind bestow),
    Thee, only Thee, resolv'd to know,
        My Saviour crucified.

8. Be it thro' life my sole delight
    The length & breadth, & depth & hei[gh]t
        Of Love to comprehend,
    And then to praise with Those above
    My Saviour's everlasting Love
        In songs that never end.

IV [24]

1. Jesus, at thy command I come,
    A sinner call'd out of my tomb
        Thy Orders to receive,
    Confirm'd by thy own Spirit's Seal,
    Enabling me to serve thy will
        And for thy glory live.

2. The only work on earth I have
    Is, as thine Instrument, to save
        The creatures of my God,
    The precious souls thy hands have made
    For whom Thou hast a ransom paid,
        And lavish'd all thy blood.

3. If by thy Spirit moved I am
    To preach redemption in thy Name
        With life procur'd for all,
    Incline the Porter by thy power
    T'admit me thro' the Sacred Door
        And recognize my Call.

4. Then, then intrusted with thy word,
    Th'acknowledg'd Servant of the Lord
        Into thy vineyard send,
    And present with thy labourers be
    Till time commence Eternity
        And faith in Vision end.

24. [MS Henderson (MS CW III[f]), p. 5.]

V[25]

1. Father, to Thee our joint request
       With meek submission we make kn[ow]n,
    Soon as thy will is manifest
       Still ready to give up our own:
    Our Friend, who on the altar lies,
       If now thy sover[eig]n mercy claim,
    We offer up the sacrifice,
       Adore thy love, and bless thy name.

2. But if, before the fixt decree
       Bring forth, we may his life desire,
    If yet thou mayst intreated be;
       The prayer thy Spirit doth inspire,
    The prayer presented thro' thy Son,
       Our *powerful* Advocate, receive,
    And send a peaceful Answer down,
       And bid the dying Victim live.

3. Were the last fatal[26] mom[en]t come,
       And death had seiz'd its willing prey,
    Father, thou canst his instant doom
       Reverse, and lengthen out his day.
    All things are possible to Thee
       To us who trust in Jesus' word,
    And suppliant in his Name agree
       And ask—Our Friend to life restor'd!

VI[27]

1.   But was it all a Dream
      When late I seem'd to stand
    Ready to pass o're Jordan's stream
      To the Celestial Land?

25. [MS Henderson (MS CW III[f]), p. 5.]
26. [Above "fatal" the word "ceasless" is written as an alternative.]
27. [MS Henderson (MS CW III[f]), p. 6.]

I hoped (alas in vain)
From earth and sin to fly
An easy victory obtain,
And like a Coward die.

2.   I have not yet receiv'd
       The grace for me design'd:
I only to myself have lived
       And not to serve mankind;
       Not to evince and prove
       My faith's sincerity,
Not to return my Saviour's love
       Who lived and died for me.

3.   My Ransomer He died:
       Expending all his blood
His Father's Justice satisfied,
       And paid my debt to God:
       But still my debt to Man,
       To Those who God revere,
I have not paid; and never can,
       Unless I pay it here.

4.   Surely the Sons of grace
       So long asham'd for me
Who saw with grief my evil days
       Shoud my repentance see:
       Before from earth I go,
       I *shoud* my faults retrieve,
Sober & just, and godly *show*
       How pardon'd sinners *live*.

5.   Wherefore with earnest cries
       On Thee, O Christ, I call,
Restore me in thy people's eyes
       Recover'd from my fall,
       To spread the joyful sound,
       'A Peace 'twixt earth & Heav'n,
'Mercy doth more than sin abound,
       'And all the world's forgiv'n!'

VII [28]

1. Father, beneath whose Hand I groan
      Submissive to thy just Decree,
   Instruct thy long-afflicted Son
      Wherefore dost Thou contend with me?
   Who dost not put to needless pain,
      Or crush a worm that feels his load,
   Thy dealings with me now explain,
      Explain the language of thy Rod.

2. What doth this grievous trouble mean
      Which on my flesh so heavy lies?
   Is it some unacknowledg'd sin
      That forces mercy to chastize?
   I fear the secret Cause to know,
      But cannot from thy sight conc[ea]l;
   Omniscient God, the evil show,
      The mysteries of Hell reveal.

3. In an angelical disguise
      If Satan did my soul deceive,
   Thou canst detect his specious lies
      And wisdom to thy Serv[an]t give:
   Against the Israelitish race,
      In vain the fiend his pow'r exerts
   Thy Spirit shall the Demon[29] chase
      And baffle all his curious arts.

4. After my L[or]d resolv'd to go
      And do whate'er thy laws require,
   I trample on th'infernal Foe,
      And cast *his* books into the fire:[30]

28. [MS Henderson (MS CW III[f]), p. 7.]
29. [Above "Demon" the word "Sorcerer" is written as an alternative.]
30. [Below this, in the hand of Sally Wesley (daughter) is written: "Before John Henderson died (on whom and for whom these Lines were written by the Revd. Charles Wesley) he earnestly entreated that all his Books on Magic might be burnt. He expressed the utmost self abasement, and whole dependence on the blessed Redeemer, without whom (He said) Heaven would be no Heaven to Him. He departed this Life in 1788, a few months after the Revd. Charles Wesley—by whom he was beloved as a Son." The scriptural reference is to Acts 19:19.]

Thy Book my Rule and Study still,
  Thy Spirit of truth, my only Guide,
Shall lead me into all thy will
  And in my loving heart reside.

DESIRING DEATH 1744[31]

1. O GOD of unlimited Power,
      Whose Rod with Amazement I hear,
    Stand by me throughout the Dark Hour
      And save from the Evil I fear:
    O do not allow me to stay,
      Till basely my Lord I deny,
    But suddenly summon away,
      And give me in Jesus to die.

2. To die is unspeakable gain
      To all in his Spirit who live:
    O grant me thy Love to obtain,
      And then to thy Mercy receive:
    Thy mercy alone I require,
      I long to recover thy Peace,
    And then to the Country retire
      Where Sorrow forever shall cease.

3. Attend to my earnest Request,
      My eager importunate Prayer,
    I never, I never can rest,
      Till Mercy hath wafted me there:
    A Man of Affliction & Strife,
      A Prophet of Evil, I pray,
    In Mercy bereave me of Life
      And take from the Sorrowful Day.

31. [MS Richmond, pp. 12–13.]

4   Ah! why shoud I longer remain,
      To see my sad Country o'rethrown,
   To feel the Perfection of Pain,
      And eccho to Sion's Last Groan?
   My Jesus, in Pity remove,
      Or hide the Distress from my Eyes,
   And pardon, & perfect in Love,
      And gather me up to the Skies.

ANOTHER[32]

1.   Why woud my cruel Friends suppress
      A desp'rate Madman's breath,
   Restrain my Passion's wild Excess,
      My fond Desires of Death?
   Why woud they curb the raging Flood,
      It's lawless Violence bind,
   Forbid the Circling of my Blood,
      Or reason down the Wind?

2.   Go bid the shipwrack'd Man forbear
      To grasp the long-sought Shore,
   The Exile charge to lose his care,
      And sigh for Home no more.
   Go bid the Wretch on yonder Wheel
      His Sense of Pain suspend,
   Or let him all his Fortune feel,
      And not desire its[33] End.

3.   In vain alas! I strive to check
      Th'Involuntary Groan,
   Yet still persist my Help to seek
      In Death, & Death alone.
   Amaz'd I ask, unhallow'd I,
      And pine for my Release,
   And start from my own Wish to die,
      Who could not die in Peace.

32. [MS Richmond, pp. 13–14. The poem is possibly incomplete as the remainder of the page has room for more than one additional verse, but apparently none was written.]
33. [Above "its" the word "the" is written as an alternative.]

4. The happy Souls who Jesus know
        May lawfully request
    A sudden Call from Things below
        To their Redeemer's Breast:
    Whose Peace is made, whose H[ear]t is pure,
        May ask the Crowning Grace,
    Of endless Happiness secure,
        And die to see thy Face.

DESIRING DEATH
WRITTEN IN N[ORTH] W[ALES], 1748[34]

1. Thou, GOD, to whom alone I live,
        For whom my All I spend,
    Thy Servant graciously forgive,
        And let my Labours end.

2. Weary alas! Thou knowst I am
        Of this sad Vale of Tears,
    Restless to die from all my Shame,
        From all my Griefs & Fears.

3. Evil & few my Days have been,
        And still Thou hearst me groan
    Impatient at my People's Sin,
        Impatient at my own.

4. Oft have I sunk orewhelm'd, opprest
        Beneath the double Load,
    And languish'd for that Land of Rest,
        Th'Inheritance of GOD.

5. Oft have I groan'd my Lot to bear,
        A Man of Grief and Strife,
    And struggled to throw off the Care,
        And burst the Bars of Life.

34. [MS Misc. Hymns, p. 24; MS Richmond, pp. 80–1, where it is entitled "Written in N(orth) W(ales)" 1748; MS Occasional, p. 83. The title "Desiring Death" appears in MS Misc. Hymns. "N.W." probably designates North Wales, since Charles Wesley was twice in North Wales during the latter part of 1748, going to and from Ireland. MS Occasional has only verses 1–8.]

6. One only Wish detains me still
   In this bleak Wilderness,
   Till mounted on thy holy Hill,
   I cannot die in Peace.

7. O might I now with calmest Haste
   From all my Griefs remove,
   Go up at once, & more than taste
   Thy Fruit of Perfect Love.

8. I pray Thee let me pass the Flood
   To yon fair Coast unknown,
   And see that pleasant Land, & good,
   That lovely Lebanon.

9. The glorious Gospel I declare
   O might I now partake,
   The Image of the Heavenly bear,
   And yield my Spirit back.

10. A Moment more I woud not stop
    To Holiness restor'd,
    But soar beyond the Mountain-top,
    But die to meet my Lord.

ANOTHER[35]

1. On Thee, Omnipotent to save,
   Thy creature tottering o're the grave,
      Thy dear-bought creature, I
   For mercy and salvation call,
   Jesus, redeem me from my fall,
      And suffer me to die.

2. Warn'd to put off this mouldring clay
   I bless Thee for my strength's decay
      And sink into the tomb;
   Welcome infirmities and pains,
   Welcome whate'er my God ordains
      To bring his servant home.

35. [MS Misc. Hymns, pp. 25–7.]

3. My days are as a shadow fled;
   And let me bow my weary head,
      Thine open face to see:
   I ask no temporal reprieve,
   I only long in Thee to live,
      And then to die in Thee.

4. O woudst Thou, Lord, thy blood apply,
   My heart to calm, and purify,
      My poor, unhallow'd heart:
   Thou knowst, I only wait for this,
   To gain the reconciling kiss,
      And then with joy depart.

5. O might my useless warfare end,
   O might my strugling spirit ascend
      And spurn the earth I leave!
   Regard my strugling spirit's groan,
   Pleading in me regard thy own,
      And now my soul receive.

6. A wretched, weak, intangled thing,
   To Thee my last distress I bring,
      Grace, only grace implore:
   Plunge in the fountain of thy blood,
   And bear me thro' the purple flood
      To that eternal shore.

7. Appear, and chase these endless sighs,
   Appear before my streaming eyes,
      And wipe these tears away;
   Thy presence is my heavenly light,
   Thy presence swallows up my night
      In everlasting day.

FOR A WIDOW
UNASSURED OF HER HUSBAND'S HAPPINESS[36]

1.   Ah! woe is me, my Friend is gone
      Silent to a World unknown,
        Without a Token given:
  He did not witness for his Lord,
  Or bid me in one parting Word
      Come after him to Heaven.

2.   O Depth of exquisite Distress!
      Is He entred into Peace,
        So suddenly remov'd?
  Who shall the Fatal Secret tell,
  The Welfare of a Soul reveal
      Whom as my own I lov'd?

3.   My other Self, to Eden borne,
      Never, never to return
        I could with Thanks resign:
  But O! to doubt his Welcom there!
  Was ever heart-distracting Care,
      Was ever Grief like Mine!

4.   Here is the Patience of the Saints!
      But my feeble Spirit faints
        Beneath so huge a Load:
  Some pitying Angel ease my Care,
  And tell me, if ye did not bear
      His Happy Soul to GOD?

5.   Or rather (if thy GOD allow),
      O, my Kinder Angel Thou,
        Forsake th'eternal Shore,
  Appear to thy poor anxious Mate,
  Assure me of thy blest Estate,
      And bid me weep no more.

36. [MS Richmond, pp. 30–33.]

6. Alas! I know not what I say—
    Lord, to Thee alone I pray,
      To Thee alone apply:
If Best it is for me to know,
The Doom of my Companion shew;
      Did he thy Servant die?

7. Bring all the Proofs into my Mind:
    Shew me why thy Goodness join'd
      That gentle Soul to me,
But that we soon might meet above
And sing the Marriage-Song of Love
      Thro' all Eternity!

8. Why didst Thou in the worst of Times
    Save him from those horrid Crimes
      Which stain the Lawless Great?
His Soul disdain'd to sit with them
Who from the Scorner's Chair condemn
      The Virtue which they hate.

9. Why didst Thou keep him all his days
    By a Miracle of Grace
      From Open Enmity?
He never dar'd oppose thy Cause,
Against Thee, Lord, who never was,
      O was he not *for* Thee?

10. Why didst Thou form him of a Mind
    Just, & generous, & kind
      To succour the Distrest?
He chas'd the needy Orphan's Fears,
And Pity at the Widow's Tears
      Resided in his Breast.

11. Did he not love the Poor & Good,
    All who for *their* Saviour Stood,
      (To Him alas unknown!)
And had he not their mournful Pray'rs?
And can the Son of all those Tears
      Be finally undone?

12. For Him Thou didst the Spirit impart,
    Pleading in thy people's Heart
      With Groans unspeakable:
Their fervent Prayer hath pierc'd the sky,
And Thou hast said, who canst not lie,
      It must, it must prevail.

13. I see the Opening Door of Hope!
    My Companion *is* caught up,
      For O! thy Word was past:
I *have* Believ'd, Thou knowst, I have,
And pray'd Thee oft in Faith to save
      His pretious Soul at last.

14. Thou heardst in me thy Spirit's Groans,
    Heardst him in thy Secret Ones,
      The Life we ask'd is given:
He never sinn'd the Sin to Death;
And sure as Thou the Prayer didst breathe,
      He *is* with Thee in H[eave]n!

TO BE SUNG BY HER FRIENDS[37]

1. Thou Helper of All in Distress,
    Our Cry for a Widow attend,
And send us an Answer of Peace,
    And Her to the Comforter send:
On Jesus's Bosom reclin'd
    Thy Fulness of Grace let her see,
And now & eternally find
    Her Heavenly Treasure in Thee.

2. Thou knowst the full Burthen she bears
    For Him Thou hast kindly remov'd,
The Doubt & Distraction that tears
    The Soul of thy Dearly-belov'd[38]

---

37. [MS Richmond, pp. 33–4. The possessive pronoun "her" in the title refers to the widow of the previous poem: "For a Widow Unassur'd of her Husband's Happiness."]
    38. [This verse is incomplete. Space has been left for four lines.]

3.   O Father of Mercies, incline
      Thine Ear to our humble Request,
  And fill with Assurance Divine
      Her tender affectionate Breast;
  The Fiery Temptation remove,
      Almighty to save as Thou art,
  And send her a Sign from above,
      And whisper a Word to her Heart.

4.   For this do we earnestly groan,
      With tenderest Sympathy grieve,
  For this we beleaguer thy Throne,
      Till Thou her Affliction relieve,
  Accept our Importunate prayer
      (With Thine if our Wishes agree)
  The Bliss of her Consort declare,
      And tell her—His soul is with Thee!

ON THE LOSS OF A FRIEND[39]

1.   Why should a living child of man
      Beneath the scourge repine,
  Or dare with impious grief to'arraign
      The righteousness Divine?
  Why should I murmur at my load,
      And farther still rebel,
  So lightly chasten'd by my God,
      And not thrust down to hell?

2.   What are the sorest plagues I bear
      To those the damn'd sustain?
  What is my temporal despair
      To their eternal pain?

39. [MS Richmond, pp.29–30. Verses 1–4 are published in *Poet. Works,* V, p. 192 together with a fifth verse. After verse 4 in the MS are a line and a half of tiny shorthand from the size of which one may suppose it was inserted after the poem was transcribed. Frank Baker notes that it seems to be a draft of a verse of a hymn but not that it is clearly the origin of verse 5 in *Poet. Works.* Baker remarks in a personal note that the second half of verse 5 "seems to be squeezed in with a slightly differing pen, and smaller; encroaches on title of following poem." Verse 7 printed here is the verse numbered 5 in *Poet. Works.* It is unclear whether Wesley is referring to the death of a friend or the turning of his son Samuel to Roman Catholicism. See *Unpub. Poetry,* I, pp. 293ff.]

My sins demand their dreadful hire,
    My sins for vengeance call
And short of that infernal fire
    'Tis grace and mercy all.

3. What though my soul with shame is fill'd,
    My heart o'erwhelm'd with dread,
What though my tender joys are kill'd,
    And every comfort fled;
What though my darling *Isaac* I
    Am forced to offer up,
And live, when all my blessings die,
    And drink the bitterest cup.

4. Shall I resent my slighted love,
    Or mourn my murder'd fame,
Worthy the hate of all above,
    And everlasting shame!
The loss of one weak, faithless friend
    Still, still shall I bemoan,
When God, whose favours never end,
    May yet be all my own?

5. GOD of my Life & refuge, hear
    A Child of misery,
And bless me with an heart sincere
    To languish after thee.
Thou, only Thou, my Thoughts engross,
    And claim my whole Distress,
Till Jesus recompence my Loss
    With everlasting Peace.

6. Confirm the gracious Wish I feel
    For Thee alone to mourn
Till Thou the ransom'd sinner seal
    And bid my Soul return,
Till Thou my Heavenly Hope app[ea]r,
    Thy glorious Face display,
And banish every Sigh & Tear
    At that Triumphant Day.

7. God of my life, to thy decree
    I humbly now submit,
Accept my punishment from Thee,
    And tremble at Thy feet:
Whate'er Thy will inflicts I take,
    Till all Thy plagues are past;
But while my soul I render back,
    O give me peace at last.

[AH! WHITHER, OR TO WHOM][40]

1.   Ah! whither, or to whom
        Should the Afflicted fly?
    Beyond the Storm, beyond the Tomb,
        To Jesus in the Sky!
        Above these Tents of Clay,
        Above these Clouds of Care,
    To Mansions of eternal Day,
        To our Redeemer there!

2.   Safe on that happy Shore
        From Sorrow, Sin, & Strife!
    The Bitterness of Death is or'e,
        The Bitterness of Life:
        The Grief with all to part
        (While Grace & Nature strove)
    The Achings of a broken Heart,
        The Pangs of Dying Love.

3.   'Tis there my Soul shall rest
        From all its Misery,
    Reclining on his loving Breast
        Who bore the Cross for me,
        Fainted beneath my Load,
        With sinless Passions torn,
    And groan'd in Death my GOD, my GOD,
        That I might cease to mourn.

40. [MS Richmond, pp. 35–6.]

4.   Come then, my Only Hope,
      My only Constant Friend,
And dry these briny Rivulets up
      And bid these Conflicts end.
      Pour in thy Mercy's Balm
      The Pangs of *Loss* to ease,
The Rage of stormy Passion calm,
      And give me back my Peace.

5.   O for one Cordial Drop
      Of pure celestial Love
To sweeten Life's afflictive Cup,
      Till Thou from Earth remove,
      Till Thou, my GOD, receive
      Thy wandring Exile home,
Where Pain & Loss can never grieve
      And Sin can never come.

6.   Thou once a Man of woe
      Indulge my sad request,
Cut short my suffering days below
      And give the Weary rest;
      For this, this only good
      I ever, ever cry,
Ah! let me feel thy sprinkled Blood,
      Ah! let me love, and die.

[WORTHY IS THE SLAUGHTER'D LAMB][41]

1.   [Worthy i]s the slaughter'd Lamb,
      [Power] and blessing to receive.
[Who for] us the world or'ecame,
      Doth the grace victorious give:
Grace and goodness infinite
      He hath to a sinner shown,
Numbred with the saints in light
      Caught her up to share his throne.

41. [MS Baker: formerly in the possession of Frank Baker, it is now located in the museum of The World Methodist Council at Lake Junaluska, NC. The MS is torn at the beginning in the upper lefthand corner and the words have been supplied by the editors at the beginning of the first three lines in verse 1.]

2. Yielding to an early call,
      Him she oft on earth pursued,
   Willing made to give up all,
      Sigh'd to feel th'atoning blood,
   Tasted the good word of grace,
      Earnest of celestial joys,
   Sat in humble Mary's place,
      Long'd to hear the Bridegroom's voice.

3. But she soon unfaithful prov'd,
      Forfeited her joy & peace,
   Far from her Redeemer rov'd
      O're the barren wilderness
   To the things of earth inclin'd,
      To the world, her Saviour's foe:
   Yet, unconquerably kind,
      LOVE refus'd to let her go.

4. Jesus sent a messenger
      (Bent his purchase to regain)
   Kindest when he seem'd severe,
      Hedg'd her round with sacred pain:
   While she frowardly [went on]
      He her broken reeds [remov'd]
   Brought by pining sickness [down]
      Chasten'd whom he dearly lo[v'd].[42]

5. Shaking the weak house of clay,
      Blasting every earthly hope,
   Sickness tore her strength away,
      Forc'd the fugitive to stop:
   Then her troubled soul awoke,
      Then she heard th'appointed rod,
   Sunk beneath his mercy's stroke,
      All renounc'd, to find her God.

6. All her happiness below,
      Pleasure, wealth, and power, and praise,
   Now she doth for Christ forego,
      All her works and righteousness.

42. [The MS is torn at the end of lines five through eight (the reverse side of p. 1) and the editors have supplied the words.]

Stript and blind and truly poor
Only sin she calls her own,
Weeping lies at Mercy's door,
Languishing for Christ alone.

7. Oft the dreadful king was seen
Justly by the guilty fear'd,
But the Friend of sinful men
Always with his foe appear'd.
Both she saw approaching fast,
Ready to resign her breath,
But she gladly own'd at last
"Love has quicker wings than Death!

8. "O how pretious is his blood
"In a dying sinner's eyes!
"Ransom'd[43]

HYMNS OF PREPARATION FOR DEATH

LX[44]

1. O Thou, to whom all hearts are known,
My latest wish, my one desire
Breath'd in the Spirit of thy Son
Accept, and grant what I require;

2. Pardon for my offences past,
Grace for a few good days to come,
Love, the sure pledge of heaven at last,
And a smooth passage to the tomb.

43. [The remainder of the MS is missing.]
44. [MS Death, p. 25; *Rep. Verse*, No. 214, p. 241.]

LXIII[45]

1.   Give me love, or else I die
        Out of thy presence cast:
  Only love can sanctify
        And save my soul at last,
  Only love can sin expel,
And change my nature into Thine,
    Make me pure, and meet to dwell
        With Holiness Divine.

2.   God in Thee, O Christ, is Love:
        To me thyself impart,
  All my evil to remove
        And fill my hallow'd heart:
  For this thing alone I live
Till Thou with my request comply;
    Holy LOVE, thy essence give,
        And grant me then to die.

LXIV[46]

1. Thee I remember on my bed
    And waking lift my heart to Thee
Whose blood for dying sinners shed
    Hath bought eternal life for me:
Thy precious blood did all procure,
    The conscious sense of sin forgiven,
The Spirit, and the nature pure,
    And Love, the antepast of heaven.

2. Still in the flesh for this I stay;
    O were I, Lord, of Love possest,
How gladly woud I drop my clay,
    And find repose in thy dear breast!
My soul, thy own acknowledg'd right,
    I woud into thy hands commend
And entring into Rest tonight
    Begin the life which ne'er shall end.

45. [MS Death, p. 28.]
46. [MS Death, pp. 28–9.]

LXIX[47]

1. All merciful, almighty Lord,
    Recall to mind thy faithful word,
       My evils to remove;
    Long have I for thy promise stay'd,
    And still I mourn the grace delay'd,
       The pardon, and the love.

2. Mercy Thou dost for thousands keep,
    For me, who at thy footstool weep
       To know my sins forgiven,
    And, loving Thee with all my heart,
    In peace triumphant to depart,
       And find my place in heaven.

LXX[48]

1. Thou to whom all hearts are known,
       Attend the cry of mine,
    Hear in me thy Spirit's groan
       For purity divine:
    Languishing for my remove,
    I wait thine image to retrieve;
       Fill me, Jesus, with thy love,
          And to Thyself receive.

2. Destitute of holiness,
       I am not like my Lord,
    Am not ready to possess
       The saints' immense reward;
    No; my God I cannot see,
    Unless, before I hence depart,
       Thou implant thyself in me
          And make me pure in heart.

47. [MS Death, p. 33.]
48. [MS Death, pp. 33–4.]

3.   Partner of thy nature then,
        And in thine image found,
      Saviour, call me up to reign
        With life immortal crown'd,
      With thy glorious presence blest
    In speechless extacies to gaze,
      Folded in thy arms to rest,
        And breathe eternal praise.

LXXIII[49]

1.   Since first my earthly course begun,
      I have pursued a God unknown,
        Attracted from above;
      I have for thy salvation stay'd,
      Thro' a long life of trouble pray'd,
        And languish'd for thy love.

2.   Why have I not my suit obtain'd,
      If with sincerity unfeign'd
        I ask'd the promis'd good?
      Why am I, Lord, at life's sad close
      Oppress'd with sins, o'rewhelm'd with woes
        And lying in my blood?

3.   The sole exception from thy grace,
      The only outcast from thy face
        If Thou hast pass'd me by,
      I to my righteous doom submit,
      And weep unpitied at thy feet,
        Till at thy feet I die.

4.   But O, if hope doth still remain,
      And mindful of thy mortal pain
        Thou thinkst on Calvary;
      Thine agony and bloody sweat,
      Thy cross unable to forget,
        In death remember me!

49. [MS Death, pp. 37–8.]

LXXV[50]

1. Ready to render up the breath
      Which I receiv'd from Thee,
   While passing thro' the vale of death,
      My God, remember me:

2. One only thing do I desire
      (Desiring all in One)
   My spirit, when Thou wilt, require,
      But give me first thine own.

LXXVI[51]

1. Take the filth of sin away,
      Give the purity of love,
   Then my loving soul convey
      To its blisful place above,
   Meet its heavenly Lord t'embrace,
   Longing to behold thy face.

2. Thee I cannot see and live:
      Let me see thee then, and die!
   Jesus, to thyself receive
      Whom Thou didst so dearly buy;
   Crown my infinite desire,
   Let me in thine arms expire!

LXXVII[52]

1. Earth to earth, and dust to dust
      While I, at thy word, return,
   O thou faithful God and just,
      Spare me who my follies mourn,
   Pardon who my sins confess,
   Cleanse from all unrighteousness.

50. [MS Death, p. 39.]
51. [MS Death, pp. 39–40.]
52. [MS Death, p. 40.]

369

2.　E'er my soul and body part,
　　　　Part, O Lord, my sin and me,
　　Lowly, meek, and pure in heart
　　　　That I may my Saviour see,
　　See with infinite delight,
　　Find my heaven in The Sight!

LXXIX[53]

1.　Keep me, Lord, by day and night
　　　　Every moment keep, and save,
　　That I may, with calm delight
　　　　Sink into a long-sought grave,
　　May for sin no longer grieve,
　　May at last myself forgive.

2.　In that land of endless rest
　　　　All things grievous are forgot,
　　Conscience doth no more molest,
　　　　Cruel, self-upbraiding thought,
　　Pangs which here my bosom tear,
　　Pangs of madness and despair.

3.　Only one faint glimmering ray
　　　　Here my drooping spirit chears,
　　Christ, the Power of God, a day
　　　　Is to Thee a thousand years;
　　Show me now thy wounded side,
　　Plunge me in the cleansing tide.

4.　Hoping against hope, I wait
　　　　The stupendous change to prove;
　　Raised to my unsinning state,
　　　　In the image of thy love,
　　Thro' the fountain of thy blood,
　　Pure I then return to God.

53. [MS Death, p. 42; MS CW III(c) 17.]

LXXXI[54]

Spirit of love, thyself impart,
   Before my Spirit I resign,
If bought for me with blood thou art,
   For me redeem'd by blood divine:
Meet for that blissful Vision make,
   And then, to share thy joys above,
The partner of thy nature take,
   The partner of thy heavenly love.

[AN ELEGIAC ODE][55]

1.   Soft! attend that awful Sound!
      Earth receives the borrow'd Clay,
      But the sky-born Soul is found
      In mansions of Eternal Day:
Borne thro' the Open Fount of Jesus' blood
He springs! he flies! he 'scapes into the arms of God!

2.   Joys all earthly joys transcending
      Never-fading, never-ending,
       Inconceivable below,
      Rivers of celestial pleasure,
      Bliss redundant above measure
       From Jehovah's Presence flow!

      There the pure inraptur'd Spirit
      Doth his Lord's delight[56] inherit,
       Doth the Father's Glory see!
      There in hymns or silent praises
      Blest on the Redeemer gazes
       Blest thro' all Eternity!

54. [MS Death, p. 44.]
55. [MSS Hendrix, Duke University; *Rep. Verse*, No. 335, pp. 376–7.]
56. [In the margin "Reward" is written as an alternative to "delight."]

3.   Mourners for ourselves alone,
     O when shall we or'etake
The saint to earlier glory gone,
And win the prize by Jesus won,
     And given for his sake!

Jesus, manifest thy grace[57]
     And pity from above,
Vilest of the apostate race
Us in thy mercy's arms embrace
     And crown us with thy Love.

[4.]   Happy in thy love reveal'd
     To the expanded heart,
Conscious of our pardon seal'd,
And thus made ready to depart
Our souls to that triumphant soul unite
And plunge in the full blaze of Everlasting Light.

57. [Between this line and the previous one the following lines are crossed through:
Jesus, Lord, to Thee we sue,
Still thy foes with pity view,
Vilest of the sinful race,
Still in mercy's [arms] embrace
And bless with pardon from above
The Objects of thy dying Love.

4.   When Thou hast thy Love reveal'd
     In every panting heart,
Conscious of our pardon seal'd,
     And ready to depart,
In the fourth deleted line "Still in mercy's [arms] embrace" there is a gap between "mercy's" and "embrace" in the first draft of this passage, but those lines are clearly the prototype of lines twenty-six and twenty-seven where "arms" appears.]

EPIGRAMS[1]

EPIGRAM[2]

Genevensis a Friend's inconsistency blames
For running with Paul, & yet holding with James,
This as knavish he notes in a free-willing brother
Saying one thing to us, & *intending* another;
But how often have *we* at *their* honesty wondred,
We cry Mercy for all, & mean One in a hundred!

N.T.[3]

Matthew, and Mark, and Luke, and John:
The Acts, and Romans follow on:
Cor. Galat. Eph. Phipp. Colo.
Thess. Tim. and Tit. and Philemo:
Heb. James and Peter, John and Jude,
With Revelation to conclude.

2. [MS CW IV, 81.]

3. [MS CW IV, 81; *Rep. Verse*, No. 276, p. 310. The poem is a mnemonic on the books of the New Testament written for his children to help them remember the order of the books.]

MISCELLANEOUS
HYMNS AND POEMS

HYMN FOR TWO PERSONS
ON THE ANNIVERSARY OF THEIR WEDDING[1]

1.   Great Author of the Mystick Grace,
     Whose Providence hath join'd our Hands,
  Hath join'd our Hearts, to seek thy Face,
     By sure, indissoluble Bands:
  Ordain'd in Life & Death to prove
  The Dignity of Nuptial Love;

2.   To Thee, great GOD of Truth & Power,
     Our Sacrifice of Thanks we pay,
  Thy Grace Unspeakable adore,
     And bless the glad revolving Day
  Which mix'd our Souls in Bliss unknown
  And made of Twain forever One.

3.   Our growing Happiness & Love
     From Thee we joyfully receive,
  Our Comforts to thy Praise improve,
     Our Body, Soul, & Spirit give
  Thee, Saviour, Thee to glorify,
  Thine, wholly Thine to live & die.

4.   For This we first together came,
     For This we still continue One,
  T'experience all thy glorious Name,
     To make thy glorious Nature known,
  To magnify the Sacred Sign,
  And prove the Ordinance Divine.

5.   For This we met, with lowly Fear,
     T'insure on Earth the Joys above,
  To work out our Salvation here,
     With chast Delight & purest Love,
  T'injoy the Sense of Sins Forgiven,
  And travel Hand in Hand to Heaven.

1. [MS Wesley Family Letters, I, p. 50. Wesley adds the note to "Two Persons": "Mr. and Mrs. B."]

6. O may we ever keep in view
        And labour tow[ar]d the Blisful End,
    In every Step the Prize pursue,
        Till Both on Angels' Wings ascend,
    Both in the Wedding Garm[en]t drest
    To share the Lamb's Eternal Rest.

TO MISS LUDLOW[2]

1. Blooming, heart-bewitching Maid,
        Lovely as an opening Flower
    Soon alas, your charms shall fade,
        Scarce outlive the morning hour:
    Tho' they scape a fever's rage,
        Envious Time they cannot fly:
    Wither'd by decrepit Age,
        You and all your charms shall die!

2. Counsel'd by a friendly Child,
        Virtue's Loveliness to win,
    Tender, affable and mild,
        Fair without, be good within,
    Study to oblige and please;
        Fair indeed you thus become,
    Real charms you thus possess,
        Charms that shall for ever bloom!

TO MISS DAVIS[3]

Gentle Inglisina, say
Can the smooth Italian Lay
Nature's ruggedness remove,
Soften Britons into love?

2. [MS CW I(p) vii. Miss Ludlow is the Harriet Ludlow mentioned in the poem, "The Lover's Complaint," *Unpub. Poetry*, I, p. 284, see footnote 16.]

3. [MS, loose sheet, Lamplough Collection; *Rep. Verse*, No. 290, p. 328. Miss Cecilia Davies was one of the most popular vocalists of the eighteenth century, and was a great success in Italy where she was known as L'Inglesina. Wesley probably wrote these lines during her first return visit to England, when she was still thoroughly italianised.]

Yes; the stocks & stones draw near,
Thy inchanting Voice to hear
And all the Savages agree
In praise of harmony & Thee!

['NOR YET FROM MY DIM EYES THY FORM RETIRES!']⁴

'Nor yet from my dim Eyes THY form retires!'
(The cold empty starving Grate before me makes me add
the following disconsolate Line.)
Nor cheering image of thine absent Fires.
No longer now on Horrel's[5] airy Van,
With Thee shall I admire the subject Plain,
Or where the Sight in neighbouring Shades is lost,
Or where the lengthned Prospect widens most:
While or the tunefull Poet's (something) song,
Or Truths Divine flow'd easy from thy Tongue.

ODE ON HANDEL'S BIRTHDAY
S. MATTHIAS DAY FEBR[UARY] 24[6]

Hail the bright auspicious Day
That gave Immortal Handel birth.
Let every moment glide away
In solemn joy and sacred mirth;
Let every soul like his aspire
And catch a glowing spark of pure etherial fire.

---

4. [Letter to John Wesley by Charles Wesley, January 20, 1727/8; John Wesley's "Miscellany Verses," pp. 39–43 (both sources are in the Colman Collection); *Rep. Verse*, No. 231, p. 257. This poem is an adaptation of some lines of his brother John, which Charles admits in the letter: "You'l pardon my turning your own Words upon you." For a full discussion see Frank Baker (*Rep. Verse*, p. 257), who points out that this is, in fact, the earliest extant piece of Charles Wesley's verse. Only the second line, however, is original with Charles.]

5. ["Hinxy's" is written above "Horrel's" as an alternative. Horrel is a plantation on a hill to the south of Stanton, Gloucestershire and Hinxey Hill is two miles south of Oxford.]

6. [MS E. T. Clark Collection, Lake Junaluska, NC; *Rep. Verse*, No. 279, p. 311. This is written on a wrapper addressed: "Rev. Mr. C. Wesley, Chesterfield Street, Marylebone."]

WRITTEN IN HANDEL'S LESSONS[7]

Here all the mystic Powers of Sound,
The soul of Harmony is found,
Its perfect Character receives,
And Handel dead for ever lives!

WRITTEN IN KELWAY'S SONATAS[8]

Kelway's[9] Sonatas who can bear?
'They want both harmony and air;
Heavy they make the Player's hand
And who their tricks can understand?   *4*
Kelway to the profound G[iardini][10]
Or B[oyce][11] compared, is but a Ninny,
A Dotard old (the Moderns tell ye)
Mad after Handel and Corelli,   *8*
Spoilt by original disaster,
For Geminiani[12] was his Master,
And taught him, in his nature's ground
To gape for Sense, as well as sound.'   *12*

'Tis thus the Leaders of our nation,
Smit with the Music now in fashion,
Their absolute decisions deal,
And from the Chair Infallible,   *16*
And praise the fine, Italian Taste,
Too fine, too exquisite to last.

7. [MS Pat. Misc., p. 5; *Rep. Verse*, No. 278, p. 311.]

8. [MS Pat. Misc., pp. 5–6.]

9. [Joseph Kelway (d. 1782) was a distinguished organist and harpsichordist of the eighteenth century with whom the gifted young Charles Wesley, Jr. studied.]

10. [Felice de Giardini (1716–96), a celebrated violinist, was known particularly for the improvization of elaborate cadenzas.]

11. [Boyce was a distinguished organist of the period and author of three volumes of Cathedral music. *Cf.* the poem on p. 279 of volume I, *Unpub. Poetry*. It is possible that Wesley meant Johann Christian Bach who was in England at the time.]

12. [Francesco Geminiani was an Italian composer (ca. 1687–1762), a writer, and brilliant performer on the violin.]

Let Midas judge, and what will follow?
A whis[t]ling Pan excels Apollo,   *20*
A Bag-pipe's sweeter than an Organ,
A Sowgelder*[13] surpasses Worgan[14]
And Kelway at the foot appears
Of Connoiseurs—with Asses ears!   *24*

MODERN MUSIC[15]

G[iardini], B[oyce][16] and all
Their followers, great and small,
Have cut Old Music's throat,
And mangled every note;   *4*
Their superficial pains
Have dashed out all his brains:[17]
And now we dote upon
A lifeless sceleton,   *8*
The empty sound at most,
The Squeak of Music's Ghost.

ANOTHER[18]

Who'er admires as Excellence
Sound unaccompanied by Sense,
Shall have my free consent to praise
The favourite Music of our days.   *4*
Still let them dance to Orpheus' Sons
Who captivate the Stocks and Stones;
And while (to Harmony's confusion)
The Masters show their execution   *8*
Attend with long transported ears,
Bad Music's Executioners.

---

13. *A maker and master of Castrato's.

14. [John Worgan (1724–90) was an organist and composer.]

15. [MS Pat. Misc., pp. 6–7; *Rep. Verse*, No. 281, p. 312.]

16. [Or Bach, i.e. Johann Christian Bach as above; see footnote 11.]

17. [Between lines five and six Wesley has written an alternative to line five: "Have quite beat out his brains."]

18. [MS Pat. Misc., p. 7.]

ON S[AMUEL] W[ESLEY][19]

Sam for his first three years the Secret kept,
While in his heart the Seed of Music slept,
Till Charles's Chissel by a carnel Stroke
Brought forth the Statue latent in the block: 4
Like Memnon[20] then, he caught the Solar Fire,
And breath'd spontaneous to Apollo's lyre,
With nature's ease th'Harmonious Summit won
The envious, and the gazing Croud outrun,   } 8
Left all the rest behind, & seized on—Barrington.[21]

ON MR. B[ARRINGTON] GIVING SAM THE PREFERENCE[22]

Judicious Barrington, whose searching eye,
Doth into Nature's close recesses pry,
Who earth in quest of excellence explores,
And the First Cause in all his works adores,   4
Skilful unnotic'd Genius to display,
And Call retiring Merit into day;
Was pleas'd thro' Fortune's envious Cloud to see
Two rising sons of heavenborn Harmony.   8
Crossing his hands, designedly he laid
His right, like Jacob, on the Younger's head;
The Elder great in harmony confest
The Younger with superior honors blest   } 12
Prince of the Tuneful Tribe, and Guide of all the rest.*[23]

19. [Ms Pat. Misc., pp. 7–8; *Rep. Verse*, No. 293, p. 330.]

20. [After Memnon's death, slain by Achilles, Zeus conferred immortality on him, and his statue was erected at Thebes which, when struck by the first rays of the rising sun, was said to give forth a sound like the snapping asunder of a chord.]

21. [Wesley has the marginal note: "al. Mornington." Like Barrington, the Earl of Mornington was an admirer of the young Wesleys.]

22. [MS Pat. Misc., p. 8. This poem also exists in a shorthand first draft with many variations.]

23. *Ephraim marched foremost of the Twelve Tribes.

THE PIANOFORTE: WRITTEN IN THE YEAR 1783[24]

Our Connoisseurs their plausive voices raise,
And dwell on the PIANO-FORTE'S praise.
More brilliant (if we simply take their word)
More sweet than any tinkling Harpsichord,   *4*
While soothing Softness and Expression meet
To make the Contrast, and the joy compleat,
To strike our fascinated ears and eyes
And take our Sense and Reason by surprize.   *8*

  'Tis thus the men whose dictates we obey,
Their taste, and their Authority display,
Command us humbly in their steps to move,
Damn what they damn, & praise what they approve.   *12*
With Faith implicit, and with blind esteem,
To own—All Music is ingross'd by Them.

  So the gay Nation whose capricious law
Keeps the whole fashionable world in awe,   *16*
Nor to Italian Airs their ear incline,
Nor to the noblest Harmony divine
But as the Sum of Excellence propose
Their own sweet Sonnets—warbled thro' the Nose!   *20*

  Yet skilful Masters of the tuneful string,
(Masters who teach the Harpsichord to—*sing*)
Tell us of Music's powers a different story,
And rob PIANO-FORTE of its glory;   *24*
Assuring us, if uncontroul'd by Fashion,
We hear, and judge, without exaggeration,
The Merit of the favourite instrument,
And all its Use and musical intent,   *28*
By the discerning Few is understood
'To hide bad Players, & to spoil the Good.'

24. [MS Pat. Misc., pp. 13–15; MS CW Letters IV, 92; *Rep. Verse*, No. 319, pp. 362–3.]

PART II

What cannot Fashion do? with magic ease
It makes the dull PIANO-FORTE please,   *32*
Bids us a triffling Instrument admire,
As far superior to Apollo's lyre:
Loud as a spanking Warming-pan its tone,
Delicious as the thrilling Bagpipe's drone.   *36*
Organs and Harpsichords it sweeps away
And reigns alone, triumphant for a day:
The Great acknowledge its inchanting power,
The echoing multitude of course adore: *40*
Ev'n Those who *real* Music dared esteem
Caught for a while, are carried by the stream,
O'er all her slaves while Fashion domineers,
And Midas lends them his sagacious Ears!   *44*

Shou'd Fashion singling out (if that coud be)
A poorer tool of modern harmony
The sanction of her approbation give;
The world polite her dictates wou'd receive,   *48*
The list'ning Herb wou'd fall with awe profound
And die transported—at a JEWS-HARP'S Sound!

OCCASIONED BY SOME ILL-NATURED REFLECTIONS
OF AN ANONYMOUS PERSON[25]

The Wesleys must be somewhat bigger,
Eer they attempt to 'soar, or figure',
Neither is yet so great a Ninny
To view with Giants, or Giardini: *4*
They now, content to be unknown,
Compare, prefer themselves to none;
None they depreciate, or despise,
Or seek by Others' fall to rise: *8*
Nor friends nor foes do they offend;
With no Competitors contend,

25. [MS Pat. Misc., pp. 15–17.]

(Whose clashing interests interfere)
For Organ, School, or Theatre: 12
They sue not for the public graces,
Pensions, or Benefits, or Places,
Nor to remoter countries roam,
But study quietly at home,   16
Unseen, unnotic'd, and unheard,
While Music is its own reward:
Their warmest wish (If that coud be)
With all of the same trade t'agree,   20
Into their friendly arms to take,
And love them all for Music's sake.

Why then shoud the Professors aim
To vilify so mean a name,   24
To crush, & nip them in the bud
(If talents *are* on them bestowed)
And clip their wings, before they try
Whither the callow birds can fly?   28

What pity that the Masters great,
Like the great Turk, their Kin shoud hate,
Envious, at worth, repine and grieve,
Nor let a younger brother live?   32
Masters of a superior spirit
Nobly rejoice in early Merit;
Worgan can good in striplings see,
And so can Arnold,[26] and Dupuis;[27]   36
Burney[28] is bold a Crutch to praise,
While Handel's head he gilds with rays:
True worth impartial he commends
In strangers, countrymen, and friends,   40
And cherishes the sons of art
All lodg'd in his capacious heart.

26. [Samuel Arnold (1740–1802) was an operatic composer, organist, and editor of Handel.]
27. [Thomas Sanders Dupuis (1733–96) succeeded Boyce as organist at the Chapel Royal and was also a publisher of piano music.]
28. [Charles Burney (1726–1814) was a musical historian and publisher of harpsichord music.]

O that the tuneful Tribe like Him,
Might excellence in all esteem,   *44*
Consent their quarrels to forget,
And candidly each other treat,
With mutual amity receive,
And, Unisons, as brethren live?   *48*
O might they all henceforward join
To vindicate their art divine,
And emulate the Quire above
Where all is Harmony and Love!   *52*

THE SPEECH OF PONIATOWSKI, KING OF POLAND, 1771[29]

Ye Nations hear! A Monarch great and good
Pleads for the Parricides who spilt his blood,
The Judges prays their sentence to suspend
And let their King his Murtherers defend: *4*
'They thought it right their Leaders to obey,
'A Tyrant, & their Country's Foe to slay;
'Mercy extend to Them that, dying, I
'With confidence may thus for mercy cry,   *8*
'Father, for Jesus' sake, the sinner save,
'Forgiving me, as I my Foes forgave!'

LUNARDI FOR EVER![30] AN AIR FOR THREE VOICES

From the poets we learn, that an Artist of Greece
On pinions of wax, flew over the seas;
And as bold an attempt we were tau[gh]t to admire,
When we saw with our eyes the Italian High-flyer;   *4*

29. [MS Pat. Misc., p. 26; *Rep. Verse*, No. 287, p. 323.]
30. [MS Pat. Misc., pp. 35–6; *Rep. Verse*, No. 331, p. 374. Vincenzo Lunardi (1759–1806) became famous for his flight in a hydrogen-filled balloon on September 15, 1784. The ascent took place near Wesley's Chapel in the City Road. See Frank Baker's note, *Rep. Verse*, p. 374.]

But when next he ascends in his airy baloon,
If himself he excels, and flies over the moon,
All Europe shall ring of an action so hardy
And the world shall be filled with the fame of Lunardi!   *8*

Chorus

Lunardi for ever!
Sing a Hero so clever
So brave and victorious,
So happy and glorious,
Sing a Hero so clever
Lunardi for ever!

[COME, PRICK UP YOUR EARS][31]

[*Nam*] *Vitiis nemo sine nascitur, optimusille* [*est*]
Qui minimis urgitur. Hor[ace][32]

[1.]   Come, prick up your ears,
         Jimmy R[33]—appears,
         In all haste to produce
         His budget of news,
         To sing or to say
         What he learnt at the play,
         And retail the bons mots
         Of theatrical beaux.

[2.]   With what glee he declares
         The pranks of the players!
         With what pleasure repeats
         The Actresses' feats!
         Or if chancing to stray
         They slip out of the way,
         He transmits their renown
         To be hawk'd thro' the town.

31. [MS Pat. Misc., pp. 36–7. *Rep. Verse*, No. 292, pp. 329–30.]
32. [No one is born without faults, and the best man is he who is beset by the least faults. *Sermones*, I, poem 3, lines 68–9.]
33. [The editors have not identified him.]

[3.]   Whene'er he thinks fit
With his delicate wit
His friends to or'epower,
His words we devour,
While by elegant chat
And similies pat
He delight us—or stuns
With a torrent of puns.

[4.]   But the Punster's vain boast
In the Painter is lost,
In a goodness of heart,
Surpassing his art:
His worth we receive,
His foibles forgive,
And true Piety own
In the Dutiful Son.

ON THE EXTENT OF THE ATONEMENT [34]

Shall man, a worm of earth, a child of dust,
Prescribe for God, the gracious, and the just?
Shall he report, how far his grace extends,
Tell where his love begins, and where it ends?   *4*
No, let our God himself his ways explain;
Let him make known his boundless love for man,
Let him unfold the purpose of his will,
And tell the world, that he is gracious still: *8*
Declare that co-extensive with the fall,
Is Jesu's death, and hath atoned for all,
That all may live accepted, through his Son,
And reap eternal joy, in worlds unknown.   *12*

34. [*Arminian Magazine* (1780), p. 455.]

ON THE MESSENGERS OF GOD[35]

A Scripture test—to tell, and try
The Messengers of the Most High—
"Servants of all"—are these on earth,
Yet Sons of God, by heavenly birth!   *4*
Godlike in temper, act, and word,
Meek imitators of their Lord;
Who seek not pleasure, profit, praise,
Which vanish with terrestrial days;   *8*
But "Honour coming from above,"
Boundless as heaven's eternal love!
"Lord, make me fruitful," is their cry,
"To prove my mission from the sky,   } *12*
"O give me children—else I die!"
    Nor labour such for souls—in vain,
While faithful—fruitful they remain;
Weeping, with zeal through crowds they roam!   } *16*
Shouting, with sheaves fly bounding home!
Wishing the world to heaven would come!
Expecting that millennial day
When earth, like heaven, shall God obey!   *20*
Nor "run they as uncertainly,"
Each know from strictest scrutiny,
By heart-felt joys, and what they see,
"I AM hath sent unworthy me."   *24*

ADDRESS TO THE CALVINISTS[36]

God has, you say, a two-fold Will,
One to Preserve, and one to Kill:
That in his Word to All reveal'd,
This from the Reprobate conceal'd: *4*
That would have All the fallen kind
Repentance and Salvation find;
To Hell's inevitable pains
This the far greater part ordains,   *8*

35. [*Arminian Magazine* (1781), p. 456.]

36. [*Arminian Magazine* (1778), pp. 383–4; *Rep. Verse,* No. 295, pp. 331–2. It is significant that the poem appears in the first volume of the *Arminian Magazine,* which was published to combat extreme Calvinism.]

Compell'd to Sin by his Decree,
And Damn'd from all Eternity.
    His written Will to All displays
Offers of Life and pard'ning Grace: *12*
His secret doth this Life deny
To most, yet asks, "Why will ye die?"
His *seeming* Will their good pretends,
His *real* their damnation sends;   *16*
Makes the devoted victims fit,
And thrusts them down into the pit.
    'Tis thus, O God, they picture Thee,
Thy Justice and Sincerity;   *20*
Thy Truth which never can remove,
Thy bowels of unbounded Love:
Thy freedom of Redeeming Grace,
"With-held from almost all the Race,   *24*
"Made for Apollyon to devour,
"In honour of thy Sovereign Power!"
    Ye weak, mistaken Worms, believe
Your God, who never can deceive;   *28*
Believe his word sincerely meant,
Whose Oath confirms his kind intent:
Believe his Tears: believe his Blood:
Both for a World of Sinners flow'd;   *32*
For those who nail'd Him to the Tree,
For those who forg'd *the dire Decree,*
For ev'ry Reprobate—and me!

WRITTEN IN MARCH 1784[37]

Who can deny the Patriots their praise?
All Order is inverted in our days;
"King, Lords, & Commons" is no more the thing
But Commons, Lords, & after that—The King:
We see the Subjects on their Sovereign tread
The Crown beneath the Mace, the RUMP above the Head!

37. [The poem is found in a letter dated March 1784 from Charles Wesley to John
Langshaw, organist of Lancaster, with the above title; Wesley Collection, Special Collections,
Woodruff Library, Emory University, Atlanta, GA.]

TRANSLATIONS FROM THE LATIN[38]

I[39]

Fuit ante Helenam mulier[40] *teterrima belli*
Causa: Sed ignotis perierunt mortibus omnes[41]
Quos Venerem incertam rapientes, more ferarum,
Viribus editior caedebat, ut in grege taurus.

Full many a war has been for woman wag'd,
Ere half the world in Helen's cause engag'd;
But unrecorded in historic verse,
Obscurely died those savage ravishers:
Who, like brute beasts, the female bore away,
Till some superior brute re-seiz'd the prey,
As a wild bull, his rival bull o'erthrown,
Claims the whole subject-herd, and reigns alone.

II[42]

Turpe pecus, glandem atque cubilia propter
Certabant pugnis, dein fustibus atque ita porro
Pugnabant armis, quae post fabricaverat usus.

The human herd, unbroken and untaught,
For acorns first and grassy couches fought;
With fists, and then with clubs, maintain'd the fray,
Till, urg'd by hate, they found a quicker way,
And forg'd pernicious arms, and learn'd the art to slay. }

38. [The poems are found in Henry Moore's *Life of the Rev. John Wesley* (1825), vol. II, pp. 366–7.]

39. [From Horace, *Satires*, I, iii, 107–10; *Rep. Verse*, No. 232, pp. 258–9.]

40. [Horace wrote "cunnus" instead of "mulier."]

41. [Horace wrote "illi" instead of "omnes."]

42. [From Horace, *Satires*, I, iii, 100–3.]

III[43]

Juppiter antiqui contraxit tempora veris,
Perque hiemes aestusque et inaequalis autumnos,
Et breve ver spatiis exegit quattuor annum.

The God of nature, and her sovereign king,
Shorten'd the primitive perennial spring:
The spring gave place, no sooner come than past,
To summer's heat, and winter's chilling blast;
And autumn sick, irregular, uneven:
While the sad year, through different seasons driven,   }
Obey'd the stern decree of angry heaven.

IV[44]

Irrupit[45] venae pejoris in aevum
Omne nefas; fugere pudor, verumque, fidesque;
In quorum subiere locum fraudesque dolique[46]
Insidiaeque et vis, et amor sceleratus habendi.

A flood of general wickedness broke in
At once, and made the iron age begin:
Virtue and truth forsook the faithless race,
And fraud and wrong succeeded in their place.
Deceit and violence, the dire thirst of gold,
Lust to possess, and rage to have and hold.

43. [From Ovid, *Metamorphoses*, I, 116–18.]
44. [From Ovid, *Metamorphoses*, I, 128–31.]
45. [Original: inrupit.]
46. [Original: dolusque.]

V[47]

Vivitur ex rapto: Non hospes ab hospite tutus:
Filius ante diem patrios inquirit in annos;
Victa jacet pietas; et virgo caede madentes,
Ultima coelestum terras Astraea reliquit.

They live by rapine. The unwary guest
Is poison'd at the inhospitable feast.
The son, impatient for his father's death,
Numbers his years, and longs to stop his breath;
Extinguish'd all regard to God and man:
And Justice, last of the celestial train,
Spurns the earth drench'd in blood, and flies to heaven again.

COME THEN, MY SOUL, THOU RESTLESS EXILE, COME
[A FRAGMENT OF AUTOBIOGRAPHY][48]

Come then, my soul, thou restless exile, come,
Suspend awhile thy languishings for home;
With backcast eye the mass of life explore,
An age of misery that returns no more.   4
Leave thy incumbent sufferings in the past,
And calmly wait the hour that brings the last.

Scarce had the morn of pining life began,
When young in days (?) *p r s*[49] of ill I ran;   8
From parents I with fatal haste remov'd,
Unseiz'd for God through nature's wilds I rov'd,
Where vice, with learning mask'd, the youth drank in,
And Babel's curse is taught, and Babel's sin;   12
Where reverend sires their labours will employ
To principle with pride the aspiring boy.
Eager he hears, pursues the glorious goal,
And emulation poisons all his soul.   16

---

47. [From Ovid, *Metamorphoses*, I, 144, 148–50; *Rep. Verse*, No. 233, p. 259.]
48. [MS Shorthand, pp. 1–5.]
49. [The intended word is uncertain.]

Here first I learnt to catch an empty name,
To idolise esteem and covet fame,
My own renown on others' fall to raise,
And gasp insatiate for distraction's praise.   20
Still in my inmost soul the fiend I find,
To vanity's eternal bonds consign'd;
Still in my inmost soul the demon reigns,
And holds me captive in a demon's chains,   24
Through all my thoughts and words his course pursues,
Steals on my verse and desecrates my muse.
From fools well *d s c d* woud rise to fame,
And glories in my aptly pictur'd shame.   28

Farther yet farther from eternal truth,
Full of the heady holiness of youth,
O'er pleasing paths of furious vice I stray'd,
As lust impell'd me, or as fancy sway'd.   32
Charm'd by the sweetly warbling wanton lyre,
I catch the pagan's with the poet's fire,
Or gaze on thundering forenacting (?) Jove,
Or loosely range through all the art of love: 36
Deep sank the poison in my tender mind,
Nor help from vain mythology I find,
While sins(?) the latter's nearer influence fills,
And memory holds it in her damned (?) seals.   40

Neglected lay the unkindled spark within,
Nor ever struggles with congenial sin:
Careless my soul slides on in nature's night,
Unfelt the darkness and unmiss'd the light;   44
Ignobly sepulchr'd in flesh remains,
Nor knows its fall from God, nor feels its chains,
Nor tames the void (?), nor stirs the quickening breath,
But all is silent, calm and cold as death.   48

Who then shall say whence second life began,
Who donn'd this prospect of the heavenly man?
Unconscious of my change I never knew
To fix the point from whence the Spirit blew,   52
So imperceptibly the stroke was given,
The power divine that turn'd my face to heaven.

Sudden o'ercome and plung'd in vast delight,
Eager I seem'd to grasp the Infinite! 56
With strong expansion swell'd my ravish'd breast
And glow'd to fain (?) impress the enticed guest:
Forever here I deem'd it good to stay
Where athletes fair bestrode the narrow way, 60
The narrow way with heedless joy I trod,
And gave my fond unwary heart to God.

Scarce had my soul fix'd her directer eye,
And aim'd at heaven, and vow'd to scale the sky, 64
When dire commenc'd the latent war within,
And feeble nature felt awakening sin.
Strong in ten thousand lusts the tyrant rose
And storm'd my bosom with ten thousand foes, 68
O'ertook my flight, mock'd my resistance vain,
Subdu'd and gall'd me with an iron chain,
Refus'd, omnipotent, to set me free,
And thought and acted, reign'd and liv'd in me. 72

Nor yet retir'd the principle divine,
Nor quite forgot the ethereal spark to shine,
Quicken'd by Thee I still renew'd the strife,
And groan'd for God, and struggling long'd for life: 76
Constrain'd to yield, yet strengthen'd to reply,
Forth with alternate pangs I rise and fly,
Sank, and resisted in unequal flight,
The indigent slave of grovelling appetite. 80

Stronger at length the heavenly instinct grew,
And just despair brought infinite hope in view:
I own'd that in my flesh sin only liv'd,
And death's sad sentence in myself receiv'd. 84
By strong temptation suffer'd to respire
Then first I felt relax'd the plaguing fire,
Then in my humbled soul the woman's seed
Victorious woke and bruis'd the serpent's head, 88
Bade inbred sin its cruel power suspend,
And in a moment's peace the internal conflict end.

But Oh how short my interval of woe,
How fierce the pangs I next am doom'd to know;   92
Pleas'd with the calm as down I sank to rest,
Nor fill'd with life divine my vacant breast,
In stronger gusts a mightier tempest rose
(In vain woud flight avoid or force oppose,   96
Nor wish'd I to resist, nor car'd to fly)
It spreads, it mounts and gains upon the sky;
Headlong I fell by passion's whirlwinds driven,
Swept from the margin of remoter heaven,   100
Down to profoundest hell my hopes it hurl'd,
Tore me from God, and interpos'd a world!

Oh what avail'd it that, from sins got free,
I gain'd a scarcely tasted liberty!   104
In vain does appetite her web remove,
Severest change of punishment I prove,
More surely chasten'd by the scorpion, love.

Distant at first my danger I survey,   108
Now idly with the nearer ruin play (?);
Refusing now the pleasing boon to shun,
I sink, I yield deliberately undone,
Gladly deceiv'd and sensibly betray'd,   112
While sweetly listening smil'd the docile maid,
Wisely admir'd the poet's sacred song,
And caught the counsel falling from my tongue.

Nor yet woud treacherous reason's timely care   116
The unstill'd mischief from my bosom tear,
My bosom, soon by reason slave (self?) thrown wide,
Receiv'd the vile affection's fatal tide;
Fed by the stream of fond benevolence,   120
And swiftly (?) rising with the torrent sense,
Resistless now the impetuous waters roll,
O'erpass their bounds and deluge all my soul.

But Oh, could longing paint the deep distress,   124
The idolising passion's just excess!
Description (?) flags, the languid colours fail—
See then thy labour, muse, and draw the veil—

No! be the veil forever cast aside,   *128*
May no false art the genuine maiden hide,
Forever stand depos'd my fond design
To augment the plenitude of love divine,
To swell the essential, all-sufficient bliss   *132*
With the poor drop of creature happiness.
Hear, ye adulterers, my warning call,
Ye who before your Maker's image fall,
With caution'd soul (?) the gradual tale pursue   *136*
Of one that languish'd, griev'd, and lov'd like you;
A God behind the covenant requir'd;
Attend and mark the rock where shipwreck'd faith expir'd.

    Vainly at first my labouring bosom strove   *140*
To heed the pain of unsuspected love,
The sad discovery lingering I delay'd
Lest shy reserve should arm the alter'd maid,
The lover manifest supplant the friend,   *144*
And friendship's offices in coldness end.
Scarce could my rising griefs at last prevail,
Or wild despair extort the written tale,
Scarce could my trembling hand perform its part   *148*
And give the token (?) of my bleeding heart.
Guiltless she read: I mark'd her conscious eyes,
Eager I saw the fluttering spirit's rise:
Soon the fair prophetess my anguish guess'd,   *152*
Sudden broke off and fear'd to read the rest,
Gently refus'd the total case (?) to explore:
'I dare pursue your fatal (?) tale no more.'
She sigh'd and sigh'd; I begg'd and urg'd in vain;   *156*
Complied at last the unfinish'd lines to explain,
Hardly I spoke, with doting transport mov'd;
And blush'd; and wondering told her that I lov'd!

    Who then can paint her soft confus'd distress,   *160*
Her sweet surprise and pitying tenderness!
The lovely soul, transparent from within,
In every motion, word and look was seen.
With kindest sympathy for me she griev'd,   *164*
For me she wept, 'Unhappily deceiv'd,
To think so mean a creature worth my care,
To prize or love or ever sigh (?) for her!

Rather she hop'd my soul from passion free   *168*
Miscall'd its own exalted charity,
A generous word mistook for low desire,
And only glow'd with friendship's heavenly (holy?) fire.'

    Mistaken comforter! Could tears remove,   *172*
Could soft compassion's balm extinguish love?
Her kind concern increas'd my tender care,
And check'd and combated my just despair.
Restless I follow'd the relenting maid,   *176*
Call'd tears and sighs and letters to my aid,
In softest accents proved my growing flame,
And weeping kiss'd the lov'd A[spasia]'s[50] name.

    Nor long enjoy'd my soul the pure relief   *180*
Of patient love and calmly pensive grief:
Rous'd by fierce jealousy's corroding smart,
And all its vipers fastening on my heart,
The helpless maid I saw with blasted eyes,   *184*
By kindred hands dragg'd on to sacrifice;
A[spasia] sentenc'd to be vilely sold,
A[spasia]'s happiness exchang'd for gold.
In horrid league the evil tribe combin'd   *188*
With lust of wealth to taint her purer mind,
Prepar'd the only good themselves desir'd,
By avarice and by curs'd ambition fir'd:
Ungenerously they urg'd their dear pretence: *192*
'Kind guardians of her orphan innocence,
The proffer'd benefit she needs must own,
Requite their care, and yield to be undone.'
In vain her tears their pity strove to engage,   *196*
In vain she started from obtruded age,
Trembling renew'd her oft-rejected plea,
The eternal bar of fix'd antipathy,
Which scarcely could his irksome form behold,   *200*
Though wealth had touch'd her lover into gold.
Basely they bore her weak resistance down,
And specious friendship help'd the ruin on;

50. [See the discussion on this name in *Unpub. Poetry*, I, pp. 18–19.]

Thrice she the *w s* torment good (?) prevail'd,   *204*
Bound to their force (?) the feeble victim fail'd,
Yielding she sank, to worse than death pursu'd;
Oh strange excess of fatal gratitude!

   Love, only love, their purpose dar'd to oppose,   *208*
A single succour(?) 'gainst a world of foes.
Inspir'd by love, I started to her aid,
I flew to rescue the devoted maid,
'Twixt fate and her resolv'd to stand alone,   *212*
And guard a safety dearer than my own.
I begg'd her stay, conjur'd herself to spare,
With all the labouring vehemence of prayer.
I warn'd her and, encourag'd by my fears,   *216*
Arm'd her with groans and fortified with tears.
Oft as she mark'd my heaving bosom rise,
And genuine sorrow bursting from my eyes,
She gently sooth'd my wildly frantic grief.   *220*
And press'd my trembling hand and sigh'd (?) relief:
To comfort me resolv'd her fate to shun,
Nor yet consent, nor haste to be undone.
Again she strove, by generous pity still'd,   *224*
And dar'd her kinsmen's rage, and scorn'd to yield:
Her generous pity stopp'd the dire decree,
And sav'd the victim but *it.* [   ] round me.

   Coud friendship self so deep concern express,   *228*
So strange an height of melting tenderness!
Surely she wept, by more than friendship mov'd,
Surely I deem'd the infected virgin lov'd.
Fir'd with the thought I chid my hasty fears,   *232*
Again gave up my heart, and hop'd for hers,
Hop'd the dear maid woud feel an answering care,
And watch'd her artless soul to find it there.
Once, as her innocence I warmly press'd,   *236*
To own my tender interest in her breast,
To grant the only bliss I liv'd to prove,
Some small return for all my waste of love,—
She sigh'd, she blush'd—confess'd my passion true: *240*
'The worthless love you ask is all your due,
Yet Oh,' she cried, 'in vain you claim a part,
Too late you claim it—I have lost my heart!'

Here, if thou darest, suffer *r m m* tell   244
What more than tortures did my bosom feel!
What more than fires or racks did I sustain,
What sad vicissitude of smarting pain!
How oft my struggling spirit groan'd to bear   248
The strong confliction of extreme despair;
How oft with sense of softer anguish mov'd,
For her I wept and trembled, pray'd and lov'd!
How oft to lonesome woods in fancy ran,   252
And hid me from the hated sight of man;
How oft impatient of continu'd breath,
Idly I call'd and rav'd and gasp'd for death!
To catch her flying soul woud life resign,   256
Rush to the grave, and die to call her mine,
As if to me by fate would soon be given
First to assert propriety in heaven!

When thus my bosom, torn by raging love,   260
Had long with the remorseless passion strove,
At length I yielded all; at length gave o'er
The contest vain and combatted no more,
But madly sank beneath the unequal load,   264
Disclaim'd my reason, and threw off my God.

No longer now my drooping hands I rear,
Or force my stubborn heart to irksome prayer;
Toward the celestial prize no longer press,   268
Plung'd in the gulf of gloomy recklessness:
My calling's hope indigent I resign,
A willing alien from the life divine,
While down the stream of headlong nature driven,   272
Nor earth I wish'd to hold, nor aim'd at heaven;
While from my centre loos'd, and dead within,
I only pant and move and live to sin,
So dear the effect of an abandon'd will,   276
So deep the fatal curse of passion's utmost ill!

Why then to heaven do I desire to bow,
Why deprecate th'Almighty's anger now?
Whence this imperfect wish my sin to mourn,   280
These faint endeavourings toward a full return?

Still can remorse this flinty bosom move?
Oh wondrous proof of unexhausted love!
Oh, Saviour, once again to Thee I call,   *284*
Bring back my struglings and retrieve my fall!
If prayer can yet find favour in Thy sight,
And stop Thy Spirit's everlasting flight,
Regard vain man, forget the outrage past,   *288*
Accept my groans, or let me breathe the last.

If while this principle for Thee remains,
Clogg'd and entangled in corporeal chains,
If haply be Thy will to make me free,   *292*
Rais'd to Thy children's glorious liberty,
From new torment change (?) thy *t s* control,
And plant Thine interest in my unborn soul;
Through all its pores renew'd from now appear,   *296*
From instant now set up Thy kingdom here,
Thy hidden sweetness give my heart to know,
And taste the Eden of Thy love below.

But if Thy sovereign will, severe yet just,   *300*
Still leaves me dark and humbled in the dust,
There let me bless Thy just-severe decree,
And in Thy secret tongues belong to Thee!
Disgust of life no more my eye repine,   *304*
But bear my nature till exchang'd for Thine;
In calm despair live out my wretched span,
Nor once depart, or struggle with my pain.
No—let me never to Thy creatures flee,   *308*
Or seek or taste a joy distinct from Thee;
Though still condemn'd to mourn my Eden's loss,
Uncheer'd my grief, uncomforted my cross,
Yet grant me strength to bear the penal load,   *312*
To want and ever hail my absent God.

So when Thy waves and storms are all pass'd o'er,
When pain torments and guilt distracts no more,
Let me aye find in Thee my long-sought heaven,   *316*
My warfare ended and my sin forgiven;
Be Thou my all, my final passion Thou,
Of this secur'd I live—I welcome judgment now.

STILLNESS
WRITTEN FOR LADY H[UNTINGDON][51]

1. O my Father, God and King,
      How shall I thy mercy praise,
   How my kind preserver sing,
      Kept from evil all my days!
   Crush'd beneath thy mercy's weight
      Far thou know'st I cannot move,
   Overwhelm'd with joy to greet,
      Lost in wonder, shame and love.

2. How hast thou my soul secur'd
      Since my earliest breath I drew,
   How my foolish heart allur'd
      Long before thy face I knew!
   From the day that I was born
      Strangely hast thou hedg'd me in,
   Fenc'd me with the legal thorn,
      Forcibly withheld from sin.

3. Born to trouble, grief and care,
      As the sparks that upward fly,
   Sin I find a cross to bear,
      Daughter of affliction I;
   But the cross to me was good,
      Chasten'd by domestic ill,
   Chang'd I was, if not subdued,
      Broke if not destroy'd my will.

4. Nature, by the cross kept down,
      Waited for renewing grace;
   In an earthly parent's frown
      Smil'd my heavenly Father's face.
   Good was out of evil brought;
      Now thy hand in all I see,
   All for good together wrought,
      All reserv'd my heart for thee.

51. [MS Shorthand, pp. 16–25.]

5. When the fiend in shape of man
    For my soul had laid his net,
Didst thou not my soul restrain,
    Turn aside my heedless feet?
Ever-watching Providence
    Baffled all the tempter's art,
Screen'd my hallow'd innocence,
    Kept my fond, unwary heart.

6. Me how often didst thou save
    From or in the fiery hour,
Long before I left my grave
    Through thy resurrection's power!
Thou didst all my foes controul
    While I knew not they were nigh;
He who touch'd this worthless soul
    Touch'd the apple of thine eye.

7. Still my soul was in thy hand
    And thou woudst not let me go,
Pluck'd each moment as a brand
    From the fiery realms of woe;
Still on snares and deaths I trod,
    Dwelt where Satan keeps his seat,
Safe in death's dark shade abode
    Standing with the lawless great.

8. Thou didst give me to despise
    All their pomps and pleasures vain,
Slaves to passion, pride and vice,
    Foul with sin's ignoble stain.
O how idly did they boast,
    Strangers to the Saviour's blood,
Poor and vile, undone and lost,
    Guilty worms that knew not God.

9. Stranger to the way of peace,
    Ignorant of Jesus' name,
Have I scorn'd their happiness,
    All their pleasures, wealth and fame;

All, I say, was vanity;
    Father, by thy only grace,
Greatness I ascrib'd to thee,
    Power and majesty and praise.

PART II

1. Praise and majesty and power,
        Jesus, now to thee I give;
    Falling, dying, every hour,
        By thy grace I rise, I live;
    O the miracle of grace!
        How shall I my God admire?
    Guardian of my early days,
        Safe with thee I walk'd in fire.

2. Now thy Spirit brings to mind
        Tongues which then I did not know;
    Never wilt thou let me find
        Ease or happiness below.
    O how miserably great
        Did I for deliverance groan,
    Languish'd to throw off my state,
        Long'd to live and die unknown.

3. Envious of the peasant's lot,
        How did I for quiet pine,
    Wish'd to be by all forgot,
        Hid from every eye but thine;
    O how set in fond desire
        Did I to the cloister fly:
    'Let me from the world retire,
        Let me in the desert die.'

4. Weary of the war within,
        Weary of my endless strife,
    Weary of myself and sin,
        Weary of a wretched life,

Harass'd with an iron yoke,
    Burden'd with an heart of stone,
All to thee I coud not look,
    Durst not then for mercy groan.

5. Tortur'd into legal fear(?),
        Long I toil'd, and toil'd in vain;
    Higher grew the storm and higher,
        Deeper my distress and pain;
    Self-condemn'd I could not rest,
        I was as the troubled sea,
    Legion-sin my soul possess'd,
        Sin is perfect misery.

6. O the grievous agonies,
        O the cruel wracking smart!
    Guilt, the worm that never dies,
        Gnaw'd and fasten'd on my heart.
    Who the anguish can declare,
        Who can know but those that fell
    All the torment of despair;
        Inbred sin is inbred hell.

7. In the toils of death I lay,
        Looking for my fearful hire.
    Satan came and seiz'd his prey,
        Hurrying to eternal fire:
    Satan came—and Jesus too!
        Just as into hell I drop,
    Jesus to my rescue flew,
        'Satan, give thy prisoner up!'

8. Jesus spoke the powerful word
        (How shall I adore the grace!
    O my dear redeeming Lord,
        Let me dwell upon his praise);
    Jesus suddenly drew nigh,
        Cast me from the lion's teeth;
    'I have found a ransom, I
        Died to save that soul from death.'

9. Satan heard, and trembling fled;
        Rescued from the fowler's snare,
    Him who lifted up my head
        Jesus I to all declare;
    Jesus is the sinner's peace,
        Jesus is our liberty,
    Jesus is our righteousness,
        Jesus liv'd and died for me!

PART III

1. Help me, Lord, thy works to praise,
        Jesus, dear atoning Lamb;
    Countless are thy works of grace
        Since I knew thee by thy name;
    Thee, my Saviour, I adore,
        Glory, strength ascribe to thee;
    Thou hast shed forth all thy power,
        Jesus prov'd indeed to me.

2. Thou hast rescu'd me from death,
        Spoil'd the lion of his prey,
    Pluck'd from the devourer's teeth,
        Tore my trembling soul away;
    Thou hast been my sun and shield,
        Sav'd me from the fowler's net,
    Still from falling hast upheld,
        Set upon the rock my feet.

3. Satan all his arts essay'd,
        Now no more a fiend in sight
    Slily his approach he made
        As a messenger of light;
    Mask'd in deep humility,
        Unsuspected he drew near;
    Who in him coud evil see,
        What coud a poor sinner fear?

4.   As a lion once he walk'd
      Seeking whom he might devour,
  Now with easy tread he stalk'd,
      Wiser now, he woud not roar:
  My destruction to ensure,
      Closely he disguis'd his skill,
  None like him so meek, so pure,
      None so tame, so smooth, so still!

5.   Weak, unarm'd, of sin afraid,
      Sick he found me, weary, faint;
  He was ready with his aid,
      He woud banish my complaint,
  He woud find me out the way,
      Sure and only way to peace,
  If I woud but him obey
      All my cares at once shoud cease.

6.   Simple love no evil thought:
      Cheated with a show of good,
  Greedily the hook I caught,
      Baited with my Saviour's blood;
  Baffled by the tempter's art
      Willing I receiv'd his yoke,
  Binding my unwary heart,
      Listening while the Serpent spoke.

7.   'Foolish child,' he suavely cried,
      'Spare thyself this needless pain,
  Cast thy zealous works aside,
      Harry not thyself in vain;
  Do not bend so much and strive,
      Do not labour up the hill,
  I a new commandment give,
      Spare thyself, I say; be still.

8.   'Run not after means of grace,
      Fancying them by God enjoin'd,
  Leave the consecrated place,
      Look at him and ye shall find:

Ordinances profit not,
    Ordinances cannot save,
Cast them by, be all forgot,
    Word and church and altar leave.

9.   'All who use, in means confide,
    Vainly ye the charge deny;
Lay them for a while aside,
    Only for a season try:
Give your prayers and reading o'er . . .
    [incomplete]

10.   'T'ward the mark ye need not press,
    Need not strive to enter in,
Following after holiness,
    Labouring to extirpate sin.
Let not sin disturb your rest,
    Sin, 'tis a mere thing of nought,
Need not be with grief confess'd;
    Sloth despise and mind it not.

11.   'Why should sin cause [   ][52] pain?
    Sin in you must always be;
Let it quietly remain,
    Sin and Christ may well agree:
Christ, you know, did all fulfil,
    Nought is left for man to do,
Freely follow your own will,
    Christ was meek and chaste for you.

12.   'Go not after empty schemes,
    Schemes of righteousness brought in,
Listen not to idle dreams,
    Dreams of living without sin:
If you once have tasted peace,
    Never can you farther go,
No inherent righteousness,
    No perfection, is below.

52. [A gap is left here in the MS.]

13. 'Safely then set up your rest,
         Where you are, in stillness keep;
     Let not casual sin molest
         Like the child when put to sleep:
     Harry poor yourself no more,
         Care not what you are or how;
     Hush, be still, all work is o'er,
         You are a poor sinner now.

14. 'Other followers of the Lamb
         Painfully deny their will;
     Call yourself ('tis all the same)
         A poor sinner, and be still;
     After Christ their cross they bear,
         You may use your liberty;
     Only cry, My Saviour there,
         He hath borne the cross for me.

15. 'Be not into bondage brought,
         What need a poor sinner do?
     Christ, I say, the work hath wrought,
         Nothing now remains for you:
     Men may bid you strive and press,
         Ask, and seek, and knock, and call;
     Works, and means, and holiness
         All are empty, legal all.

16. 'Lay your zealous scruples by,
         Be not to yourself severe,
     With the world you may comply,
         Little tongues you need not fear:
     Put your gold and jewels on,
         You are born to high estate;
     Pride in baser minds is shewn,
         You are truly good and great.'

17. Here my spirit took the alarm,
         Half-perceiv'd the naked snare,
     Started from the apparent harm,
         Flattery too gross to bear (?);

411

Back recoil'd my frighted heart,
  Satan his advantage knew,
Left within his poison'd dart,
  Dropp'd his feignings and withdrew.

18. Sure he went and came again,
      Watch'd me with an evil eye,
    Sent me many an humble man,
      Smooth retailers of his lie;
    All my goings they beset,
      Soothing me with nicest skill,
    Hunting me as with a net,
      Sweetly whispering, 'Be still.'

19. Willingly I heard them speak
      Of my dear Redeemer's blood,
    (Men so loving, mild, and meek,
      All they said must needs be good!)
    Long'd my judgment to submit,
      Lov'd them for their dying Lord,
    Kiss'd the ground beneath their feet,
      Honour'd and almost ador'd.

20. How then, O my simple heart,
      Didst thou 'scape out of their toils?
    Christ the tempted took my part,
      Woud not quit his lawful spoils,
    Woud not let me wholly yield,
      Blest for ever be his name;
    Me he forcibly withheld,
      Kept me till the rescue came.

21. God who sends by whom he will,
      God the good, the mighty God,
    Baffled all their strength and skill,
      All his power in weakness shew'd,
    Sent from out their host of foes
      One in sin and stillness drown'd;
    Where the rankest poison grows
      There the antidote is found.

22.   *Mene tekel!*[53] here the days,
          Here the reign of stillness ends;
      I disclaim the faithless race,
          Hold no fellowship with fiends.
      Thou art in the balance weighed,
          Wanting art thou found at last;
      Stillness, all thy hell's display'd,
          All thy hour of darkness past.

23.   Now I see with other eyes
          What before I woud not see,
      Froward (?) holiness (?), disguise,
          Close (?) serpentine subtilty,
      Shy reserve that shuns the light,
          Devil-heart and devil-tongue,
      Wisdom dark and deep as night,
          Deep as hell from whence it sprung.

24.   Who the cunning can declare
          Of thy silent, simple ones?
      Simple, yet surpassing far
          Loyola and all his sons!
      O how skilful to o'erthrow
          Altar, church, foundations, walls!
      None suspects the secret blow
          Till the sudden ruin falls.

25.   Who can all their virtues paint!
          Tell me, which shall I commend?
      Say, ye mighty to supplant,
          Wise to undermine, your friend;
      Shall I praise your magic art?
          Exquisite dissemblers, say;
      Dearest friends your whispers part,
          Steal the unwary heart away.

26.   O how winning your address,
          When the first approach ye make!
      Every carnal taste ye please,
          Every shape and colour take;

53. [See Daniel 5:25–8.]

Now your brother dear ye praise,
   Now your brother dear exclude,
In his fall yourselves to raise,
   Cunning German gratitude!

27. Gainers ye by others' loss,
   Ye like Persian monarchs reign,
All into your hands engross,
   All besides yourselves disdain;
All to you for faith must come,
   All beside yourselves are blind,
Closely keeping after Rome,
   Popes ye are of all mankind.

28. Such ye were too long to me,
   But I now reject your sway,
Guile and I can ne'er agree,
   All your cords I cast away:
Now the full divorce is made,
   Now the gulf is brought between,
Ordinances disobey'd,
   Pleaders for the world and sin.

29. Will ye claim my friendship now
   More than heathen Turks or Jews?
Do ye stiffneck'd rebels bow
   God's appointed means to use?
Use because by God enjoined,
   Seek the ancient Christian way,
Undefil'd and unrefin'd,
   Now repent, believe, obey.

30. Haste, ye advocates for sin,
   Haste, ye foes to holiness,
Rent, O rent, your hearts unclean,
   All your guile and sin confess;
All your blasphemies abjure,
   Turn and sue to be forgiven,
Turn in time, ye sinners poor,
   Turn, and we may meet in heaven.

414

PART IV

1. Glory, honour, thanks and praise,
       Dearest Lord, I render thee,
   Strong to succour, rich in grace,
       Thou hast got the victory;
   Hewn in pieces all their snares,
       Glory, praise to thee I give,
   Sav'd me from my sins and fears,
       Bade me stedfastly believe.

2. Thou art king, and reign'st alone,
       Scatt'ring evil with thine eyes,
   Tumbling sin and Satan down,
       Conquering all my enemies;
   Thou hast sav'd my soul from hell,
       Thou dost still my soul defend,
   Thou shalt save (I know, I feel)
       Thou shalt save me to the end.

3. Thou hast made my terrors cease,
       Thou hast made my sins depart,
   Stablish'd me in righteousness,
       Arm'd with love my faithful heart;
   Evil now I cannot fear,
       Satan, death, the world, and sin,
   Let them to my soul draw near,
       Christ my Saviour stands between.

4. Still he bids me look to him,
       Looking I am sav'd from all;
   Jesus mighty to redeem,
       While he stands I cannot fall;
   He my helpless soul defends,
       He my strength and fortress is,
   Christ the Rock his shade extends,
       Christ, th'eternal Rock of peace.

5. Now I dare my hellish foe,
       Challenge thee to take the field,
   All thy fiery arrows throw,
       Can they pierce this sacred shield?

Tremble thou when this appears,
   Lo, I lift it up on high,
See the dreadful sign it bears,
   See the bloody cross, and fly.

6. When their chief I put to flight,
     Dare his soldiers turn their face?
Can the world withstand my might,
     When their prince and god I chase?
What if here I trouble have,
     There is still the victory,
From this evil world to save
     Jesus liv'd and died for me.

PART V

1. Lo, again the silent fiend
     Calls for my extorted lays!
Thou whose witchcrafts never end,
     Lovely monster, shew thy face!
Stand in all thy charms display'd,
     Skulk no more in deepest night,
Let me draw thee from the shade,
     Drag thy modesty to light.

2. See we then the sinners poor,
     Poor as Popish mendicant!
No design have they, be sure,
     Christ and only Christ they want.
What if rich ones they respect?
     Rich ones do the greatest good;
What if beggars they reject?
     Beggars only turn for food.

3. From the poor they turn away,[54]
   Where there is not store of wealth,
Bigots still may fast and pray,
   Are not worth the charge (?) of health.
But if riches wave her hand,
   Here they follow day and night,
Fly to compass sea and land,
   Seize the important proselyte!

4. When the prey is in their net,
   Surely then they merit praise
G n r[55] their captivating[56] threat,
   Lead him in their flowery ways.
Easy is their yoke and light;
   Nothing need their convert do,
Need not stand on wrong or right,
   Let him his own way pursue.

5. He may enter into life,
   Ignorant (?) of God's commands,
Spare himself the toil and strife,
   All is ready to his hands:
God's commands he need not mind,
   Holy Church so he obey,
Heaven he now with us may find,
   Wide the gate and broad the way.

6. Say, ye prophets smooth and still,
   Answer if I do you wrong
Please ye not the carnal will?
   Tell me with your silver tongue.
Who can captivate the heart,
   Who like you the beasts can soothe?
Say, ye masters of your art,
   Say, ye prophets still and smooth!

54. [Wesley originally wrote "aside."]

55. [Wesley's abbreviation is unclear but "g n r" is all that is decipherable. The editors cannot suggest what these consonants mean.]

56. [Wesley's abbreviation is again unclear, but "captivating" seems most likely.]

7. You like Rome with laws dispense,
    Human duties and divine,
  Trample on man's ordinance,[57]
    When your happy praise ye join.
  Gath and Askelon rejoice
    O'er your bridegroom and his bride,
  Hellish shouts confirm your choice,
    Blasphemies on every side.

8. Heathen scoff the Saviour's name
    Whom ye still with guile confess,
  Silent, ye enjoy your shame,
    Fed, your churches take their ease;
  Marry whom or how ye will,
    Or if weary of your lives
  Cast away the cross, be still,
    Sell your livings,—or your wives!

9. Hail, ye nursing fathers' god (?),[58]
    Take the praise to virtue due!
  Who so careful of the good (?),
    Who can cherish self like you?
  Ye your churches' ease secure,
    Feed them with convenient food,
  For their every want procure,
    Flood the church with flesh and blood.

10. Hail, successful levellers,
    Ye your happy arts employ
  Arms and titles to reverse,
    Ranks and orders to destroy:
  Ye can compass your design,
    Undistinguish[59] high and low,
  Strangest contraries ye join,
    Yoke the coronet with the plough.

57. [The MS clearly reads "man's ordinance." It would appear to be a slip either for "God's ordinance" or "man's innocence." The latter may be more likely, since the word "man's" comes first.]

58. [The interpretation is uncertain, as the last word in lines one and three is identical in the shorthand, i.e. "god" and/or "good."]

59. [If the interpretation of the shorthand is correct, the verb "Undistinguish" is a coinage of Charles Wesley.]

11. Advocates (?) with flesh and blood,
         Wrong in you alone is right;
     Appetite to mix with mud,
         Grovelling, downward appetite.[60]
     Pride and avarice and lust
         Yours may follow, if they please,
     Sin commences good and just,
         Licens'd by your holiness.

[WITH HUMBLE, MEEK, SUBMISSIVE FEAR]
MATT. 19:11–12[61]

1. With humble, meek, submissive fear,
        Dark, foolish, blind to what is best,
    To thee, my Jesus, I draw near,
        And trembling urge my fond request.

2. Give me thy saying to receive,
        Thy innocence to emulate,
    In every point like thee to live,
        To live and die in thy estate.

3. Not that I dare my God blaspheme,
        Or blithely slight the nuptial tie,
    Holy and just and good I deem
        The great tremendous mystery.

4. Worthy the pure primeval man
        Before he touch'd the mortal tree,
    Worthy by thee, O Christ, to reign,
        Fit emblem of thy Church and thee.

60. [This strange phrase is justified by line 356, "A downward Appetite to mix with Mud," in "An Epistle to a Friend," *Unpub. Poetry,* I p. 180.]

61. [MS Shorthand, p. 26. This poem was clearly written before Charles Wesley had met Sarah Gwynne and reflects his attitude toward personal celibacy prior to marriage. It is included here with other poems from MS Shorthand rather than with biblical poems in volume II of *Unpub. Poetry.*]

5. Yet O my soul would fain decline
   The marriage-yoke, I know not why;
   I bless the ordinance divine,
   But as I am, exist to die.

6. Lord, if thou didst the wish inspire,
   The breathings of thy spirit own,
   Fulfil my trembling heart's desire
   And let me live with thee alone.

7. Let me from men forever cease,
   Let all my creature-comforts die;
   Be thou my soul's immortal pleas (?),
   Thou only all my wants supply.

8. Fairer than all the sons of men,
   Fairest among ten thousand thou,
   I pant thy only love to gain,
   And all my soul requires thee now.

9. Come, thou, dear pardoner (?) of my soul,
   Thou the Desire of Nations, come;
   Come, take posession of the whole,
   Fit and receive my spirit home.

10. Bear my affections all above,
    Where thou my heavenly haven art;
    Take the poor treasure of my love,
    And keep, O keep, my virgin heart.

11. Mark every thought that rises there
    Nor let me for a moment stray;
    Watch over me with jealous care,
    And lead me in thy perfect way.

12. Lover of souls, on thee I call,
    Save me from every love but thine,
    And let me on thy bosom fall,
    And rest within the arms divine.

TO MISS MARTHA WESLEY[62]

When want, and pain, and death besiege our gate
And every solemn moment teems with fate;
While cloud and darkness fill the space between,
Perplex th'event, and shade the folded scene: *4*
In humble silence wait th'unuttered voice,
Suspend thy will, and check thy forward choice;
Yet wisely fearful for th'event prepare;
And learn the dictates of a brother's care.   *8*
How fierce thy conflict, how severe thy flight,
When Hell assails the foremost sons of light;
When he, who long in virtue's paths had trod,
Deaf to the voice of conscience and of God,   *12*
Drops the fair mask, proves traitor to his vow;
And thou the temptress and the tempted thou!
Prepare thee then to meet the infernal war,
And dare beyond what woman knows to dare;   *16*
Guard each avenue to thy flutt'ring heart,
And act the sister's and the Christian's part.
Heaven is the guard of virtue; scorn to yield,
When screened by Heaven's impenetrable shield.   *20*
Secure in this, defy th'impending storm,
Though Satan tempt thee in an angel's form.
And, Oh! I see the fiery trial near;
I see the saint, in all his forms, appear.   *24*
By nature, by religion, taught to please,
With conquest flushed, and obstinate to press,

---

62. [Adam Clarke, *Memoirs of the Wesley Family* (1823), pp. 518–19. Martha (Patty) Wesley, Charles's sister, while staying with her uncle Matthew Wesley in London, met a Westley Hall who was one of John Wesley's pupils. He paid his addresses to her and they became betrothed, without the knowledge of her parents. Some time later he accompanied John and Charles to Epworth and there he met Kezia, became attracted to her, and obtained her and and her parents' consent to marriage. At the last moment he seems to have had twinges of conscience and declared he had a revelation from heaven that he should marry Martha. She, of course, had no knowledge of his engagement to Kezia, and on her marriage to him incurred the censure of her parents and her brothers who accused her of stealing her sister's promised husband—hence the mention of incest. This poem must date between 1730, when he first met Martha, and 1735, when he married her. Though a clergyman, Westley Hall became a deist and a polygamist with several illegitimate children, and later deserted his wife. Both sisters behaved with exemplary charity towards him.]

He lists his virtues in the cause of Hell,
Heaven, with celestial arms, presumes to assail;   28
To veil with semblance fair the fiend within,
And make his God subservient to his sin!
Trembling I hear his horrid vows renewed,
I see him come by *Delia's*[63] groans pursued,   32
Poor injured Delia! all her groans are vain;
Or he denies, or listening mocks her pain.
What though her eyes with ceaseless tears o'erflow,
Her bosom heave with agonizing woe;   36
What though the horror of his falsehood near
Tear up her faith, and plunge her in despair;
Yet can he think, (so blind to Heaven's decree,
And the sure fate of curs'd apostasy)   40
Soon as he tells the secret of his breast,
And puts the angel off—and stands confess'd;
When love, and grief, and shame, and anguish meet
To make his crimes and *Delia's* wrongs complete,   44
That then the injured maid will cease to grieve;
Behold him in a Sister's arm, and live!
Mistaken wretch—by thy unkindness hurl'd
From ease, from love, from thee, and from the world;   48
Soon must she land on that immortal shore,
Where falsehood never can torment her more:
There all her sufferings and her sorrows cease,
Nor saints turn devils there to vex her peace!   52
Yet hope not then, all specious as thou art,
To taint with impious vows her Sister's heart;
With proffered worlds her honest soul to move,
Or tempt her virtue to incestuous love: 56
No—wert thou as thou wast, did Heaven's first rays
Beam on thy soul, and all the Godhead blaze,
Sooner shall sweet oblivion set us free
From friendship, love, thy perfidy, and thee;   60
Sooner shall light in league with darkness join,   ⎫
Virtue and Vice, and Heaven and Hell combine.   ⎬
Than her pure soul consent to mix with thine;   ⎭

63. [Delia is a classical name used by Latin elegiac poets and is presumably found here to avoid the use of Kezia's name directly.]

To share thy sin, adopt thy perjury,   *64*
And damn herself to be revenged on thee;
To load her conscience with a Sister's blood,
The guilt of incest, and the curse of God!

POEMS FROM MS DREW

III[64]

1.   Father, thou know'st whate'er we need
     Before our wants we own;
    Nor wilt refuse thy children bread,
     Or mock us with a stone;
    If nature's gifts thou dost bestow
     They speak the Giver kind;
    Not hurtful presents of a foe,
     But for our good design'd.

2.   The talents to my offspring lent
     I thankfully confess;
    O may they answer thy intent,
     And use them for thy praise!
    What to put on, and drink, and eat,
     Hard toiling to procure,
    But more laborious for the meat,
     Which always shall endure.

3.   Thou seest my fears lest thee their God
     They shoud forget and slight;
    Follow the unregenerate crowd,
     And in the world delight;

64. [The following poems numbered III–IX are from a group of Wesley poems at Drew University copied in a mid-nineteenth century hand. They are designated here by MS Drew. The above poem is found on two pages of the MS. The genuineness of the poems is authenticated by their style and by the fact that they form part of a bundle of poems, all in the same hand, entitled "60 Unpublished Hymns of Revd. Chas. Wesley." In point of fact, most of the sixty had already been published. This poem clearly expresses Charles Wesley's well-justified concern lest his sons' musical talents should prove a snare. The last line seems to be based on Alexander Pope's *An Essay on Man*, i. 294: "One truth is clear, whatever is is right." It is reminiscent also of Voltaire's *Candide*, chapter 30: "All is for the best, in the best of all possible worlds." It is a theme frequently used by Charles Wesley.]

To evil with the many run,
    Fantastic man to please,
By lawful means, alas, undone,
    And thro' their own success.

4.   But thou canst turn aside the ill,
    And pluck them from the flame;
Canst from their rash designs conceal
    And blast their surest aim;
Or from, or in, the dangerous hour
    Ready to save thou art,
To guard from pride and passion's power
    Their unsuspicious heart.

5.   The thing whose consequence unknown
    I tremble to foresee,
Or let it in thy name be done,
    Or let it never be.
To thee the matter I resign,
    And in thy pleasure rest;
For order'd by the will divine,
    Whatever is, is best.

IV [65]

1.   O God, from whom our blessings flow,
    Orderer of all events below,
    With gracious smile thy children see
    Who hope success from none but thee.

2.   But if thou favour our design
    Tho' men and fiends against us join,
    They cannot thy decree repeal,
    They cannot contradict thy will.

3.   The counsel of the Lord shall stand,
    For all bow down to thy command;
    It must be done, whate'er it be,
    And lo! we wait our work to see.

65. [MS Drew.]

4. Thou wilt not let us hence remove
    Without the convoy of thy love;
    And if thy love our steps attend,
    Our toil on earth in heaven shall end.

V[66]

1. Prosper, for our Redeemer's sake,
    What in his name we undertake,
    Who our appointed task fulfil,
    And serve thy providential will.

2. The gift thou hast on us bestow'd,
    Productive of our needful food,
    As a sure token of thy grace,
    We use it to the Giver's praise.

3. And if we lawfully pursue
    What thou commandest us to do,
    Let it thy approbation meet,
    Or else our surest hopes defeat.

4. A thousand ways thou canst prevent
    The deed that hath not thy consent;
    And O! forbid it to be done,
    If ours, O Lord, is ours alone.

VI[67]

1. Except the Lord conduct the plan,
    We put forth all our powers in vain;
    We waste our utmost strength and skill
    For something must be wanting still.

66. [MS Drew.]
67. [MS Drew.]

2. Something unmark'd by human eye
Shortsighted man cannot supply;
But God, who makes our deed his own,
And speaks the word, Let it be done.

3. If God upon the action shine
And stamp it with the stamp divine,
And graciously vouchsafe to bless,
His blessing ascertains success.

4. Then all th'opposing mountains flow,
And God's intent we plainly know;
And thankful at his feet approve
The fiat of Almighty love.

VII [68]

1. Man, sinful man, to labour born,
    And urg'd by the divine command,
Till, dust he doth to dust return,
    Idle on earth shoud never stand;
But still his six days' work pursue,
And do what God appoints to do.

2. The work, the time, the manner show,
    And if we now our path mistake,
No farther suffer us to go,
    But warn, and stop, and turn us back,
Who would in thee alone confide,
And into all thy counsel guide.

68. [MS Drew. This poem together with the next one is written confusedly on one sheet
of paper, so that the order of verses is uncertain.]

VIII[69]

1.   With readiness and lowly fear
      We come, O God! to serve thy will,
   Sentenc'd to toil incessant here,
      And then to rest on Sion's hill.
   But while thy justice we obey
   O let thy love point out our way.

2.   Our way by reason's glimmering light
      Unable clearly to perceive,
   Teach us to think and act aright,
      A more distinct direction give;
   And let thy providence declare
   The work it doth for us prepare.

3.   Infinite in thy means and ways
      The wants of nature to supply,
   Thou canst maintain the chosen race,
      By making windows in the sky,
   Canst in the barren desert feed,
   Or bid the ravens bring us bread.

4.   O might we seek the kingdom first,
      Th'unutterable joy and peace,
   For God the living fountain thirst,
      And hunger after righteousness,
   We then should by thy promise prove
   The all-sufficient power of love.

69. [MS Drew.]

IX[70]

1.   Safe in all events and blest
            The man who trusts in Thee;
        What shall violate his rest,
            And calm serenity?
        Loss he cannot dread, or pain,
    He cannot disappointment know,
            Confident, the Lord doth reign,
            And orders all below.

2.   While on Thee, my God, I wait,
            And on thy word rely,
        Blind, inexorable fate
            And fortune I defy.
        Not by destiny compell'd
            Not by chance at random driven,
        In the hand Almighty held,
            And kept by watchful heaven.

3.   Him who for his servant cares
            In all things I respect;
        Him who numbers all my hairs,
            And doth my paths direct:
        He demands my utmost love,
    And loving him with all my heart,
            Neither men nor fiends can move,
            Nor life nor death can part.

4.   Jesus, shelter'd in thy name,
            My adamantine tower,
        Thee I joyfully proclaim,
            Supreme in love and power;
        Power that earth and hell controuls,
            Love which none can e'er explain,
        Love that reigns in faithful souls,
            And shall for ever reign.

70. [MS Drew. The second verse is crossed out vertically, presumably as an indication that the copyist did not intend to use it. Note: line six in verses 2 and 4 is in a different metre from the corresponding line in verses 1 and 3.]

SECTION X

FRAGMENTS

ON THE SPRING[1]

How chearful among the gay mead
The daisies and cows

I AM STRUGLING IN THE TOILS OF DEATH[2]

(I am strugling in the Toils of Death)
Who shall tell me if the Strife
In Heaven or Hell shall end!

IN THE BEGINNING OF A RECOVERY[3]

Jesu, thro' whom again I breathe,
Uplifted from the Gates of Death,

[HEB. 4:16], COME BOLDLY TO &C.[4]

1. Lord, Thou dost for ever live
      The sinner's Cause to plead,
    Rais'd by God's right hand to give
      The blessings which we need.

1. [MS Cheshunt, p. 218.]
2. [This fragment is in a letter to John Wesley of March 16, 1740.]
3. [MS Thirty, p. 122.]
4. [MS Preachers (MS CW I[q]) xiii. Above the title appears in shorthand, "Obadiah Chadwick." These fragments of two verses of a poem in 7.6.7.6.7.8.7.6 metre, beloved by Charles Wesley, may illustrate his method of composing verse: the use of a scriptural verse, the jotting down of initial thoughts at times with gaps to be filled in later.]

2.

Still for grace and mercy cry
Till all my course is run;
Mercy which the heavens transcends
And lands my happy soul above,
Grace that in full glory ends,
And crowns me with thy love.

REV. 3:19, BE ZEALOUS [THEREFORE], & REPENT.[5]

1. Humble, penitential zeal
Lord, Thou only canst bestow;
Now with fear my spirit fill,
Sharp remorse & contrite woe,
Self-reproach & self-despair,
Shame too deep for life to bear.

[FATHER, WE THRO' THY FAVOURITE SON][6]

Phil. 4:6–7, *Be careful for nothing; but in everything by prayer and supplication with thanksgiving let your requests be made known unto God. And the the peace of God, which passeth all understanding, shall keep your hearts and minds through Christ Jesus.*

1. Father, we thro' thy favourite Son
Approach thy mercy-seat,
Our suits in everything make known
Howe're minute or great:
The least are not below thy care;
And if we still believe,
Above what we can ask in prayer,
Thou ready art to give.

5. [MS Preachers (MS CW I[q]), p. iii.]
6. [MS CW Letters II, 118, sheet 33.]

2. Thy mercies which for ever last
Our prostrate souls adore,
And humbly thankful for the past
We boldly ask for more:

[PROPHET DIVINE, WHO KNOWST ALONE][7]

Prophet Divine, who knowst alone
The dread Paternal Deity,
Who only canst to us make known,
Reveal his Will concerning *me*,
And guide

[ME, AND MY WORKS CANST THOU APPROVE][8]

12. Me, and my works canst Thou approve
All good, all gracious as Thou art?
What is Obedience without Love?
A sacrifice without an heart?

[SHE DIES ON EARTH TO DIE NO MORE][9]

4. She dies on earth to die no more,
Whom landing on the heavenly shore
Her faithful comrade greets;
But who the impious sin can paint
Whose breast a des[   ] saint
A kindred spirit meets.

7. [MS CW Letters I, p. 33. The verse is incomplete and crossed out.]
8. [MS CW III(a) No. 12.]
9. [This fragment appears in shorthand on the inside cover of an old notebook.]

5.   Mocked with her comrades in distress,
      With joy an [   ] she [   ]
          To   n   h s t   sent down
      Her [   ] spirit [   ] to bear
      (On earth so long their [   ] care)
          To the eternal throne.

6.   Her smiling Lord appoints his bride
      To await, with [   ] spirit reside (?)
          The [   ] mystery
      The [   ] complete
      When all around his throne shall meet
          And God forever see!

[O THOU WHO HANGING ON THE TREE][10]

1.   O Thou who hanging on the tree
      Didst pray for Those that murther'd Thee
          And mock'd thy mortal Smart,
      Inspire me with thy patient love,
      For those that now thy servant prove,
          And tear my bleeding Heart.

2.   My bitter persecuting Foes,
      The Authors of my Griefs and woes,
          I beg Thee, Lord, to spare;
      Evil for good who still return,
      For these I sigh & weep & mourn
          And agonize in prayer.

[3.] [   ]
      [   ]
        [   ]
      Master, the promised grace we claim,
      We boldy now confess thy name,
          And suffer for thy cause.

10. [MS Richmond, p. 126.]

[4.]   Send down Thy Spirit on us to rest,
         And give our ravished souls to taste, `
             The sweetness of Thy love.
         [   ]
         Afflicted for Thy Gospel's sake.
             [   ]

         [   ] thy faithful heart.
         [   ]
         Panting for full conformity.[11]

[AH, WOE IS ME, WHOM THRONES SURROUND][12]

1. Ah, woe is me, whom thrones surround,
        Who still with powers and [   ] dwell,
    With [   ] men of [   ] profound,
        Whose thoughts are set in fear of hell,
    Who see their t[   ] as sh[ining] swords,
    And shout as darts their bitter words.

2. The man who meek and upright seems,
        As sharper than a two-edged stake,
    Himself he seeks, himself esteems,
        And havoc of our faith would make,
    His own importance to secure,
    And make his gain and party sure.

[WHILE THE CITY WALLS ARE SPARKLING][13]

15. [   ]
     [   ]
     While the city walls are sparkling
     With meridian glory bright:
         How stupendous
     Are the glories of the Lamb!

11. [Verses 1 and 2 are followed by three and one half lines of shorthand. The above is a transcription by Elijah Hoole of the shorthand.]

12. [MS CW IV, 75. The verses are transcribed from shorthand.]

13. [MS CW IV, 92, pp. 5–6; the earlier verses are lost.]

16. On his throne of radiant azure,
   High above all height he reigns;
Reigns amidst immortal pleasure,
   While refulgent glory flames:
      How diffusive
   Shines the golden blaze around!

17. All th'angelic pow'rs adoring,
   Circle round his orient seat;
Ransom'd saints with seraphs soaring,
   Loudest praises to repeat:
      How exalted
   Is his praise, & how profound!

18. Every throne, & every mansion,
   All th'empyrean arches ring,
Echo, 'To our God, salvation,
   Glory to our glorious King;
      High & Holy,
   Holy, holy, holy Lord!'

19. Praise be to the Father given,
   Praise to the incarnate Son;
Praise the Spirit, One, & Seven,
   Praise the mystic Three in One;
      Hallelujah,
   Everlasting praise be Thine!

CHAOS[14]

Adverse to Brothers, when we seem'd to stray
In wild excursions from the ancient[15] way,
Thy vigilant fidelity reprov'd,
And own'd us less than England's Church belov'd.

14. [Lamplough Collection.]
15. [Below "ancient" the word "beaten" is written as an alternative.]

[THOU WOULDST NOT HAVE CUT OFF IN LIFE'S DECAY][16]

Thou wouldst not have cut off in life's decay
And cast me as a sh[   ] crumb away;
His pitiful insinuating art
Could tear me from Thy arms but not Thy heart.

[COMMEMORATIVE HYMN][17]

But how have I, alas, repaid
  The blessings from above,
What grateful retribution made
  For all thy waste of love!

Thy goodness placed my parents good
  As guardian angels near;
Armed with Thy flaming sword they stood
  T'inspire me with Thy fear.
Paternal or Fraternal care
  I see was only Thine;
The power of Godliness declare
[   ]

[WE THUS TO MEET OUR GOD PREPARE][18]

We thus to meet our God prepare,
Labouring and watching unto prayer.

16. [This fragment is on the cover of an old notebook in shorthand.]
17. [MS CW IV, 66. These two fragmentary verses are presumably part of drafts for the "Commemorative Hymn" which appears in *Poet. Works*, VIII, pp. 390–4. The first four lines of the second verse appear in Part II, verse 3 of this hymn with variants.]
18. [MS CW IV, 75.]

[HOW DID I EV'N CONTEND TO LAY][19]

How did I ev'n contend to lay
  My limbs upon that bed!
I ask'd the angels to convey
  My spirit in his stead.

[IF THOU CANST PARDON ME ONCE MORE][20]

If Thou canst pardon me once more,
  Once more so great Compassion shew,

[BUT NOW WE FEAR, HE WOUD MUCH RATHER][21]

But now, we fear, he woud much rather
Pluck out the eyes of his old Father.

ANOTHER[22]

Martin woud have pluck'd out, we own,
His eyes, and given them once to John:
But

---

19. [MS CW Letters, I, p. 95. The poem was written from Moorfields on the death of S[ister] Pearson in a diary letter to Mrs. James, July 3.]
20. [MS Clarke, p. 216.]
21. [MS Pat. Misc., p. 23.]
22. [MS CW IV, 81.]

HYMNS AND POEMS
OF DOUBTFUL AUTHORSHIP

PARAPHRASE ON THE LORD'S PRAYER[1]

1.   Father of all, Eternal mind,
    In uncreated light enshrin'd,
       Immensely good & great;
    Thy children form'd, & blest by thee,
    With filial love & homage we
       Fall prostrate at thy feet.

2.   Thy name in hallow'd strains be sung,
    Let every heart & every tongue
       The solemn concert join:
    In loving, serving, praising Thee,
    We find our chief felicity,
       But cannot add to thine.

3.   Thy righteous, mild, & sovereign reign,
    Throughout creation's ample plain
       Let every being own;
    Lord, in our hearts where passions rude
    With fierce tumultuous rage intrude,
       Erect thy peaceful throne.

4.   As angels round thy seat above,
    With joyful haste & ardent love,
       Thy blest commands fulfil;

1. [MS CW IV, 92, p. 8. The poem is incomplete. In a personal note Frank Baker questions Charles Wesley's authorship and wonders whether it could be by James Hervey.]

FOR THE MAGDALENE[2]

1. Blest Redeemer, bow thine ear,
   To our humble fervent prayer;
       Thus adoring,
       Thus imploring,
   Mercy bids us not despair.

2. Though our crimes of deepest dye
   Swell the aching heart and eye,
       Yet relying
       On the dying,
   Faith relieves the throbbing sigh.

3. By all-saving grace we know
   Scarlet sins grow white as snow:
       Vain our merit,
       If the Spirit
   Did not through repentance glow.

4. Freed from shame, reproach, and taunt,
   Lawless vice, and grinding want,
       Here accepted,
       Here protected,
   For celestial bliss we pant.

[VORACIOUS LEARNING, OFTEN OVERFED][3]

Voracious Learning, often overfed,
Digests not into sense its motly meal.
This Forager on others' Wisdom leaves
His native Farm, his Reason, quite untill'd,

2. [MS CW Letters, p. 487. Though written in Charles Wesley's handwriting on the verso of a letter of Sir Edward Walpole, it is probably a hymn or poem for the Magdalene Hospital, London, by Walpole and possibly altered by Wesley. John Wesley supported the hospital (*cf.* Sermon LII, I, paragraphs 8–9) and the unfortunate Dr. William Dodd was for a time its chaplain. *The Works of John Wesley*, vol. II: Sermons II, 34–70, ed. by Albert Outler (Nashville: Abingdon, 1985), p. 307.]

3. [MS CW Letters, p. 482. The verse appears in a letter to his (Charles's) daughter Sally, September 17, from Bristol. Is it perhaps from the classics or a translation by Wesley? If it is indeed by him, it is the only example of blank verse by Charles Wesley.]

With mixt Manure he surfeits the rank Soil,
Dung'd but not drest, & rich to beggary:
A Pomp untameable of Weeds prevails:
His Servant's Wealth encumbred Wisdom mourns.

[WHO IS THE TREMBLING SINNER, WHO?][4]

Who is the trembling sinner, who
That owns eternal death his due,
Waiting his fearful doom to feel,
And hanging on the mouth of hell?
Peace, troubled soul, thou need'st not fear;
Thy Jesus saith, Be of good chear;
Only on Jesus' blood rely,
He died that thou might'st never die.

SOME VERSES OCCASIONED BY THE SEVERE ILLNESS
OF THE REV. MR. JOHN WESLEY
TO THE TUNE OF OLIVER'S[5]

I

See the *Star* of England clouded,
How the dreadful Fever preys,
By all Human Art *deserted*!
Number'd are *his* useful days;
But the Spirit—but the Spirit
In his num'rous Offspring *prays*!

4. [MS CW Family Letters, II, p. 13. It is written in the body of a letter by Charles Wesley. Is it by him or a quotation?]

5. [From a Broadsheet originally classified as Book Room MS 303. The full title of the Broadsheet reads: "Some Verses occasioned by the severe Illness, much fear'd dissolution, and a most mirac'lous restoration of the Rev. Mr. John Wesley, at Lisburne in Ireland, July 2, 1775. (London: Printed for W. Kent, No. 116, High-Holborn, MDCCLXXV)." M. Riggall thought the poem was probably by Charles Wesley, though "Not one of his best." In a personal note Frank Baker "can't agree that it is by Charles Wesley, from printer & format, quite apart from internal evidence," e.g. the un-Wesleyan rhymes. Cf. *Proceedings*, VI (1908), p. 50 for a reference to a poem by John Ryley on Wesley's recovery from fever in 1775. Is this perhaps the poem?]

II

Faithful, urgent Intercession,
　　Storm the hideous low'ring Skies,
SPARE—O SPARE a Nation's Blessing!
　　HEAR—O HEAR our plaintive Cries!
　　　　Heaven listens—Heaven, &c.
　　Chides our Fears and wipes our Eyes.

III

From the threat'ning Cloud emerging,
　　See the *Luminary* come!
Brighter *now* and brighter shining;
　　JESUS *hath* revers'd his doom!
　　　　Boundless Mercy—boundless, &c.
　　Bids him to *our* Help return.

IV

Thankful let us take the Blessing,
　　Which His Goodness now repays,
By united Pray'rs unceasing,
　　MORE improve *his* future Days;
　　　　Still contending—still, &c.
　　GOD in *all* our ways to please.

V

May his gracious Restoration
　　More unfold the Gospel Word!
'Till all know that FULL Redemption
　　Purchas'd by a bleeding Lord;
　　　　Rise triumphant—rise, &c.
　　Fully, finally restor'd!

WROTE BY J[OHN] H[ENDERSO]N [6]

Thine wholly, thine alone I'l be,
My song shall always be of Thee;
My willing fingers ne'er shall move,
But on the subject of thy love.   *4*
My well-tun'd heart, touch'd by thy hand
Shall ready play at thy command;
Thy Spirit within shall form my lays,
And every breath of mine be praise.   *8*
My love's soft tears shall sweetly flow,
Nor will I other passion know,
But endless strains of melody
Strike out, my dearest Lord, of Thee.   *12*
I with the early lark will vie,
And mount to Thee my fav'rite Sky,
And ever, at the fall of night,
Impassion'd songs to Thee indite.   *16*
Under the shelter of thy wing
Happily shall I sit & sing:
And when I in the night awake,
Thy love my sweetest subject make;   *20*
And when I die, or late or soon,
My last-fetch'd gasp shall be in tune.

"WE LOVE HIM BECAUSE HE FIRST LOVED US"
PART OF ST. BERNARD'S HYMN ALTER'D BY MR. WESLEY [7]

1. Of him who did Salvation bring
    I cou'd for ever think and Sing.
    Arise, ye Guilty, he'll forgive:
    Arise, ye Poor, he will relieve.

6. [MS CW III(a) No. 6. "J. Hn." is John Henderson, see MS Henderson, above, pp. 344–52. In spite of the title, the poem is in Charles Wesley's handwriting and immediately follows one of his own poems.]

7. [MS Gwynne, pp. 7–8. The line "alter'd by Mr. Wesley" was added later to the title. MS Gwynne contains poems in the writing of Sarah Gwynne, Charles Wesley's wife, some of which may not be by Charles. The MS dates from about 1747, i.e. before their marriage. Are some of the poems perhaps early works of Charles? This translation of *Jesu dulcis memoria* is listed in Julian's *Dictionary of Hymnology* as being from Madan's *Hymns* (1760). Madan, who used many Wesley hymns, printed only verses 1, 3, and 6 and heads the poem "Eph. 2:13."]

2. Ask but his Grace, and lo! 'tis given;
   Ask, and he turns your Hell to Heaven:
   Tho' Sin and Sorrow wound my Soul,
   Jesu, thy Balm will make it whole.

3. Eternal Lord, almighty King,
   All Heaven doth with thy Triumphs ring:
   Thou conquer'st all beneath, above;
   Devils with Force, and Men with Love.

4. The wounding Spear pierces my Heart;
   When thou art nail'd I feel the Smart:
   Thy Groans my echoing Sighs display;
   Thou bow'st thy Head, I faint away.

5. Ye Hearts of Stone, come, melt, to see
   This he endur'd for you and me:
   He suffer'd: all our Guilt's forgiven;
   And on his blood we Swim to Heaven.

6. To shame our Sins he blush'd in Blood,
   He clos'd his Eyes to shew us God.
   Let all the World fall down, and know
   That none but God Such Love cou'd show.

7. O let my Mouth thy Sweetness taste,
   My Nostrils with thy Odours feast;
   On thee I rest, of thee I boast;
   Who sav'd the World won't see me lost.

8. 'Tis thee I love, for thee alone
   I shed my Tears and make my Moan;
   Where'er I am, where'er I move,
   I meet the Object of my Love.

9. Insatiate to this Spring I fly;
   I drink, and yet am ever dry:
   Ah, who against thy Charms is Proof;
   Ah, who that loves can love enough.

Finis.

A HYMN FROM THE GERMAN[8]

1. Behold the Saviour of Mankind
   Patient & good, and meek of Mind;
   How on his Throne He now does grieve,
   That ah! so few on Him believe.

2. The Work was finish'd long ago;
   Man is redeem'd from Sin and Woe;
   Freedom there is, & Life and Peace;
   When Jesus dy'd, He purchas'd these.

3. Yet who among us lives by Faith?
   Who the true Peace and Sweetness hath?
   Who from his Bondage is set free?
   And who, O Jesu! follows Thee?

4. How dark is all the World & dead,
   With this Delusion over-spread;
   Seeking to be devout and good
   By other Ways than Jesu's Blood!

5. We, all our lives, Where have we been?
   Have we the Lord's Salvation seen?
   No: For we sought it not this Way;
   Lord! Shew us the true Path To-Day.

ANOTHER[9]

1.   My Saviour, Thou didst shed
      Thy precious Blood for me;
      O dwell within my worthless Heart,
      And let me live to Thee.

8. [MS Gwynne, p. 16. Extensive research has failed to trace the German origin of this and the next three hymns. If these are indeed early compositions by Charles, it means that he knew enough German perhaps to have translated some of the German hymns, the English versions of which have hitherto been attributed to John.]

9. [MS Gwynne, pp. 16–17.]

Thou callest all, O Lord,
To come to Thee and live;
I therefore come with all my Sins,
I know Thou can'st forgive.

2.   My Lamb, and Saviour dear!
I long to see Thy Face,
To know Thee more & more by Faith,
I pray Thee give me Grace.
And when this Life is o'er,
O may I dwell with Thee,
Still worshipping the Blessed Lamb,
Who liv'd and dy'd for me.

ANOTHER[10]

1.   The Cross, the Cross, O that's my Gain!
Because on that, the Lamb was slain;
'Twas there my Lord was Crucify'd;
'Twas there the Saviour for me Dy'd.

2.   What wondrous Thing cou'd move Thy Heart,
To take on Thee my Curse and Smart?
When Thou foreknewest I should be
So cold and negligent t'wards Thee.

3.   The Cause was Love, I Sink with Shame
Before Thy Sacred Jesu's Name,
That Thou should'st bleed & slaughter'd be,
Because, because Thou lovedst me.

4.   Thou lovedst me: O boundless Grace!
Who can such wondrous Mercy trace?
I, who Unfaithful, foolish am,
Yet find Thee still a patient Lamb.

10. [MS Gwynne, pp. 17–19.]

5. To thy red Cross I lift mine Eyes,
   That is the Tree will make me wise;
   That, that's a Tree of Knowledge good,
   Evil was drown'd in Jesu's Blood.

6. The bloody Cross, That bears a Fruit,
   Which does poor hungry Sinners suit:
   It is a Tree of Life for all,
   Who're doom'd to Death in Adam's Fall.

7. See what a deep-dy'd red it bears!
   Look how that Nail my Saviour tears;
   Stain'd & besmear'd with Blood divine,
   There hangs the King f[ro]m David's Line.

8. Here will I stay & gaze awhile
   On Thee, Thou Friend of Sinners Vile;
   I'll look & see what I have done,
   To GOD's Eternal gracious Son.

9. Lord, what is Man, & what am I,
   That Thou should'st such a Creature buy;
   And Seal my Ransom with thy Blood,
   Languishing, melting on the Wood.

10. Here is an Ensign on a Hill!
    Come hither, Sinners, look your Fill;
    To look aside is Pain & Loss,
    I'll glory only in the Cross.

11. I'll live & dwell by this blest Flood;
    The flowing Stream of Jesu's Blood!
    That Blood which he in tender Love
    To shed, did leave his Throne above.

12. Here in a Glass I fix my Eye,
    The Glory of the Lord t'espy;
    'Tis by beholding I shall be
    Chang'd to his Image who lov'd me.

13. His Glory did the Lord proclaim,
    When Moses pray'd to see the Same:
    "Before Thee shall my Goodness pass,
    "But thou can'st not behold my Face."

14. But we with open Face behold
    The Glory which before was told
    Should be reveal'd when Jesus dy'd;
    We look upon him, Crucify'd.

15. No Flaming Sword doth guard this Place,
    The bloody Cross proclaims Free Grace;
    No other Way can Heaven win:
    All by the Cross must enter in.

ANOTHER[11]

1. Beloved Saviour, Prince of Life,
       To us thy Spirit give;
   We pant to hear that sacred Voice
       Which bids poor Sinners live.

2. Open to us those living Springs,
       Which from thy Wounds do flow;
   Dart down thy bright refreshing Beams,
       To us Thy Goodness shew.

3. 'Tis thy Desire to save the Lost,
       To ease them of their Pain!
   Therefore we come to Thee, blest Lamb,
       Who for our Sins wast slain.

4. O'erstream our Souls with thy rich Grace,
       To us reveal thy Will;
   O be Thou our Immanuel,
       Thy work in us fulfill.

11. [MS Gwynne, pp. 19–20.]

HYMN 1ST
AN HYMN ON THE BIRTH DAY
OF THE REVD. MR. J[OHN] W[ESLEY]
JUNE THE 17TH (TO MY BATH TUNE)[12]

1. Ye gratefull Souls your Voices Raise,
     Lift up your Hearts to Christ your King;
   With humble Adoration Praise
     The God that gives you Power to sing;
   O thank him for this Blessed Morn,
   On which our Minister was Born.

2. Hail, this Glad Day, let every tongue
     Sing Praises for this Blessing given;
   The Angel Quire will catch the Song
     And Join our Chearful Lay in Heaven;
   Let Thanks and blessings Crown the Morn,
   On which our Minister was Born.

3. O Bless the great Creator's Name,
     Praise Him with all your Noblest Powers;
   Who Called our Shepherd to Proclaime
     His Son, the Dear Redeemer ours;
   In Distant Lands the Songs repeat,
   To make the Harmony Compleat.

4. The Great Jehovah spake the Word,
     And Sent the Herald forth to Prove
   The Goodness of our Dying Lord,
     A Witness of Redeeming Love:
   Glory to God forever give:
   On this Glad Day he bad Him Live.

5. Sent him to shake the Gates of Hell,
     The fiends Alarmed exert their Power;
   Feeling their Tottering Kingdom reel,
     They Roar aloud and Curse the Hour;
   But we will bless the Happy Morn
   On which that Blessed Son was Born.

12. [MS CW IV, 67. The title is in Charles Wesley's handwriting, but all the rest is in another hand. In spite of the title, there is perhaps a little doubt as to whether the poem is by Charles Wesley. In verse 8 the words "Earth" and "Death" do not read like his rhyme, unless these poems are very early compositions.]

6.   May it in Each Revolving Year
      With some Peculiar Gift be Bless't;
    Singled from all the Rest appear
      On every Grateful Heart Impresst;
    Let Thanks and Praise our Time employ,
    And keep this Day with solemn Joy.

7.   O may the Spirit from above
      Guide and pronounce our Shepherd blesst;
    Fill all his Soul with Perfect Love,
      And on him ever let him Rest,
    Still we shall Bless this Happy Morn,
    On which our Minister was Born.

8.   On this thy favourite bestow
      The Blessing of a Constant Heaven:
    The Greatest Good he here can know
      Be to our faithfull Shepherd given;
    Still let Him soar above this Earth,
    Conquerer o're Sin, & Hell & Death.

9.   With Double Splendour may the Sun
      Arise, and all his Charms display,
    And finish Bright as he begun,
      To Crown and bless this Happy Day
    On Him his brightest Influence shed,
    Till Hoary Age adorn his Head.

10.   Then when the Glorious work is done,
      The Glorious work of faith with Pow'r,
    Call Home at Last thy favour'd son;
      And make him more than Conqueror;
    Like Moses to thyself Convay,
    And Kiss His Raptur'd Soul away.

HYMN 2ND
ON THE BIRTHDAY OF THE REVD. MR. C[HARLES] W[ESLEY]
DECEMBER THE 18[13]

1.   Rejoice with solemn Joy,
        And Tune your Hearts to sing;
      Your every hour Employ,
        To Praise the Eternal King;
      Who called our Pastor to Proclaim
      Our Int'rest in the bleeding Lamb.

2.   To God who reigns above
        Let us the Glory give;
      In Tooken of his Love
        He bids our Shepherd Live;
      O Bless Him for this Happy Morn
      On which our Minister was Born.

3.   Sing to the Builder's Praise,
        Ye Heavens of Purest Light,
      Let us Resound his Lays
        And Catch the sweet Delight;
      With Praises usher in the Morn
      On which our Minister was Born.

4.   Break forth, ye Riseing Hills,
        Ye Mountains, Praise the Lord;
      Whilst he with Plenty fills
        Who formed you by his Word:
      Dance to the Sound of Joy, & Pay
      Your gratefull Tribute on this Day.

5.   Our Pastor was sent Down
        Embassador from Heaven;
      Glad Tidings to make known,
        Peace & your Sins forgiven:
      Let cheerful song employ this Morn
      On which our Minister was born.

13. [MS CW IV, 67. This poem is almost certainly the work of the same author who composed the previous poem. Would Charles Wesley write of himself in the third person?]

6.   Thus the Almighty said
          To His adopted Heir,
       "Fear not, nor be dismay'd,
          "To Hurt thee none shall Dare,
       "Go forth, the gates of Darkness shake,
       "And bring the wandering Sinners back.

7.   "Fear not the darkest Hour
          "That may thy Soul assail,
       "I'll guard Thee by my Power
          "Nor shall thy foe Prevaile;
       "In suffering I'll My Strength increase,
       "Speak on, nor Dare to Hold thy Peace.

8.   "Nor Fire nor Plague nor War
          "Thy steady Soul shall fright;
       "For still thou art secure,
          "Supported by my Might,
       "Tho' Thousands fall at thy Right Hand,
       "Thy Safety is at my Command."

A PROPHECY OF SIR EDWARD NEWLITE'S
IN THE REIGN OF CHARLES II[14]

When a Branch of the Thistle gets o're the Atlantic,
And in the New World its seed doth get planted,
When it doth arrive t'a degree of perfection
It surely will breed a great Insurrection: 4
In seventy and four its Root will get polished,
And in Eighty and six it will be quite demolish'd.

14. [MS Pat. Misc., p. 128. While the poem may not be Charles Wesley's original composition, the fact that he included it among his poems suggests that he probably amended it.]
    This prophecy was found by an American lady, now in Philadelphia, of undoubted character and veracity (when on a visit to England in 1766) among her Great-Grandfather's papers. When the First Congress met in 1772, she thought the first part of the prophecy seemed to be fulfilling. She then gave copies of it to her friends, and One to an intimate Acquaintance in America, now in London. (Mr. Joseph Galloway, who gave this copy to Charles Wesley.)

In that year its seed will be hot in rebellion,
Of them will be slaughter'd above half a million: *8*
The Lilly and Thistle that year will unite,
But the Lion and Dun Cow will put them to flight,
The Eagle will eagerly join in the fray,
But Luna will clip all their wings in one day.   *12*

O Thistle, O Thistle, your wounds shall be sore,
And you'l be abridg'd of all civil power,
And Kirk, and Kirk-Government shall be no more.   }

[THE DOCTRINE OF OUR DYING LORD][15]

1. The doctrine of our dying Lord,
    The faith he on mount Calvary seal'd,
   We sign; and every steadfast word
    Within his testament reveal'd
   We firm believe; and curse we they[16]
   Who add thereto, or take away.

2. And now before this awful crowd
    Of brethren militant on earth!
   Before the firstborn church of God!
    We hearty own the second birth;
   We constantly consent to this,—
   Who hath not Christ is none of his.

---

15. [Thomas Jackson, *The Centenary of Wesleyan Methodism*, (London: J. Mason, 1839), pp. 302–4; (New York: T. Mason & G. Lane, 1839), pp. 188–9. Jackson notes that the poem was originally published in the form of a handbill. He provides this descriptive background of the poem: "On the fourth of November, 1744, when the Wesleyans, Moravians, and Calvinistic Methodists had become so many distinct bodies, they held a 'general love feast' at the Tabernacle in London, when they unitedly sung the following 'Confession of Faith,' composed unquestionably by Mr. Charles Wesley." (p. 187) Since there is no documentary evidence, however, for Jackson's claim, the poem is included here with "Hymns and Poems of Doubtful Authorship."]

16. [Jackson suggests that this is a misprint for "and cursed be they."]

3.   Also to blood we this maintain,
     That none are righteous, no, not one,
  But those for whom the Lamb was slain,
     Who're justified by faith alone:
  And whoso in his name believes,
  Himself and all Christ hath receives.

4.   Our works and merits we disclaim,
     We trample on our righteousness;
  Our holiest actions we condemn,
     As dung and dross; and this confess,
  They are but sand; who builds thereon
  Denies and slights the Corner Stone.

5.   No other doctrine dare we hear,
     But Christ alone our Saviour is;
  To all besides we stop our ear,
     And shun as dangerous heresies:
  This truth to death we will proclaim,—
  There is no Saviour but the Lamb!

6.   He is the only Lord and God!
     The fulness of the Three in One!
  His name, death, righteousness, and blood,
     Shall be our glory, this alone:
  His Godhead and his death shall be
  Our song to all eternity.

7.   On him we venture all we have,
     Our bodies, souls, and spirits too:
  None will we ask besides to save,
     Nought but the Saviour will we know:
  This we subscribe with heart and hand,
  Resolved through grace by this to stand.

8.   This now, with heaven's resplendent host,
     We echo through the church's bounds;
  And 'midst the heathen make our boast
     Of our Redeemer's blood and wounds:
  And loud like many waters join
  To shout the Lamb, the Man Divine!

9. By this our mark will we be known
        In heaven, and in the earth abroad,—
    That every doctrine we disown,
        And every faith, and every god;
    But Christ Emmanuel, and that faith
    Which apprehends his blood and death.

INDEX
OF
FIRST LINES
IN VOLUMES I – III

INDEX OF FIRST LINES[1]

1. Entire first lines in italics indicate "Hymns and Poems of Doubtful Authorship" (see Section X). Occasionally the initial part of the second line of a poem is noted immediately following the first line for the sake of clarity, for example:

O Thou to whom all hearts are known / My latest

O Thou to whom all hearts are known / Who dost.

In this instance both first lines are identical and the second line differentiates clearly between the two poems.

2. Not by Charles Wesley.

3. There is a question as to whether this line begins a new poem or is a continuation of the previous lines.

Extensive research has not produced the texts of the following poems which are thought to exist at The Methodist Archives (Manchester):

> Father, Son & Spirit come
> Have I not then misspent my souls fond fears
> I live, not I, but Christ in me
> Let earth & heaven together join
> O what shall dust & ashes say
> On God's great bounty we dependent live
> The Lord himself, the mighty Lord

INDEX
OF
PERSONAL NAMES
IN VOLUMES I – III

INDEX OF PERSONAL NAMES

1. Wesley wrote also Burgoine.

2. See Sarah Wesley.

3. Wesley wrote "Sacheveril" to rhyme with "ill."

INDEX
TO
SCRIPTURAL PASSAGES
IN VOLUMES I AND III

INDEX OF SCRIPTURAL PASSAGES[1]

OLD TESTAMENT

NEW TESTAMENT

1. For an index to the scriptural passages found in volume II of *The Unpublished Poetry of Charles Wesley*, see p. 475 of that volume.